O9-AJO-609

Laissez Les bons
temps rouler

Also by Rima and Richard Collin

The Pleasures of Seafood
The New Orleans Restaurant Guide

Also by Richard Collin

The New Orleans Underground Gourmet

THE NEW ORLEANS COOKBOOK

THE
NEW ORLEANS
COOKBOOK
CREOLE, CAJUN, AND
LOUISIANA FRENCH RECIPES
PAST AND PRESENT
by Rima Collin & Richard Collin
ALFRED A. KNOPF, NEW YORK, 1995

THIS IS A BORZOI BOOK
PUBLISHED BY ALFRED A. KNOPF, INC.

 Published in the
United States by Alfred A. Knopf, Inc.,
New York, and simultaneously in Canada by Random House
of Canada Limited, Toronto. Distributed
by Random House, Inc., New York.

Library of Congress Cataloging in Publication Data
Collin, Rima (date)
The New Orleans cookbook.
1. Cookery, American—Louisiana. 2. Cookery,
Creole. I. Collin, Richard H., joint author.
II. Title.
TX715.C713 1975 641.5'9763'35 74-7729
ISBN 0-394-48898-9
ISBN 0-394-75275-9 (pbk.)

Manufactured in the United States of America
Published March 14, 1975
Reprinted Five Times
Seventh Printing, April 1995

For the city and the people of New Orleans

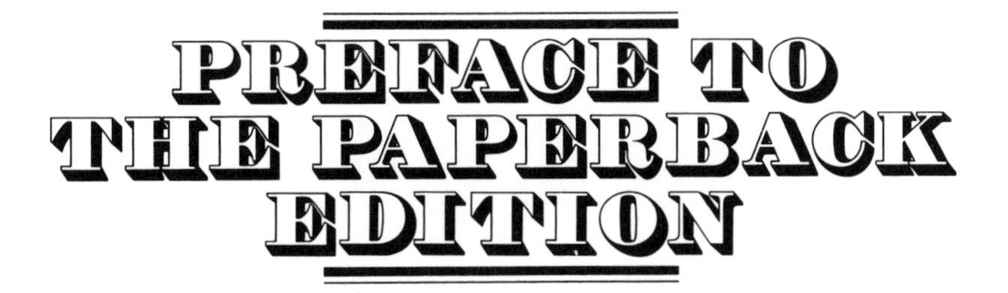

PREFACE TO THE PAPERBACK EDITION

In the eleven years and ten printings since *The New Orleans Cookbook* was first published in 1975, New Orleans' unique cooking style has become nationally famous, as "Creole" and "Cajun" restaurants have made spicy chicken and blackened fish national staples. We view the proliferation of nationalized New Orleans cooking with mixed feelings, especially when the menus of the so-called Cajun restaurants in other parts of the country bear little resemblance to historic local food. The new Cajun-Creole craze is as new to New Orleans as it is to most of the rest of the country, and owes most of its prominence to the way the food media promote new restaurants and successful chefs.

The pioneers of the national New Orleans food styles, Al Copeland and Paul Prudhomme, however, fall squarely within the old New Orleans tradition of dramatic culinary pyrotechnics that produced the famous Creole dishes such as pompano en papillote, shrimp Creole, and oysters Rockefeller. Popeye's spicy and crispy fried chicken transformed bland and often soggy American franchise fried chicken into a fiery and unmistakably different dish, hot enough to shock even some New Orleans palates. Blackening a fish in a highly seasoned pepper marinade extends the old New Orleans style of restaurant spectacle that flames desserts or coffee. Nothing could be farther from the staid old American restaurant standby of Dover sole in a butter sauce than Prudhomme's peppery blackened fish.

Blackened redfish made in the home will not only suffuse the palate with spices, it will fill the home with smoke. Putting pompano in a paper bag does little for the pompano, but it sure gets attention. New Orleans cooking has always been dramatic. It is a measure of the newly adventuresome American palate that blackened fish and spicy chicken are finding an enthusiastic reception throughout the country.

The new national New Orleans food is primarily restaurant fare. Although we offer a recipe for blackening, we advise you to cook the dish outdoors or let a restaurant handle it. Spicy fried chicken is clearly a fast food restaurant preparation. New Orleans' basic food has changed little in the last decade. The new interest in American regional cooking has brought more food from the rest of America to New Orleans, especially mesquite grilled fish, but the new restaurants have also reintroduced many old local staples. So red beans and mesquite grilled fish are found side by side with more traditional steaks and continental dishes. New Orleanians are always willing to try new dishes, but poor boys, red beans, barbecued shrimp, soft shell crabs, baked oysters, trout (fried, amandine, meunière), fried and boiled seafood still remain unique local favorites. In New Orleans, where change is traditionally slow to appear, the more things change, the more they stay the same. New Orleans (urban Creole) and Southeastern Louisiana's (country Cajun) cuisine are still intact, unchanged by the national attention, constituting two of the nation's hardiest and most intriguing regional American cuisines.

September, 1986

THE NEW ORLEANS COOKBOOK

New Orleans is an old city. Its layers of history form as strange a configuration as the eighteenth-century French buildings of the Vieux Carré, with their splendid Spanish courtyards hidden just behind the gates. New Orleans began as a French settlement in 1718, became Spanish in 1762, then French again briefly just after 1800 and, with the Louisiana Purchase in 1803, American. But people do not change simply because diplomatic papers are signed. By 1803 New Orleans was already a thriving cosmopolitan center with a culture and character of its own.

From its earliest days New Orleans was prosperous. The city and the surrounding region had valuable sugar and rice crops and unparalleled supplies of seafood and game. The Mississippi River and the Gulf of Mexico made New Orleans the natural port for the entire mid-American continent, and the river linked New Orleans with Canada, the other, more remote French outpost in the New World. Frenchmen from the north migrated south, driven by the British dominance over an area they had hoped would be a New World France. Spaniards seeking wealth, Frenchmen in pursuit of religious freedom or in flight from the guillotine, blacks driven from their Caribbean islands by revolutions—all came to this city of many cultures.

Throughout much of the nineteenth century New Orleans was largely a French city. French cafés and coffeehouses dotted the Vieux Carré, or French Quarter. The Café des Émigrés opened in 1791 and became a meeting place for Haitian refugees exiled after Toussaint L'Ouverture's rebellion. Political and economic exiles from Paris and the French provinces sought refuge and fortune in this spiritual capital of the French New World, while wealthy New Orleans families sent their children to be educated in Paris. And from France and Canada came the Acadians, farmers and fishermen who settled in southwestern Louisiana and quietly developed a cohesive, authentic French provincial culture with its own customs and language—a culture that has remained intact for over two hundred years.

The Creoles of New Orleans, those who settled here before the Louisiana Purchase, comprised a mixed group, economically and socially. Some of them were wealthy; many were poor. All of them considered themselves the "natives"—as opposed to the "Americans," the new arrivals who settled "uptown," on the other side of Canal Street from the French Quarter. Creole culture had many of its roots in French culture, but it developed on New World soil. New Orleans food as we know it today originated with the Creoles, who combined French cooking traditions and techniques with seasonings and new ingredients introduced to them by the Spanish, the Indians, and the many blacks who lived in the old part of the city.

During the first half of the nineteenth century, when New Orleans was a thriving commercial center and a haven for strangers, it became a significant center of culture in still-young America. Le Théâtre d'Orléans, the French Opera House, built in 1859, housed the oldest opera company in the United States. And most attractive of all to visitors, New Orleans had remarkably good food—food that was quite different from what was found anywhere else in the country. Businessmen came to New Orleans for practical reasons; they also stayed on a bit to enjoy the life of the city, its lively cafés, its relaxed pace, and its excellent dining rooms. Early in the nineteenth century, in New Orleans as in the rest of the country, most major dining rooms were connected with hotels. By 1820 the food prepared by the owner-chef at the Tremoulet Hotel, facing the Place d'Armes (Jackson Square), had a considerable reputation. In the late 1830s three major hotels were built: the St. Charles Hotel, on the "American" side of Canal Street, which became a leader in establishing New Orleans' reputation for lavish dining and cosmopolitan atmosphere; the nearby Verandah, less opulent, also famous for the quality of its table; and, in the French Quarter, the St. Louis Hotel, where wealthy visitors enjoyed what was considered a model of Creole elegance.

Of course, not all visitors to New Orleans and not all natives wanted to eat elaborate meals every time they ate out, and consequently pensions or boarding hotels, taverns with free lunches, simple eating houses, and market restaurants began to flourish. In all these modest eating places New Orleans' native cooking—Creole cooking—was the mainstay. At the grand hotel dining rooms, the food was a mixture of French, Continental, and Creole. Antoine's, New Orleans' oldest French Creole restaurant, opened in 1840 as a French boarding hotel, then moved in 1874 to its present location on St. Louis Street in the French Quarter.

By the time the Civil War and Reconstruction were over, New Orleans' wealthy Creoles were clearly on the decline, both in numbers and in influence. The bustling, prosperous Americans had become the city's economic and political leaders. Then a New Orleans writer, George Washington Cable, published two books—*Old Creole Days* (1880), a collection of stories, and *The Grandissimes* (1881), a novel—that had a curious impact. Cable portrayed the Creoles realistically—not as exclusively wealthy or expensively educated aristocrats, but as the mixture of classes and human types he saw around him. Most readers found Cable's portrait of the Creoles sympathetic, but Creoles on many levels were outraged by his suggestion that they were not all members of the social aristocracy. A violent controversy developed over what Creole culture really was, and as a result Creole culture was defended and, in the process, defined as simply what was indigenous to New Orleans. Even some of the more recently settled Americans rose to defend the Creole heritage, which they sensed was the very spirit of the city that had become their home.*

Just about this time the Cotton Exposition of 1884-1885 took place in New Orleans and helped to solidify the movement of self-definition, once and for all time establishing the unique identity of New Orleans as "Creole." Many groups and individuals prepared souvenir books, pamphlets, and guides for visitors to the Exposition. William H. Coleman, a New York publisher who loved New Orleans, persuaded Cable and a gifted young writer named Lafcadio Hearn, then living in the city, to collaborate with others in the writing of the *Historical Sketch Book and Guide to New Orleans.* Coleman's *Guide* covered all the good eating New Orleans offered at all prices—from a ten-course meal including oysters, turtle soup, broiled pompano, beef or game with two vegetables, a second entrée of duck or turkey, a soufflé, a pastry, dessert, and coffee at one of the grand hotels such as the St. Charles, for twenty dollars a person, which in 1885 the wealthy could enjoy, to a seven-course meal at a first class restaurant for six dollars plus wine. And for an ordinary dinner,

*For a full discussion of the origins and historical development of the term "Creole," see Joseph G. Tregle, Jr., "Early New Orleans Society: A Reappraisal," *Journal of Southern History,* 18 (February, 1952), 20-36.

the *Guide* noted: "A hungry man, dropping casually into a restaurant, should take a soup and some fish; then an *entrée*, say a sweetbread or a lamb chop; then say a spring chicken, or roast beef, or roast mutton or veal, with one or two dishes of vegetables. For dessert, some fruit or jelly, and cheese, and a cup of coffee. With a half bottle of claret, this would cost from $1.50 to $2.50."

In the same year two cookbooks were published that reflected the city's private eating: *The Christian Women's Exchange Creole Cookery Book* and Lafcadio Hearn's *La Cuisine Creole*. Both books emphasized dishes indigenous to New Orleans, dishes prepared in homes or served in the eating houses and market restaurants—and from that moment Creole cuisine became fashionable. In wealthy New Orleans homes most of the older cooks were blacks, whose ancestors had contributed some of the earliest important Creole dishes, such as gumbo. These black cooks had inherited a love of spicy food and were adept at preparing the old dishes; now they were encouraged by their employers to follow the "new" fashion. Frequently, when wealthy New Orleanians dined out, they would taste a dish they liked and then transmit it to their black cooks at home with instructions from a cookbook. Black cooks moved freely from job to job, in homes, boardinghouses, and cafés, cooking vigorous versions of favorite local specialties; their skill was the most important thread of continuity in the fabric of Creole cuisine.

Finally, in 1900, New Orleans' leading newspaper, the *Picayune*, published *The Picayune Creole Cookbook*, a collection of recipes interspersed with commentary on the character of New Orleans society at the turn of the century. The group that compiled the recipes, moved by the new spirit of the era, identified the food New Orleanians ate as Creole. They included a number of dishes obviously imported from France well after 1803, as well as recipes copied directly from French cookbooks and virtually unknown in New Orleans. However, despite such flaws, the book was a landmark in the history of New Orleans cuisine; it erased the dividing line between "downtown" and "uptown" cooking and made the term "Creole" synonymous with New Orleans.

Today, as anyone who has visited New Orleans knows, Creole cuisine is still very much alive. Of course, many of the special dishes that have been a tradition in local households haven't been written down and are disappearing. And in some restaurants fine local dishes have been so carelessly or badly prepared, with inferior ingredients, that visitors who expected so much of our famous cooking have often been sadly disappointed. They have also had little success in duplicating at home dishes they enjoyed here. New Orleanians have always loved to cook, to eat, and to talk about food, but they have seldom been moved to explain it. Older local recipe books abound with charmingly vague instructions—"Take a nice fish, season to taste, cook until done, and serve."

Because we love this food, we wanted to translate to paper accurate recipes for the dishes that seem to us to represent the best of Creole cooking. It is a style of cooking that has few rigid rules and, as you will see, often contains many different versions of the same dish. In the final analysis, we have had to let our own taste and taste memory be our guides in the selection and conception of the dishes included here. We'd travel eighty-five miles to taste a filé gumbo that a friend from the Cajun country told us was the best in the world, and if we loved it as much as he did, we'd cook it again and again until it tasted like the one we sampled; we'd prepare many different versions of favorite local specialties and work out a careful recipe for the version we liked best; we'd offer our recipes to friends so that they could cook them and see if the recipes worked for them in their own kitchens. And so this book has evolved, by a slow process but one we feel gives dependable results. We've tried to keep in mind, too, the many people who have tasted something superb in New Orleans and want to duplicate it when they get back home; whenever possible we have suggested good alternatives for ingredients that are only available locally, alternatives that work very well and produce good New Orleans style dishes.

The style of Creole and Cajun cooking is what makes it special; the techniques are the most essential ingredients. Once you understand these techniques—and we have tried to make them very clear in these recipes—you will enjoy preparing this food and also creating variations of your own, in the true spirit of Creole cooking. We hope that you will come to love our food as we do and to share with us the excitement of New Orleans eating, from gumbos and jambalayas to oysters Rockefeller and red beans and rice.

DEFINITIONS AND SPECIAL INGREDIENTS

ABSINTHE: An anise-flavored liquor banned in 1912 because the wormwood used in its distillation was judged dangerous. Absinthe is now used as a generic term for any liqueur with an anise or licorice flavor. Herbsaint, Pernod, Ojen, and Raki are the most common ones.

AMANDINE, ALMONDINE: A style of cooking using toasted almonds. For examples, see Amandine Sauce (page 114), Trout Amandine (page 87).

ANDOUILLE: A local pork sausage. See page 139.

BOUDIN: A local rice sausage. See page 140.

BOUILLI: Meat used to prepare soup, which is then served as a separate course. See Vegetable Soup (page 25) and Boiled Brisket of Beef (page 124).

BUSTERS, BUSTER CRABS: The crab at the point it molts its hard shell and begins to grow a new one; frequently used to denote any very small soft shell crab.

BUTTER: All recipes calling for butter in this book require lightly salted stick butter; sweet butter is made differently and should not be substituted. Clarified butter is not used in New Orleans cooking; the milk solids that brown during cooking are an important part of New Orleans meunière sauce.

CANE SYRUP: Brown sugar cane syrup made and used locally in place of maple syrup.

CAYENNE: See Pepper and Tabasco, below.

CHICORY, CHICORY COFFEE: The chicory in New Orleans chicory coffee comes from a particular white chicory root and is different from the chicory used as a vegetable. The chicory used in coffee is dried, roasted, and ground in the same manner as coffee beans. See New Orleans Chicory Coffee (page 237).

CORN FLOUR: See Fish-Fri.

CRABS, HARD SHELL AND SOFT SHELL: Crabs evolve from soft shell crabs into hard shell crabs. They molt, lose their shells, then begin anew to grow a hard shell. In Louisiana they are caught in either stage and cooked in a variety of ways.

*CRAB AND SHRIMP BOIL:** A bouquet garni of spices for seafood court-bouillons; it is packaged and sold in New Orleans in net bags or in concentrated

*If you cannot obtain crab boil, add a mixture of the following ingredients to 4 quarts of water before boiling:

1 c. salt
Juice of 2 large, fresh lemons (about 6 Tbs.)
¾ tsp. Tabasco
1 tsp. allspice
10 whole cloves
4 sprigs fresh thyme or 1 tsp. dried thyme
5 whole bay leaves, broken in half
1 tsp. celery seed
½ tsp. dry mustard
1½ tsp. freshly ground black pepper

liquid form, and is used to flavor the water in which crabs, shrimp, or crawfish are boiled.

CRAWFISH, CRAYFISH: A small edible crustacean. The universal local pronunciation is "crawfish," and this has become the preferred spelling. Elsewhere "crayfish" is the accepted spelling, and the word is pronounced accordingly. In French, *écrivisses.*

CREOLE (adjectives): Locally used to indicate the finest regionally raised products, such as Creole garlic (extra large pods, highly pungent), Creole tomatoes (large, ripe, very juicy), etc. Generally used to describe a style of cooking associated with New Orleans (see Introduction).

CREOLE CREAM CHEESE: The only indigenous New Orleans cheese, made somewhat like cottage cheese and packaged in similar containers. The curds are pressed together and packed solid, then surrounded by heavy cream. See Creole Cream Cheese Evangeline (page 198).

CREOLE MUSTARD: A distinctive, locally made mustard using spicier and darker mustard seeds than average; the seeds are marinated before preparation. See the Shopping Guide (pages 239-40) for suppliers.

CREOLE SAUSAGE: Any locally made smoked or hot sausage. See Chapter Nine, Meats and Sausages.

CREOLE TOMATOES: The preferred locally grown premium tomato, resembling beefsteak and Jersey tomatoes.

ÉCRIVISSES: French for "crawfish."

ETOUFFÉE: Étouffée is a method of cooking something smothered in a blanket of chopped vegetables over a low flame in a tightly covered vessel—popular in Louisiana Cajun country for making crawfish or shrimp.

FILÉ: A powder made from dried wild sassafras leaves used as a flavoring and a last minute thickening agent in one form of gumbo, gumbo filé. See Chapter One, Gumbos and Soups.

FISH-FRI, FISH-FRY: Pure corn flour is marketed in New Orleans under this trade name, which has also become the local generic name.

FRENCH, NEW ORLEANS (AND CAJUN ENGLISH): New Orleans is primarily a French city, and its language, both spoken and written, reflects an intermingling of French and English. French names often mean different things here (see Meunière Sauce, page 113) and many of them are pronounced in ways odd to the French ear (CHAR-ters Street for Chartres Street). French words which are part of common New Orleans usage are not italicized. In this book we give the common New Orleans names for dishes and ingredients; these names may be French, English, or a mixture of the two.

FRENCH BREAD: The local generic name for New Orleans' version of French bread, prepared in loaves from one to nine feet long.

GREEN ONIONS: See Shallots (New Orleans), below.

GUMBO CRABS: Hard shell crabs too scrawny to yield good lump crabmeat, packaged and sold for making gumbo as gumbo crabs.

JAMBALAYA: A group of Spanish Cajun rice dishes, made with chicken, ham, and shellfish. See Chapter Two, Red Beans and Rice! and Jambalaya.

LAGNIAPPE: An old Creole word (pronounced *lah-nyahp*) for "something extra." Soup meat is the lagniappe from the preparation of vegetable soup; the thirteenth oyster you get when you order a dozen is lagniappe.

MEUNIÈRE: A New Orleans butter sauce resembling a French *beurre noisette*; also, another New Orleans sauce with a beef stock roux. Both are used on trout and shellfish. See Trout Meunière, Galatoire Style (page 86), and Trout Meunière, Arnaud Style (page 86); see also Meunière Sauce (page 113).

MIRLITON: A local vegetable resembling a pale green squash, also occasionally called a vegetable pear.

MUSTARD: See Creole Mustard.

OKRA: A vegetable locally popular for making gumbo and also eaten as a vegetable. Originally imported from Africa, where it is called "*gombo*."

OLIVE OIL: We use a French olive oil, Plagniol, which is lighter than Italian, Spanish, or Greek olive oils. Plagniol is marketed nationally; it can also be ordered from sources listed in the Shopping Guide (pages 239-40).

ORANGE FLOWER WATER: A derivative of the orange tree blossom essential in making the authentic Ramos (New Orleans) gin fizz. See Ramos Gin Fizz (page 235).

PEPPER: All the recipes use white and black pepper freshly ground from pepper mills. White pepper is milder than black and invisible when ground into most food; it is therefore excellent for light-colored sauces. We use telicherry pepper wherever black is called for; pungent, aromatic, and less sharp than many other black peppers, it is marketed nationally in fancy food stores. Cayenne or red pepper is only sold already ground or in liquid form as Tabasco. It is important that cayenne or Tabasco used in cooking be fresh.

PICKLED PORK, SWEET PICKLED PORK: A locally popular seasoning meat sold packaged in supermarkets and used for gumbos and bean dishes. It is fatty pork shoulder marinated in brine. *The Picayune Creole Cookbook* gave instructions for preparing a year's supply; twenty-five pounds of pork, "which should be pickled about twenty hours after killing," and which took "ten to twelve days" to prepare. Practically no one makes it at home any more. If pickled pork is not available in your area, substitute salt pork, slab bacon, country or Smithfield ham or bacon, and eliminate all other salt from the recipe.

PONTCHARTRAIN: A culinary term for seafood with a cooked soft shell crab on top of the dish as a garnish. See Redfish Pontchartrain (page 96).

POOR BOY: The generic name for the standard New Orleans sandwich made with French bread. See Roast Beef Poor Boy (page 135).

RICE: The rice universally used in local dishes is long grain white rice, which cooks up fluffy and is widely available nationally. Most locally used rice is Louisiana grown. Quick and instant rice are not recommended; the cooked texture is different and the time saved is not appreciable.

ROUX: The flour and butter (or oil) sauce that is the basis of the heartier New Orleans French dishes. See the introduction to Sauces (page 111).

SAUSAGE: See Creole Sausage, above.

SCALLIONS: See Shallots (New Orleans), below.

SEASONING HAM: The bits and pieces left over after a ham has been prepared for market are packaged and sold in New Orleans as seasoning ham, for many bean and other dishes. Because these scraps of ham would otherwise be wasted, they are sold more cheaply. Where seasoning ham is called for, any baked ham cut into pieces can be used. Country hams are apt to be too strong.

SHALLOTS (NEW ORLEANS): A linguistic confusion. What we call "shallots" in New Orleans are called "scallions" or "green onions" everywhere else. In the recipes we specify New Orleans shallots—that is, scallions—to avoid any confusion.

SHALLOTS (FRENCH): "Shallots" outside New Orleans means French shallots, tiny bulbs with a flavor somewhere between small white onions and chives. Sold in fancy food stores nationally, they are harder to obtain in New Orleans and much more rarely used here than in the rest of the country. French shallots are grown in New Jersey and sold extensively by mail.

SHRIMP BOIL: See Crab and Shrimp Boil, above.

SWEET PICKLED PORK: See Pickled Pork, above.

TABASCO: A nationally marketed liquid form of cayenne made from red peppers grown on Avery Island, Louisiana, and bottled by the McIlhenny Company. Tabasco and cayenne are specifically indicated in the recipes; they serve the same function but are used in different quantities and cook differently.

TOMATOES: See Creole Tomatoes, above.

YAM: A highly prized, locally grown strain of sweet potato. In much of the South the word "yam" is used interchangeably with "sweet potato."

USEFUL COOKING TECHNIQUES

These techniques are described in detail within individual recipes. The following is designed as a helpful summary:

BOILING: When boiling seafood, first prepare the courtbouillon with its spices and let it come to a boil. Boil about 10 minutes before putting in the shellfish. This enables the seasoning to permeate the shellfish without overcooking them. Crabs are cooked for 15 to 20 minutes, shrimp 5 to 7, and crawfish for about 10 minutes.

BROILING: One of the best ways to prepare fish, if properly done. Simple broiling requires a preheated oven and a buttered broiling pan. The fish should be basted with butter, placed between 3½ to 4 inches from the heat, and cooked no more than 5 to 7 minutes. Only very large fish whose fillets are quite thick require longer cooking or need to be turned over during broiling.

CHOPPING: There is no real shortcut to chopping vegetables, and they cannot be chopped hours ahead without losing much of their flavor and aroma. Blenders tend to puree rather than chop, and mechanical spring-mounted devices require too much precutting to make them real time savers. All you need is a large wooden surface and a sharp cleaver or large knife. The Chinese cleaver, which can be held with both hands, works very well.

FRYING: Frying has an ignoble reputation in cooking that it does not deserve. It can produce very light food if you follow some simple rules. Use an electric deep fryer or a deep electric frying pan with a thermostatic control. It is essential to maintain the correct degree of heat, 375° for most foods. (Even a bit below that will give you the greasy food too many restaurants serve.) With the new polyunsaturated vegetable oils, frying is one of the healthiest ways of cooking. The cooking oil must be clean, at least 2 to 3 inches deep in the pan, and should fill the fryer no more than half full to allow for bubbling up. Frying is best done in small batches to prevent radical lowering of the oil temperature when the food is added.

Vegetable oil works quite well; peanut oil is more fattening but has a fine flavor; lard also has an excellent flavor, but is not markedly better than pure vegetable oil. Butter cannot be used for frying no matter what any cookbook says—it simply will not maintain a proper frying temperature without burning.* After use, the cooking oil should be allowed to cool, then strained through cheesecloth or a fine mesh strainer, covered, and refrigerated. Add a little fresh oil (about 1/3 cup) each time you fry to keep it fresh, and discard the entire batch after using it ten or twelve times or when it gets very dark in color.

POACHING: Cooking in a small amount of seasoned liquid at a low boil. Used for eggs, fish.

SAUTÉING: Sautéing means frying slowly in a small amount of fat, oil, or butter, a perfect way to brown or glaze (just short of browning) vegetables and some shellfish, especially shrimp. One can combine cooking oils—butter and vegetable oil, bacon drippings and oil or butter—to vary the flavor. An all-butter mixture tends to burn more easily than one mixed with oil. (Soft crabs can be sautéed, but they will be less crisp than deep fried crabs, and much oilier. Sautéed fish will fall apart before becoming crisp and chicken will not cook through.) We find sautéed food much richer than fried, since at lower temperatures more cooking oil is absorbed; high temperatures seal and prevent absorption, so that there is less taste of oil in the food. The special flavor of butter and oil, often used with onions, other vegetables, and seasoning, is meant to permeate sautéed food; frequent stirring, preferably with a wooden spoon or spatula, is important to distribute the flavor evenly and to prevent scorching.

SMOTHERING: Smothering, a technique often used in New Orleans French as well as in Southern cooking, means cooking slowly in a covered pot or skillet, with a little liquid added to a sautéed mixture. Smothered greens are simply washed and shaken lightly before cooking; the water that clings to them provides sufficient liquid for cooking. Smothering produces a tender dish permeated with whatever seasonings are used, and is a particularly effective technique for cooking chicken, meat, and vegetables.

UTENSILS

POTS: The battery of pots and saucepans in local kitchens can be prodigious. Several pots and saucepans of varying sizes are essential for Creole and Cajun cooking. In recipes calling for rouxs and sautéed ingredients, since it is difficult to empty a pan, reserve its contents, and use the pot again for another stage of the cooking, using separate pans is more efficient. Still popular in New Orleans are the old iron pots, some of enormous size, that have been handed down through generations of family cooks. New iron pots are inexpensive, heavy, and easily available in hardware stores. Except for their tendency to discolor delicate sauces, they are ideal for New Orleans cooking. Our own favorite cooking utensils are copper lined with stainless steel; they hold the heat as evenly and are easier to care for than tin-lined copper, which has to be relined periodically. European pots and skillets of cast iron coated with porcelain are excellent (Le Creuset, Descoware, and so forth); they are sufficiently heavy, wash easily, and won't discolor some foods the way iron or aluminum

*In some of the old cookbooks butter is called for in frying directions. We suspect the writers simply felt butter sounded more respectable than lard, which was generally used—just as they sometimes said "sauté" when they meant "fry."

will. For pot dinners of large proportions a heavy aluminum pot (professional weight, indicated by the NSF rating on the bottom) is ideal.

FRYERS: As already noted, electric fryers and deep skillets with accurate thermostats are best. Nonelectric fryers work well, but the task of keeping a manual thermometer attached and making sure the oil temperature doesn't change demands a great deal of attention.

PEPPER MILLS: Among the least expensive of investments are good pepper mills. We keep one for white pepper and one for black. Using a pepper mill ensures fresh pepper each time.

KNIVES: We prefer stainless steel knives to carbon steel, since our climate creates a considerable rust problem. Contrary to widely published opinions, we have found that stainless steel Sabatier and Henckels knives work just as well as carbon steel, and can be cleaned in a dishwasher. All knives used in cooking should be sharpened on a sharpening steel just before use. The most useful sizes include 8- and 10-inch chef's knives, a Chinese cleaver for chopping, and a long serrated French bread knife.

SPATULAS AND SPOONS: A nice selection of inexpensive wooden spatulas and spoons is very useful for a variety of cooking tasks.

MISCELLANEOUS: Two or three ladles; tongs; hand graters (the French Mouli is excellent); a long-handled wooden mallet; mortar and pestle; skewers; a hand rotary beater; several wire whisks; an electric blender; mixing bowls of stainless steel or porcelain (plastic tends to retain food odors); a manual or electric meat grinder; a sieve; an 8-inch black iron crêpe pan (measured across the top) and a flambé pan for preparing crêpe dishes; a brûlot set for café brûlot. The usual assortment of serving dishes, soufflé dishes, and baking dishes is useful.

THE SPICE SHELF

MOST WIDELY USED PEPPERS: powdered cayenne, Tabasco (liquid), crushed red pepper pods, chili powder, black peppercorns (telicherry), white peppercorns

SPICES AND HERBS: whole bay leaves, sweet basil, dried thyme, oregano, dried rosemary leaves, dried marjoram, ground mace, whole cloves, whole allspice, ground allspice, nutmeg, ground mustard, gumbo filé

FREQUENTLY USED: ground bay leaves, ground thyme, fines herbes, ground rosemary, ground marjoram, tarragon leaves, ground cardamom, coriander, cloves, cinnamon, ground cumin

OCCASIONALLY USED: chopped chives, chervil, turmeric, sage, saffron, whole dill seed, caraway seeds, celery seed, anise seeds, cream of tartar, dried ground chicory, capers

BASIC MIXTURES: crab and shrimp boil (Yogi or Zatarain's), Worcestershire sauce (Lea & Perrins), French wine vinegar, olive oil (Plagniol), orange flower water, Pickapeppa Sauce, beef tea concentrate (Bovril or Wilson), bouillon cubes, Creole mustard, prepared horseradish

NOTE: Bottled spices deteriorate once they are opened, at varying rates. Check your spices fairly regularly; if their aroma is faint, throw them away and buy fresh ones. Stale spices add nothing to one's cooking except perhaps a slightly bitter, stale taste.

CULINARY NOTES

RECIPE PORTIONS AND ADAPTABILITY OF COURSES

Portions are generally given for four, and unless otherwise indicated, dividing the recipes in half or multiplying them should cause no problems. When doubling or tripling quantities for pot dinners, increase the total cooking time by 15 to 30 minutes. In certain recipes we have indicated individual portions or portions for two, since this is the simplest way to approach them.

We have not made the usual distinctions between appetizers, entrées, and side dishes in organizing this cookbook; in New Orleans, courses are often interchangeable. Oysters Rockefeller make a marvelous main course, as well as a grand appetizer; red beans and rice are often served as a side dish, as well as a complete pot dinner; gumbos are used as soup courses and also as full meals. We seem to eat things we like, when we want them, and in portions that suit our mood.

1

GUMBOS AND SOUPS

The steaming aroma of fresh caught crabs, shrimp, and oysters; the smell of butter and flour browning slowly in a large iron pot over an open fire; the sizzle of freshly chopped onions, green peppers, and "shallots" added at just the moment the flour and butter turn a rich brown; the scent of chicken or duck slowly cooking into the mixture of onions, vegetables, and roux; the taste of good fresh okra or exotic sassafras—this adds up to a good Louisiana gumbo. Pour the finished gumbo over hot, fluffy, long grain white rice and serve the bowls steaming.

There are many varieties of gumbo, but every kind uses certain fundamental cooking techniques. First, gumbos all have a roux base, a mixture of butter and flour slowly cooked to a rich brown, which gives gumbo much of its characteristic thick texture and smoky taste. And further, all gumbos are thickened with okra or with filé. In fact, it is the okra that gives gumbo its name—*gombo* being an African word for okra. Filé is a powder made from dried sassafras leaves originally discovered by the Choctaw Indians. In New Orleans the most popular gumbo is one made with seafood and okra;

the Cajun favorite is oyster and sausage filé gumbo.

Gumbo seems to please everyone, perhaps because it blends and balances all the varied ethnic influences that have shaped present-day Louisiana cooking—the Spanish love of rice and spices, the Southern fondness for okra, the French technique of making roux, the Caribbean gift for combining seasonings. Readily available local ingredients such as okra, filé, and rice (Louisiana's basic cash crop), along with whatever the hunter or fisherman catches, are used, all combined in a dish infinitely variable in its ingredients and adaptable in its uses. A simple Sunday supper, a one course pot dinner, a fine first course—gumbo has remained a favorite of the rich as well as the poor. A noted society banquet held in New Orleans in 1803 featured twenty-four different kinds of gumbo. Today the most common gumbo ingredients are crabs, shrimp, chicken, sausage, and game. But Cajuns happily use squirrel and armadillo, and a Frenchman recently settled in New Orleans is working on a snail gumbo. Clams, mussels, conch, abalone, venison, king crab are all potential elements for exciting new gumbos.

We have selected some of our favorite gumbos; preparing them will give you an idea of how gumbo is made. Once you get the hang of it, try some variations of your own. A local Creole cook may tell you that your gumbo variation just isn't the real thing; she also says that to her next door neighbor who uses filé instead of okra, shrimp instead of crab, or fails to put some fresh oysters in the gumbo just before serving. There are really no hard and fast rules beyond the basics. All you need is a good roux, some okra or filé, a mound of freshly chopped vegetables, and imagination, to make this glorious soul-satisfying dish.

BOILED RICE

Firm, fluffy, freshly prepared boiled rice is the essential accompaniment to so many of our dishes that we felt this recipe belonged first. Rice is served with gumbos, bean dishes, crawfish bisque, étouffées, and many other dishes. Preparing it this way takes only 15 minutes, very little more than any precooked convenience rice, and gives you the superb texture and flavor only freshly cooked rice has. The tiny amount of butter keeps the grains from sticking together. *(for 4)*

---

1 c. long grain white rice
2 c. cold water
1 tsp. salt
1 tsp. salt butter

Combine all the ingredients in a heavy 3-quart saucepan with a tight-fitting cover and bring to a boil over high heat. Stir once with a fork, then cover tightly and reduce the heat to very low. Cook covered for exactly 15 minutes. Do not lift the cover during cooking. Remove the pan from the heat, uncover, and fluff the rice gently with a fork.

Note: The rice will keep warm enough for serving second helpings if you use a heavy saucepan and keep it covered after serving. Another way to keep the extra rice warm is to put the covered saucepan in a preheated 175° oven. Do not keep it warm for more than about 25 minutes; if you need more, make it from scratch.

SHRIMP AND CRAB OKRA GUMBO

The basic New Orleans seafood gumbo. Gumbo crabs are the hard shell crabs we use for cooking; any hard shell crab available in your area can be used. Whether you eat the cooked crab served in the gumbo is a matter of taste—some of us do and some of us don't. A delightful and slightly extravagant variation is to use lump crabmeat in addition to or as a substitute for hard shell crabs. We like chopped smoked sausage in this gumbo because it adds a fine, smoky flavor. Reserve half of the shrimp, and if you use it, half the lump crabmeat, then add them just a few minutes before the end of cooking time. This way your gumbo will have both the cooked-in taste of shrimp and also some good firm shrimp for eating. Be sure to have everything else ready before you start the roux because you can't do all that chopping and tend the roux at the same time. *(for 8 or more)*

THE GUMBO BASE

2 c. chopped onion
¾ c. chopped green pepper
⅓ c. thinly sliced green shallot (scallion) tops
2 Tbs. finely minced fresh parsley
1 Tbs. finely minced garlic
1½ c. coarsely chopped Creole (beefsteak, Jersey) tomatoes (2 medium)
2 Creole (Polish, French garlic) smoked sausages, chopped fine (page 23)
2 lb. whole fresh shrimp, peeled and deveined
1 lb. gumbo crabs, broken in half
2 lb. fresh okra, stems and tips removed, sliced ⅜ inch thick

THE ROUX

¾ c. vegetable oil
¾ c. flour

THE LIQUID AND THE SEASONINGS

2½ qt. cold water
3 whole bay leaves, crushed
1½ tsp. dried thyme
5 tsp. salt
1¼ tsp. freshly ground black pepper
¼ tsp. cayenne
4 tsp. fresh lemon juice
10 whole allspice
½ tsp. mace
8 whole cloves

After you have assembled the ingredients for the gumbo base, heat the oil in a heavy 7- to 8-quart pot or kettle over medium heat. Make the roux by gradually adding the flour to the oil, stirring constantly. Cook over low heat, always stirring, until a medium brown roux is formed. (This will take from 20 to 30 minutes. The roux should be the color of pecan shells or hazelnuts.) Immediately add the onion, green pepper, shallot tops, parsley, and garlic. Continue cooking for about 10 minutes longer, stirring constantly; the chopped vegetables should be lightly browned at this point. Add the chopped tomatoes and smoked sausage and mix thoroughly. Add 2 quarts of the cold water, 1 pound of the raw shrimp, the crabs, the okra, and the seasonings. Raise the heat slightly and bring the mixture to a boil, then lower the heat and simmer for 1 hour. Stir from time to time and scrape down the sides and across the bottom of the pot with a wooden spoon or spatula to prevent scorching. At the end of the hour, still keeping the gumbo at a simmer, add the remaining ½ quart water and stir. Remove the pot from the heat and let stand at room temperature.

Before serving, bring the gumbo to a boil and add the remaining pound of shrimp. Simmer just until the shrimp turn pink, about 10 to 12 minutes. Stir thoroughly, turn off the heat, and cover the pot. Let it sit, covered, for about 15 minutes before serving. Serve by ladling the gumbo over mounds of boiled rice in gumbo bowls or deep soup bowls.

CHICKEN AND SAUSAGE FILÉ GUMBO

One of the richest Cajun gumbos, this makes a hearty and unusual dinner. Be sure to include plenty of sausage from the pot along with a piece of chicken in each serving.

(for 8)

THE GUMBO BASE

1¼ lb. Creole (Polish, French garlic) smoked sausage, sliced ½ inch thick (page 23)
½ lb. lean baked ham, cut into ½-inch cubes
1 fryer, 3½ to 4 lb., cut up
½ c. chopped green pepper
½ c. thinly sliced green shallot (scallion) tops
2 Tbs. finely minced parsley
1 Tbs. finely minced garlic
2 c. chopped onion

THE ROUX

⅔ c. vegetable oil
½ c. flour

THE LIQUID AND THE SEASONINGS

2 qt. cold water
3 tsp. salt
1 tsp. freshly ground black pepper
⅛ tsp. cayenne
1¼ tsp. dried thyme
3 whole bay leaves, crushed
2½ to 3 Tbs. filé powder

After assembling the ingredients for the gumbo base, in a heavy 7- to 8-quart pot or kettle heat the oil over high heat. Brown the chicken parts in the hot oil, turning them several times to ensure even browning. Remove to a heated platter and place in a preheated 175° oven to keep warm. Make the roux by gradually adding the flour to the oil, stirring constantly. Reduce the heat and cook, always stirring, until a medium brown roux (the color of hazelnuts) is formed. When the roux reaches the right color, immediately add the sausage, ham, onion, green pepper, shallot tops, parsley, and garlic. Continue cooking over low heat for 10 minutes more, still stirring, then add ¼ cup of the water, the reserved chicken pieces, and all the seasonings except the filé powder; mix thoroughly. Gradually stir in the rest of the water. Raise the heat and bring to a boil, then lower the heat and simmer the gumbo for 50 minutes to 1 hour, or until the chicken parts are tender. Stir frequently, taking care not to break the pieces of chicken. Remove the pot from the heat and let the simmer die down, then add the filé powder and stir.

Let the gumbo stand in the pot for 5 minutes after adding the filé, then serve in gumbo bowls or deep soup bowls over boiled rice.

OYSTER AND SAUSAGE FILÉ GUMBO

Oysters and smoked sausage are an irresistible flavor combination. We use Creole smoked sausage (see page 138, if you want to make your own), but any country or smoked sausage may be substituted. Polish sausage and French garlic sausage are ideal. (Italian sausage tends to be too sweet.) This gumbo can be prepared a day in advance, but since oysters and filé cannot be reheated, simply add the oysters and filé just before serving. *(for 8 or more)*

THE GUMBO BASE

2 c. chopped onion
⅔ c. chopped green pepper
½ c. thinly sliced green shallot (scallion) tops
1 Tbs. finely minced garlic
2 Tbs. fresh parsley, finely minced
½ lb. lean baked ham, cut into ½-inch cubes
1 lb. Creole (Polish, French garlic) smoked sausage, half cut into ½-inch cubes and half sliced ½ inch thick (page 23)

THE ROUX

6 Tbs. salt butter
¼ c. vegetable oil
½ c. flour

THE LIQUID AND THE SEASONINGS

2 qt. cold water
3½ tsp. salt
1¼ tsp. freshly ground black pepper
⅛ tsp. cayenne
1 tsp. dried thyme
3 whole bay leaves, crushed
⅛ tsp. mace
2½ to 3 Tbs. filé powder

---

1 pt. fresh shucked oysters (about 2 doz. medium-sized) and their liquor (about ½ c.)

After assembling the ingredients for the gumbo base, make the roux by melting the butter in a 7- to 8-quart pot or kettle over low heat. Add the oil and mix well. Heat for 2 minutes more, then gradually add the flour, stirring constantly. Cook over low heat, always stirring, until a medium brown roux (the color of hazelnuts) is formed. As soon as the roux reaches the right color, quickly add the onion, green pepper, shallot tops, and garlic. Stir thoroughly, then add ¼ cup of the water, the diced ham, and the diced ½ pound of Creole sausage. Mix thoroughly and continue browning over low heat, stirring constantly, for 10 minutes more. Add the parsley, oyster liquor, the ½ pound sliced Creole sausage, and all seasonings except the filé powder. Gradually pour in the remaining water. Bring the gumbo to a boil, lower the heat, and simmer for 1 hour, stirring frequently. At the end of the hour add the oysters and cook for 4 to 5 minutes more, just until the oysters begin to curl at the edges. Remove the pot from the heat and let the simmer die down, then add the filé powder and mix well.

Let the gumbo stand for 5 minutes after the filé powder has been added, then mix thoroughly and serve in gumbo bowls or deep soup bowls over boiled rice.

SHRIMP FILÉ GUMBO

The richest, smokiest, most delicious shrimp filé gumbo we ever tasted was served in the very seedy coffee shop of a decidedly unprepossessing hotel in a small Cajun town. There we learned the secret of so many superb Cajun gumbos—the chicken cooked into the base. You remove the chicken before serving the gumbo, but its aroma remains to permeate the gumbo and the shrimp. Chill the leftover chicken along with about 1/3 cup of sausage from the gumbo. It makes a marvelous meal in itself (see page 147), the perfect example of what we call "lagniappe." Reheat it in a covered saucepan with about 2 tablespoons of water over low heat until warmed through, or serve it chilled. *(for 8 or more)*

THE GUMBO BASE

1 lb. Creole (Polish, French garlic) smoked sausage, sliced 1/4 inch thick (page 23)
2 c. chopped onion
2/3 c. chopped green peppers
1/2 c. thinly sliced green shallot (scallion) tops
2 Tbs. finely minced fresh parsley
1 Tbs. finely minced garlic
1 fryer, 3 to 3 1/2 lb., cut up
2 lb. whole fresh shrimp, peeled and deveined

THE ROUX

2/3 c. vegetable oil
2/3 c. flour

THE LIQUID AND THE SEASONINGS

2 qt. cold water
3 1/2 tsp. salt
1 1/4 tsp. freshly ground black pepper
1/8 tsp. cayenne
1 tsp. dried thyme
3 whole bay leaves, crushed
2 1/2 to 3 Tbs. filé powder

After assembling the ingredients for the gumbo base, heat the oil in a heavy 7- to 8-quart pot or kettle over high heat. Brown the chicken parts in the hot oil, turning several times to ensure even browning. When the chicken is brown, remove it to a heated platter and place, uncovered, in a preheated 175° oven to keep it warm. Make the roux by gradually adding the flour to the oil in the pot, stirring constantly. Cook over low heat until a dark brown roux (the color of milk chocolate) is formed. When the roux reaches the right color, quickly add the sausage, onion, green pepper, shallot tops, parsley, and garlic. Continue cooking over low heat for 10 minutes more, stirring constantly. Then add 1/4 cup of the water, the browned chicken parts, and all the seasonings except the filé powder; mix gently but thoroughly. Keeping the heat at low, gradually add the rest of the water and bring the gumbo to a boil, stirring gently. When it boils, reduce the heat to low and simmer for about 45 minutes, or until the chicken is quite tender.

Remove the chicken and some of the sausage slices with a slotted spoon to a deep bowl. Cover the bowl with plastic wrap and refrigerate for another meal. Add the shrimp to the gumbo and cook for about 8 minutes longer. Remove the pot from the heat and let the simmer die down. Add the filé powder and stir. Let the gumbo stand in the pot for 5 minutes after adding the filé, then serve in gumbo bowls or deep soup bowls over boiled rice.

GUMBO Z'HERBES (GREEN GUMBO)

Gumbo z'herbes breaks all the rules of gumbo. It uses neither okra nor filé; it is the only gumbo in which the roux is not prepared first; originally it contained no meat, seafood, or game.

A Lenten dish, it was traditionally served on Good Friday. Legend had it that you would make as many friends as the number of different greens you put in the gumbo. Seven greens, seven new friends. The flavor that comes from combining many different greens is what makes this gumbo so delicious—the number is unimportant. No longer exclusively a Lenten dish, gumbo z'herbes is often prepared with meat, as in the recipe we give here. We include it because it is good to eat and because the first time we served it we made seven new friends. *(for 8 or more)*

GREENS (AS MANY OF THESE AS ARE AVAILABLE: A MINIMUM OF 5 IS ADEQUATE, 7 OR 8 ARE PERFECT)

1 bunch collard greens
1 bunch mustard greens
1 bunch turnip greens
1 bunch shallots (scallions)
1 bunch parsley
1 bunch watercress
1 bunch spinach
1 bunch beet tops
1 bunch radish tops
1 small head green cabbage
1 bunch chicory
1 bunch carrot tops

THE GUMBO BASE

1c. chopped onion
½ lb. lean baked ham, cut into ½-inch cubes
½ lb. Creole (Polish, French garlic) smoked sausage, cut into ½-inch cubes*
½ lb. lean veal, cut into ½-inch cubes
1 large ham bone, sawed into 3- to 4-inch lengths

THE ROUX

½ c. vegetable oil
⅔ c. flour

THE LIQUID AND THE SEASONINGS

2 qt. plus ⅓ c. cold water
1 tsp. salt
¼ tsp. freshly ground black pepper
⅛ tsp. cayenne
2 whole bay leaves, crushed
½ tsp. dried thyme
½ tsp. dried marjoram
2 whole cloves
6 whole allspice

Wash all the greens thoroughly, taking care to remove all sand and to trim off any tough stem ends or discolored outer leaves. Place the washed greens in a colander and rinse under cold running water. Let the excess water drain off, then shake the colander lightly. Place the damp greens in a heavy 3- to 4-quart saucepan, add the ⅓ cup cold water, and turn the heat to high. When the liquid at the bottom of the pan begins to boil, cover the pan tightly, reduce the heat to medium, and cook the greens for 12 to 15 minutes, or until just tender. Remove the pan from the heat and drain the greens by dumping them into a colander placed over a large bowl to catch the liquid formed during cooking. Reserve the liquid. Chop the cooked greens fine and set them aside.

In a large 7- to 8-quart heavy pot or kettle, heat the oil over high heat. Reduce the heat to low and gradually add the flour, stirring constantly. Cook over low heat, always stirring, until a golden brown roux (the color of peanut butter) is formed. Quickly add the chopped onion, stir thoroughly, and continue browning for 5 minutes longer, still stirring. Add the ham, sausage, veal, and the liquid reserved from cooking the greens; mix well, then gradually stir in the chopped cooked greens. Add the ham bone and the seasonings. Keeping the heat at low, gradually add the 2 quarts cold water, stirring to mix thoroughly. Raise the heat to high, bring the gumbo to a boil, then lower the heat again to low and simmer for 1¼ hours. Serve over boiled rice.

NAVY (WHITE) BEAN SOUP

New Orleans' most popular bean soup, this is cooked with a ham bone and smoked sausage and served with lots of whole beans in it. *(for 8)*

---

2 lb. dried white navy beans, soaked overnight in cold water to cover

---

1 c. chopped onion
1 c. thinly sliced shallots (scallions)
½ c. chopped green pepper
¼ c. chopped celery
2 Tbs. finely minced fresh parsley
1 Tbs. finely minced garlic
2 large ham bones with some meat on them, sawed into 4- to 5-inch lengths
½ lb. Creole (Polish, French garlic) smoked sausage, chopped fine*
4 qt. cold water
1 tsp. salt
½ tsp. freshly ground black pepper
⅛ tsp. cayenne
⅛ tsp. crushed red pepper pods
¼ tsp. dried thyme
2 whole bay leaves, crushed
¼ tsp. dried basil

When you are ready to cook, drain the beans in a colander and put them, along with all the other ingredients, into a heavy 8- to 10-quart pot or kettle. Bring to a boil over high heat, then lower the heat and simmer for 2¾ to 3 hours; the beans should be very soft and the soup quite thick. Remove the ham bones and visible chunks of meat with a slotted spoon, and discard, then strain the soup through a coarse sieve. Remove about 2½ cups of whole beans from the solids remaining in the sieve and put them, along with the soup, back into the pot. Warm over low heat for about 8 minutes and serve.

*Because most commercially sold sausage is very fatty these days, pan grill the sausage briefly and drain well before using in recipe.

RED BEAN SOUP

Red bean soup is the richest soup we know, a thick velvety puree with a subtle smoky flavor. It's cooked with lots of meat and takes about 5 hours to prepare. This soup tastes like the essence of New Orleans red beans. And as lagniappe, the ham and some still-solid beans left over after you puree the soup make another meal—ham and red bean stew. To reheat the stew, put it in a pot with about 1/3 cup of water, add a pinch of salt, and warm it over low heat for about 10 minutes. *(for 4)*

---

2 lb. dried red beans, soaked overnight in cold water to cover

---

- 1 1/4 lb. seasoning (baked) ham, cut into large chunks
- 1 1/4 c. chopped onion
- 1 c. thinly sliced shallots (scallions)
- 1/3 c. celery
- 3 Tbs. finely minced fresh parsley
- 2 tsp. finely minced garlic
- 1/2 c. chopped green pepper
- 2 large ham bones
- 4 qt. water
- 1 tsp. salt
- 1/2 tsp. freshly ground black pepper
- 1/8 tsp. cayenne
- 1/8 tsp. crushed red pepper pods
- 1/4 tsp. dried thyme
- 3 whole bay leaves, crushed

When you are ready to cook, drain the beans in a colander and put them, along with all the other ingredients, into a heavy 8- to 10-quart pot or kettle. Bring to a boil over high heat, then lower the heat and simmer for 4 1/2 to 5 hours. Turn off the heat. Remove the ham bones with a large slotted spoon and discard. Scoop out the pieces of ham with the slotted spoon and put them into a large bowl. Strain the soup through a coarse sieve or a conical-shaped passoire into another large bowl, mashing through most of the still-whole beans with a pestle or the back of a wooden spoon. Remove about 3/4 cup of bean solids from the sieve and put them in the bowl with the pieces of ham; cover with plastic wrap and refrigerate for later use. Put the thick creamy soup back into the pot and warm it over low heat for about 5 minutes, stirring to keep it smooth. Serve piping hot.

VEGETABLE SOUP AND BOUILLI (SOUP MEAT)

This rich Creole vegetable soup is served with chunks of soup meat. It takes about 4 hours to prepare, but the remaining soup meat makes several additional meals. *The Picayune Creole Cookbook* devoted an entire chapter to *Le Bouilli*, explaining: "The Creoles long ago discovered, or rather brought over with them from the mother country, France, the delightful possibilities for a good entrée that lurked within the generally despised and cast aside bouilli, and these possibilities they improved upon in their own unique and palatable styles. . . . In France the 'bouilli' is always served at the home dinner, and so with the new France, New Orleans."

To reheat the bouilli, put it in a heavy saucepan with about 1⁄3 cup of water, cook over high heat until the water boils, then cover the pan tightly, lower the heat, and cook until the meat is warmed through, about 12 to 15 minutes. To serve, cut it into slices about 3⁄4 inch thick. We like it with the creamy horseradish sauce we use for brisket or with hot mustard. *(for 8 or more)*

THE SOUP BASE

- 1 end round or shoulder roast of beef (4 to 5 lb.)
- 2 or 3 soup bones (optional)
- 2 medium onions, quartered
- 4 carrots, cut in half, then quartered lengthwise
- 1⁄4 c. chopped carrot tops
- 3 stalks celery, cut in half, then quartered lengthwise
- 1⁄4 c. chopped celery leaves
- 2 large Creole (beefsteak, Jersey) tomatoes, quartered
- 3 small turnips, quartered
- 1 parsnip, quartered
- 6 shallots (scallions), cut into 3- to 4-inch lengths
- 6 sprigs parsley, stems included, cut into 4-inch lengths
- 1 large Irish potato, quartered

THE SEASONINGS AND THE LIQUID

- 1 1⁄4 tsp. salt
- 1⁄2 tsp. freshly ground black pepper
- 1⁄4 tsp. crushed red pepper pods
- 1⁄2 tsp. dried thyme
- 2 whole bay leaves, broken in half
- 6 qt. cold water, more if necessary

In a heavy 8- to 10-quart stock pot or kettle, put the beef, soup bones if you use them, vegetables, and seasonings. Add the water. Turn the heat to high and bring to a boil. Reduce the heat to allow the liquid to simmer very slightly. Simmer for 4 hours, from time to time skimming off any scum that rises to the top with a long-handled spoon. If necessary, add a cup or so of water toward the end of the cooking time. When the soup is done, turn off the heat and remove the meat with a large fork, allowing the excess liquid to drain off before putting the meat on a platter. Cut off about a third of the meat. Reserve the larger piece for other meals. (Let it cool, then wrap in foil or plastic wrap and refrigerate.) Cut the smaller pieces into large chunks and put them back into the soup pot. Let the soup stand for a few minutes, then mix and serve.

Note: When fresh corn and snap beans (very young string beans) are in season, add 2⁄3 cup freshly shucked corn kernels and 1 pound snap beans, broken into 3-inch lengths, 45 minutes before the end of cooking time.

CREAM OF NEW ORLEANS SHALLOT SOUP

In New Orleans green onions, or scallions, are universally called "shallots." They are found in almost every local dish and help give our cooking its special flavor. We felt the noble New Orleans shallot deserved a dish all its own, so we created one. This cream vegetable soup in the French manner features a vegetable unknown in France.

Pureeing the soup through a sieve rather than using an electric blender will give you just the right texture, thick and creamy with tiny bits of shallot still intact. As for the flavor, it's pure New Orleans. *(for 4)*

---

5 Tbs. salt butter
6 bunches shallots (scallions) (about 3½ c.), cleaned and thinly sliced
2 Tbs. flour
1 c. rich chicken stock
½ c. heavy cream
½ c. milk
2½ c. water
1/16 tsp. cayenne
¼ tsp. freshly ground white pepper
Salt, if necessary

To cook this dish you will need one large and two small saucepans. In a heavy 4- to 6-quart saucepan, melt 3 tablespoons of the butter over low heat. Sauté the sliced shallots in the butter for 10 minutes, or until just golden but not brown. Remove the pan from the heat and set aside. In a 2- to 3-quart saucepan, melt the remaining 2 tablespoons butter over low heat. Gradually stir in the flour and mix until a smooth white roux is formed. Immediately remove the pan from the heat. In a third small saucepan combine the chicken stock, cream, and milk. Heat just to a boil, then add slowly to the roux, stirring constantly. Place the pan over low heat and cook slowly until slightly thickened (about 5 minutes), continuing to stir; pour the contents of this pan into the large pan containing the glazed shallots. Mix well.

Place the large saucepan over low heat and gradually add the water, stirring evenly to keep the mixture quite smooth. Add the cayenne and white pepper, then raise the heat to high and bring the soup to a boil. As soon as it begins to boil, reduce the heat to low and simmer gently for 30 minutes, stirring frequently. Taste and add a bit of salt if necessary. (This will depend on how salty your chicken stock is.) After the soup is cooked, pass it through a sieve, pureeing the pieces of cooked shallot with a pestle or the back of a wooden spoon. (Do not use an electric blender. You will get too fine a puree.) Scrape into the soup any solids that have passed through the sieve but still cling to the sides, then stir the soup and put it back into the pan. Reheat for a minute or two before serving. It tastes best very hot.

TURTLE SOUP

Good homemade turtle is a hearty, festive delicacy. Fresh turtle is available in many American coastal markets; huge green sea turtles produce the meat prized for turtle stews, while the smaller terrapin and snapper turtles are the usual base for soups. Turtle meat freezes well but is perishable, so buy it from a reliable source and keep it carefully refrigerated. For soup, canned turtle is an acceptable compromise.

The New Orleans version of turtle soup uses a roux and tomato base. Sherry should be used very sparingly; we prefer it cooked into the soup rather than added at the last minute. Turtle soup takes about 4 hours to prepare, but requires little attention after the first hour. It is best made in large quantity; you can refrigerate it and reheat as much as you plan to serve each time over a period of 3 days. Do not reheat any of it twice; it tends to turn sour. If you notice the soup getting a bit thick, add just a little cold water when reheating. *(for 8 or more)*

THE SOUP BASE

½ lb. lean ham, cut into ½-inch cubes
1 c. chopped onion
2 large Creole (beefsteak, Jersey) tomatoes (about 1½ c.), coarsely chopped
2 Tbs. chopped celery tops
2 Tbs. finely minced fresh parsley
1 Tbs. finely minced garlic
2 lb. turtle meat, cut into ¾-inch cubes and kept refrigerated

---

THE ROUX

¾ c. (1½ sticks) salt butter
½ c. flour

THE SEASONINGS AND THE LIQUID

2 tsp. salt
1 tsp. freshly ground black pepper
⅛ tsp. cayenne
3 whole bay leaves, broken into quarters
½ tsp. dried thyme
½ tsp. cloves
½ tsp. allspice
¼ tsp. mace
3 c. rich beef stock
1¼ c. water

---

1 Tbs. Worcestershire sauce
1 Tbs. fresh lemon juice
1 Tbs. dry sherry

In a large 7- to 8-quart heavy pot or kettle, melt the butter over low heat. Gradually add the flour, stirring constantly. Cook over low heat, always stirring, until a light brown roux (the color of light peanut butter) is formed. When the roux reaches the right color (after about 25 to 30 minutes), quickly add the ham, onion, tomatoes, celery tops, parsley, and garlic. Mix thoroughly and continue cooking over very low heat, still stirring, until the vegetables are browned; this should take another 20 to 30 minutes. Add the seasonings and mix well, then add the turtle meat, beef stock, and water, stirring as you do so to keep the soup smooth. Raise the heat to high, bring to a boil, then lower the heat again and simmer for 3 hours. At the end of 2 hours add the Worcestershire, lemon juice, and sherry. Stir from time to time with a wooden spoon or spatula and scrape down the sides and across the bottom of the pot to prevent scorching.

When the cooking is done, let the soup stand for 5 to 10 minutes in the pot. Stir thoroughly before you ladle out the portions to distribute the solids evenly.

CRAWFISH BISQUE

Crawfish bisque is considered by many of us to be the highest test of a great Louisiana cook. Crawfish bisque is a thick soup containing pureed cooked crawfish, firm crawfish meat, stuffed crawfish heads, chopped vegetables, and a great deal of pungent cayenne pepper. For Louisianians crawfish bisque offers the same sense of satisfaction and involves the same kind of ritual preparation as Thanksgiving turkey with all the fixings.

Making crawfish bisque the traditional way is a time-consuming job—catching the live crawfish, purging them, boiling them, picking the meat from the tails and the fat from the heads: it helps to have a large Cajun family to share the work. We prefer to buy the picked meat, fat, and shells already separated and frozen in supermarkets. (Langenstein's, 1310 Arabella Street, New Orleans, carries all of these regularly, or they may be ordered by mail from the sources listed in the Shopping Guide, pages 239-40.) We have prepared crawfish bisque the hard way and in the simpler form given here. They are equally good. But by using the packaged ingredients one can make bisque in a few hours, rather than spending a weekend at it.

(for 6 to 8)

THE ROUX

5 Tbs. lard or bacon drippings
1 c. flour

THE BISQUE BASE

2 Tbs. salt butter
1 c. chopped onion
¼ c. chopped shallots (scallions), white part only
3 Tbs. thinly sliced green shallot (scallion) tops
2½ Tbs. chopped celery tops
2 Tbs. finely minced fresh parsley
1 Tbs. finely minced garlic
½ c. chopped crawfish tails (about 24 tails)
¼ c. crawfish fat
1½ c. whole crawfish tails (about 30 tails)

THE LIQUID AND THE SEASONINGS

1½ to 2 qt. cold water (depending on how moist the crawfish tails are)
1 Tbs. salt
¼ tsp. freshly ground black pepper
½ tsp. cayenne (or ⅝ tsp., if you like your bisque very hot)
2 whole bay leaves, broken in half
1 tsp. dried thyme
4 whole cloves
12 whole allspice
½ tsp. mace

---

2 to 3 doz. stuffed crawfish heads
or 1 lb. crawfish tails

In a large 5- to 6-quart heavy pot or kettle, melt the lard over low heat. Gradually add the flour, stirring constantly, and cook over low heat until a medium brown roux (the color of rich peanut butter) is formed. In a skillet or sauté pan, melt the butter and in it slowly brown the chopped onion and white parts of the shallots. (It is possible to make the roux and sauté the onion and shallots at the same time on adjoining burners. It takes about 15 to 20 minutes to slowly brown the onion and shallots and about 30 minutes to make the roux. The roux will not be left unattended; you simply stop stirring it for a minute from time to time, except during the crucial last 10 minutes. Keep a second spoon handy to stir the sautéing vegetables.) When the onion and shallot bottoms are browned, turn off the heat and let them sit in the skillet. As soon as the roux reaches the desired color, add the contents of the skillet to it, stirring rapidly, then add the shallot tops, celery tops, parsley, garlic, and all the seasonings; mix very thoroughly. Add the ½ cup chopped crawfish meat and the crawfish fat and mix.

Keeping the heat low, very gradually add the water, stirring constantly to keep the mixture smooth. Raise the heat to high and bring the bisque to a boil, then lower the heat and simmer for 1 hour. After 15 minutes of simmering, add the whole crawfish tails. Five minutes before serving, add 2 to 3 dozen stuffed crawfish heads or 1 pound crawfish tails. Serve in gumbo bowls or deep soup bowls over boiled rice.

Note: Any leftover bisque can be refrigerated and served within a day or two. Reheat it slowly over low heat, stirring frequently. Do not let it come to a boil; it is only necessary to get it hot—boiling it will tend to overcook the stuffed heads or crawfish tails.

OYSTER SOUP

The two basic forms of oyster soup eaten in New Orleans include a simple broth and this richer version made with milk and cream which resembles Eastern oyster chowders.

(for 4)

1½ c. milk
½ c. heavy cream
1½ pt. fresh shucked oysters (about 2½ doz. medium), liquor (about ¾ c.) reserved
1½ tsp. salt
¼ tsp. freshly ground black pepper
⅛ tsp. cayenne
3 Tbs. salt butter
2 Tbs. thinly sliced green shallot (scallion) tops

Combine the milk, cream, and oyster liquor in a 2- to 3-quart saucepan, and warm over low heat. Add the salt, pepper, and cayenne and raise the heat to high. Bring just to a boil, then quickly lower the heat and add the oysters. Cook just below a simmer for 4 to 5 minutes, just until the oysters begin to curl at the edges. Remove the pan from the heat and add the butter and shallot tops. Stir to mix thoroughly and serve immediately.

BOUILLABAISSE

When Thackeray visited New Orleans in 1856 he proclaimed the bouillabaisse he had at Boudro's on the lake the best he had ever tasted. Gumbo far outstrips it in local popularity, but bouillabaisse is fun to cook, especially when the family fishermen bring in a big catch. We like a bouillabaisse with at least two kinds of fish and two kinds of shellfish in it. The way to get a good hearty fish soup taste without overcooking the fish is simple: cook only a fourth of the fillets in the soup and add the rest about 15 minutes before the end. Shrimp and oysters go in even later, just 6 minutes before you take the pot off the stove. *(for 8 or more)*

THE ROUX

¼ c. (½ stick) salt butter
¼ c. olive oil
½ c. flour

---

1 c. chopped onion
1 Tbs. finely minced garlic
3 Tbs. chopped celery
1 c. coarsely chopped fresh Creole (beefsteak, Jersey) tomatoes
3 whole bay leaves, broken into quarters
2 Tbs. finely minced fresh parsley
1 pt. fresh shucked oysters (about 2 doz. medium), liquor reserved (about ½ c.)
½ c. dry white wine
2 lb. redfish fillets
1 lb. trout (croaker, drum) fillets
2 qt. cold water
2 tsp. salt
½ tsp. freshly ground black pepper
⅛ tsp. cayenne
⅛ tsp. saffron
2 Tbs. fresh lemon juice
¾ c. lump crabmeat
1 c. crawfish tails (in season)
1 lb. whole fresh shrimp, peeled and deveined
8 half-inch-thick slices of stale French bread

In a heavy 7- to 8-quart pot or kettle, melt the butter over low heat. Mix in the olive oil, then gradually stir in the flour and cook over low heat, stirring constantly, until a light brown roux (the color of light peanut butter) is formed. When the roux reaches the desired color (after about 25 minutes), quickly add the onion, garlic, and celery. Mix well and continue cooking over low heat, always stirring, until the vegetables begin to brown (about 8 minutes more). Add the tomatoes, bay leaves, parsley, oyster liquor, wine, ½ pound of the redfish fillets, and ¼ pound of the trout. Raise the heat, bring to a boil, then lower the heat and simmer for about 20 minutes, gradually adding the water, remaining seasonings, and lemon juice after the simmer has begun. After the 20 minutes, add the remaining fish fillets, the crabmeat, and the crawfish tails if used; cook for 8 minutes more. Then add the shrimp and oysters and cook 6 minutes more.

Remove the pot from the heat and let it stand for 5 minutes before serving. To serve, place several pieces of fish, some of each kind of shellfish used, and a slice of stale French bread in each gumbo or soup bowl, then pour about 1 cup of liquid from the pot over the contents of the bowl.

2

RED BEANS AND RICE! AND JAMBALAYA

Louis Armstrong signed his letters, "Red beans and ricely yours," which expresses perfectly the attachment New Orleanians feel for their favorite dish. Like gumbo, red beans (and white) originated as enormous dinners cooked in iron pots over an open fire. *The Picayune Creole Cookbook* in 1900 observed: "In all the ancient homes of New Orleans, and in the colleges and convents, where large numbers of children are sent to be reared to be strong and useful men and women, several times a week there appear on the table either the nicely cooked dish of Red Beans, which are eaten with rice, or the equally wholesome White Beans à la Crème, *or* Red or White beans boiled with a piece of salt pork or ham."

We give here recipes for the original slow-cooked versions of the great New Orleans bean dishes; in complexity and texture they resemble the classic bean dishes of other cuisines such as French *cassoulet*, Brazilian *fejoida*, and Texas chili. Red beans were traditionally cooked while the Monday wash was drying on the line, and since New Orleans humidity made that an all-day job, the beans cooked for many hours. Bean dishes, like gumbo, suited the local temperament. They took seasoning well, were inexpensive, were served with rice, and the quantity of meat could be varied according to one's budget. These dishes were enriched by the arrivals of such immigrants as black chefs from the Caribbean with their love of seasoning, and Italian chefs, whose way with *fagioli* made them masters of Creole bean cooking.

Today we love our red beans as passionately as ever, but frequently eat lighter versions in workingmen's restaurants throughout the city, always on Monday. These thinner, less elaborately seasoned red beans are generally accompanied by meat in the form of sausage, pork chops, or New Orleans style hamburger. But unless somewhere, sometime, you have tasted the incredibly rich old-time version, you may wonder what all the fuss is about. Beans whose gravy is thickened with flour, beans without large quantities of meat cooked into them, beans without a ham bone will never convince anyone.

The "real red beans" and the white are still with us, in private homes where the tradition endures, in the kitchens of grand restaurants such as Le Ruth's or Galatoire's, where huge pots of beans to feed the chef and the staff simmer, unseen by visitors. The rich taste of authentic slow-cooked beans comes from the careful balance of spices, from the marrow of the ham bone seeping into the natural gravy which forms slowly, filling the kitchen and the whole house with an aroma you never forget. The following recipes will enable you to prepare New Orleans bean dishes at home, where the greatest versions are traditionally served.

RED BEANS AND RICE

This is the way red beans and rice were cooked in the old days—loaded with meat and steeped in a rich, natural gravy. You must include a large ham bone, whose marrow gives the beans that creamy texture and distinctive smoky flavor. Many supermarkets now carry only preboned hams, and you may have difficulty finding ham bones. Ask your local packer which butchers still bone their own hams and buy the bones in large batches. Ham bones freeze well, and a good supply in the freezer will enable you to prepare red beans the right way whenever you wish. If you have any left over, red beans freeze beautifully. Just add a little water and perhaps a pinch of salt when you reheat them.

Be sure to use baked rather than country or smoked ham in this and all other New Orleans beans dishes. Smoked ham is too salty and will unbalance the seasonings. Pickled pork is pork shoulder marinated in brine for over a week; New Orleans markets regularly carry it, but elsewhere you probably will not find it. A good substitute for pickled pork is salt pork; with salt pork eliminate all other salt in the recipe.

(for 8 or more)

---

2 lb. dried red (kidney) beans, soaked overnight in cold water to cover

---

- 2 c. chopped onion
- ½ c. thinly sliced green shallot (scallion) tops
- ½ c. chopped green pepper
- 1⅓ Tbs. finely minced garlic
- 2 Tbs. finely minced fresh parsley
- 1 lb. seasoning (baked) ham, cut into 1-inch cubes
- 1 lb. pickled pork (page 9), cut into large chunks
- 1 large ham bone with some meat on it, sawed into 4- to 5-inch lengths
- 1 Tbs. salt
- ½ tsp. freshly ground black pepper
- ⅛ tsp. cayenne
- ⅛ tsp. crushed red pepper pods
- 2 whole bay leaves, broken into quarters
- ½ tsp. dried thyme
- ⅛ tsp. dried basil
- 2 qt. cold water, approximately
- Boiled Rice (page 17—double the recipe)

Drain the soaked beans in a colander and put them, along with all the other ingredients, into a heavy 8- to 10-quart pot or kettle, adding just enough of the cold water to cover. Bring to a boil over high heat, then lower the heat and simmer on low heat for 2⅓ to 3 hours, or until the beans are tender and a thick natural gravy has formed. Add about 1 cup of water toward the end of cooking if the mixture appears too dry. During cooking, stir frequently and scrape down the sides and across the bottom of the pot with a wooden spoon or spatula to prevent scorching. (If you use a heavy pot and very low heat—just high enough to keep the barest simmer going—you should have no problem with beans sticking to the pot during cooking.) Stir the entire mixture thoroughly just once about every half hour.

When the beans are cooked, turn off the heat. To serve, ladle about 1½ cups of beans, with meat and gravy, over a portion (about ⅔ cup) of boiled rice.

WHITE BEANS, RICE, AND SMOKED SAUSAGE

The classic New Orleans version of white beans, slow-cooked with plenty of seasoning meat and slices of smoked sausage. *(for 8 or more)*

---

2 lb. dried white (navy) beans, soaked overnight in cold water to cover

---

2 c. chopped onions
½ c. chopped green pepper
½ c. thinly sliced green shallot (scallion) tops
2 Tbs. finely minced fresh parsley
1½ tsp. finely minced garlic
1 lb. seasoning (baked) ham, cut into 1-inch cubes
1 large ham bone with some meat on it, sawed into 4- to 5-inch lengths
1 tsp. salt
½ tsp. freshly ground black pepper
⅛ tsp. cayenne
⅛ tsp. crushed red pepper pods
2 whole bay leaves, crushed
½ tsp. dried thyme
¼ tsp. dried basil
3 qt. cold water
6 Creole (Polish, French garlic) smoked sausages
Boiled Rice (page 17—double the recipe)

Drain the soaked beans in a colander and put them, along with all the other ingredients except the sausages, in a heavy 8- to 10-quart pot or kettle. Bring to a boil over high heat, then lower the heat and simmer for 2 to 2½ hours, or until the beans are tender. Stir from time to time and scrape the sides and bottom of the pot to prevent scorching. Add more water toward the end of the cooking if the mixture begins to appear too dry.

While the beans are cooking, pan grill the sausages in a heavy skillet for about 12 to 15 minutes, turning them frequently, until they are well browned on all sides. Drain on paper towels, then cut them into slices ½ inch thick. Add them to the beans about 1¾ hours after the simmering begins. Serve over boiled rice.

BUTTER (LIMA) BEANS AND RICE

Butter beans cooked with slab bacon and ham have been a New Orleans favorite for over a hundred years. We cook them without a ham bone because they make a creamy natural gravy so easily. Butter beans taste best when you let them steep in the pot for about 2 hours after you turn off the heat. They freeze very well, but should never be reheated twice; store leftover beans in several smaller freezer containers if you plan to feed only a few people at a time. *(for 8 or more)*

---

2 lb. dried butter (lima) beans, soaked overnight in cold water at least twice the depth of the beans

---

- 2 c. chopped onion
- 2 tsp. finely minced celery leaves
- 2 Tbs. finely minced fresh parsley
- 1 Tbs. finely minced garlic
- 1 lb. slab bacon, cut into 3/4-inch cubes
- 1 lb. seasoning (baked) ham, cut into 1-inch cubes
- 4 3/4 tsp. salt
- 1 tsp. freshly ground black pepper
- 1/8 tsp. cayenne
- 3 whole bay leaves, broken into quarters
- 3/4 tsp. dried thyme
- 1/8 tsp. dried marjoram
- 1/8 tsp. mace
- 2 1/2 qt. cold water, approximately
- Boiled Rice (page 17—double the recipe)

Drain the soaked beans in a colander and put them, along with all the other ingredients, in a heavy 8- to 10-quart pot or kettle, using just enough cold water to barely cover. Bring to a boil over high heat, then lower the heat and simmer for about 1 1/2 to 2 hours, or until the beans are tender but not mushy. (If they have absorbed plenty of water during soaking, they should be done in less time than the maximum indicated. Taste a bean to find out if they are done; it should be creamy in texture, but still have enough solidity to chew on.) Stir frequently and scrape the sides and bottom of the pot to prevent scorching. When the beans are cooked, remove the pot from the burner and let it cool for about 15 to 20 minutes. Then cover the pot and let it stand at room temperature for 1 1/2 to 2 hours.

When you are ready to serve, ladle just the amount of beans you plan to serve into a heavy saucepan and heat them slowly over low heat, stirring frequently, until they are quite hot. (About 1 1/2 cups per portion is a safe estimate.) You can reheat more if necessary. (Discard any leftover reheated beans. If you put them back with the others, they will spoil the flavor and texture of the whole batch.) Add a bit of water if the mixture seems too dry. Serve over boiled rice.

BLACK EYED PEAS, PIG TAILS, AND RICE

Black eyed peas have a long history. Still a staple in their native Africa, they are also known in American cooking as "cowpeas" and in old Creole recipes as *congri*. Black eyed peas are actually beans, and we cook them as we do red and white beans. The seasoning meats and accompaniments used with bean dishes are often interchanged—sausage, ham, pig tails, pork chops, pickled pork, hamburger.

(for 8 or more)

2 lb. dried black eyed peas, soaked overnight in cold water to cover

1½ c. chopped onion
1 c. thinly sliced shallots (scallions)
⅔ c. chopped green pepper
⅓ c. chopped celery
3 Tbs. finely minced fresh parsley
2 tsp. finely minced garlic
1½ lb. pig tails, cut up
1 lb. lean baked ham, cut into 1-inch cubes
1 large ham bone, sawed into 4- to 5-inch lengths
1 tsp. salt, more if necessary
¾ tsp. freshly ground black pepper
Scant ⅛ tsp. cayenne
¼ tsp. crushed red pepper pods
3 whole bay leaves, broken into quarters
½ tsp. dried thyme
½ tsp. dried basil
¼ tsp. dried marjoram
⅛ tsp. mace
3 qt. cold water, approximately
Boiled Rice (page 17—double the recipe)

Drain the soaked beans in a colander and put them, along with all the other ingredients, into a heavy 8- to 10-quart pot or kettle. Bring to a boil over high heat, then lower the heat and simmer for 1¾ to 2¼ hours, or until the peas are tender and a natural gravy has formed. Add a bit more water toward the end of cooking time if the mixture appears too dry. Taste and if necessary add ¼ teaspoon salt before serving. Serve over boiled rice.

CREOLE CROWDER PEAS (PURPLE-HULLED PEAS)

Crowder peas are also really beans—the only beans we cook fresh rather than dried. Their season is short, so in the summer and early fall, when they are plentiful, we buy them by the bushel at the French Market and invite friends over to help with the shelling and stay on for the eating. Crowder peas cook more quickly than most other beans and have an unusual and delicate flavor. This recipe is primarily for local cooks who welcome a seasonal variation in their bean dishes. If crowder peas are marketed in your area, try them. You can shell the peas in advance; they will keep for a week in the refrigerator in a tightly closed plastic bag. Cooked crowders keep two to three days under refrigeration; they should not be frozen. If you double or triple the recipe, increase the cooking time from 10 to 20 minutes. *(for 8 or more)*

---

3 lb. crowder or purple-hulled peas (about 5 to 6 c. shelled)
2 c. chopped onion
1 c. chopped green pepper
3 Tbs. finely minced fresh parsley
¼ tsp. finely minced garlic
1 lb. seasoning (baked) ham, cut into 1-inch cubes
1 ham hock, heavy rind trimmed off
¼ tsp. salt
¾ tsp. freshly ground black pepper
1 whole bay leaf, crushed
¼ tsp. dried thyme
¼ tsp. dried marjoram
¼ tsp. dried basil
⅛ tsp. cayenne
⅛ tsp. mace
6 to 7 c. cold water, approximately
¼ c. (½ stick) salt butter
Boiled Rice (page 17—double the recipe)

Rinse the shelled peas under cold running water in a colander. Put them, along with the chopped vegetables, seasoning ham, ham hock, and seasonings, in a heavy 8- to 10-quart pot or kettle. Add cold water just to cover. Bring to a boil over high heat, then lower the heat and simmer for about 1¾ to 2¼ hours, or until the peas are tender and a natural gravy has formed; add the butter after the beans have simmered for an hour. Stir frequently and scrape the sides and bottom of the pot during cooking to prevent scorching. Add about ⅔ to 1 cup of water near the end of cooking time if the mixture appears too dry. Serve over boiled rice.

JAMBALAYA

On the old Airline Highway between New Orleans and Baton Rouge lies a small spanish Cajun town, Gonzales, the Jambalaya Capital of the World. Everyone has heard of jambalaya, but few persons outside of Gonzales know how delicious the authentic version of this dish can be. Every June the inhabitants of Gonzales compete for the annual jambalaya cooking championship. Huge three-legged iron pots are hauled to the center of town, where they are hung over open wood fires and stirred slowly and watchfully. Jambalaya is eaten year round in Gonzales and each cook has his own favorite form of jambalaya and special jambalaya secrets.

A rice dish descended from Spanish *paella*, jambalaya is seasoned with chili powder as well as cayenne; it is rare among local dishes to cook rice right in with the main ingredients. One of the secrets of great jambalaya is the way the hot chicken or sausage fat coats and seals the rice, so it keeps its texture during long cooking while absorbing the flavors that surround it. By using the right blend of seasonings you can prepare a jambalaya on a home range as pungent as the ones cooked over wood smoke.

Included here are three jambalayas we particularly like. They make marvelous one dish meals, and will also give you a good idea of the basic principles of jambalaya. Like gumbo, jambalaya is fun to experiment with. A word of warning, however: good jambalaya disappears at a prodigious rate, so be sure to double the recipes if you plan to feed more than four. If you have any jambalaya left over, refrigerate it and reheat it the next day, adding a tablespoon or two of water.

CREOLE JAMBALAYA (PORK, HAM, AND SAUSAGE)

This basic meat jambalaya is enriched by using beef stock in place of water. If you have no stock on hand, you can easily prepare some from a good quality beef concentrate. As in the preparation of gumbo, chop the vegetables and cut up the principal ingredients before beginning to cook. We like our jambalaya very rich, but if you need to stretch it, double the amount of rice and water and add ½ teaspoon salt and ¼ teaspoon black pepper—you'll have enough jambalaya to feed eight. For a more delicately flavored variation, substitute lean veal for the pork. *(for 4)*

- 2 Tbs. salt butter
- 4 c. chopped onion
- ⅔ c. chopped green pepper
- ⅓ c. thinly sliced green shallot (scallion) tops
- 1 Tbs. finely minced garlic
- 2 Tbs. finely minced fresh parsley
- 1 lb. lean pork, cut into ¾-inch cubes
- 1 c. finely chopped baked ham
- 6 Creole (Polish, French garlic) smoked sausages, sliced ½-inch thick and kept refrigerated (page 23)
- 1½ c. long grain rice
- 3 c. rich beef stock
- 2½ tsp. salt
- ¼ tsp. freshly ground black pepper
- ⅛ tsp. cayenne
- ½ tsp. chili powder
- 2 whole bay leaves, crushed
- ¼ tsp. dried thyme
- ⅛ tsp. cloves

In a heavy 7- to 8-quart pot or kettle, melt the butter over low heat. Add the vegetables, parsley, pork, and ham; continue to cook over low heat, stirring constantly, for about 15 minutes, or until the vegetables and pieces of meat are browned. Add the sausage and seasonings and continue cooking and stirring over low heat for 5 minutes more. Add the rice and beef stock and mix well, then raise the heat to high and bring to a boil. Cover the pot, turn the heat to very low, and cook 45 minutes, uncovering from time to time to stir. Uncover the pot during the last 10 minutes of cooking and raise the heat to medium to allow the rice to dry out, stirring very frequently. Serve immediately.

CHICKEN JAMBALAYA

This is our favorite version of chicken jambalaya, richer than the basic chicken jambalaya all contestants in the annual jambalaya contest at Gonzales are required to prepare. Buy a good fat fryer because the fat it renders during browning gives the dish its marvelous flavor and aroma. You can stretch this jambalaya in the same way suggested for the preceding recipe, although the result will be markedly less pungent. For grand occasions, we prefer to double everything in order to feed eight. *(for 4)*

- 2 Tbs. vegetable oil
- 1 fryer (3 to 4 lb.), cut up, rinsed, and thoroughly dried
- 4 c. chopped onion
- ¾ c. chopped green pepper
- ¾ c. thinly sliced green shallot (scallion) tops
- 1 Tbs. finely minced garlic
- 3 Tbs. finely minced fresh parsley
- ½ c. finely chopped lean baked ham
- 1 lb. lean pork, cut into ½-inch cubes
- 6 Creole (Polish, French garlic) smoked sausages, sliced ½-inch thick and kept refrigerated (page 23)
- 3½ tsp. salt
- ½ tsp. freshly ground black pepper
- ¼ tsp. cayenne
- ½ tsp. chili powder
- 2 whole bay leaves, crushed
- ¼ tsp. dried thyme
- ⅛ tsp. cloves
- ¼ tsp. dried basil
- ⅛ tsp. mace
- 1½ c. long grain white rice
- 3 c. water

In a heavy 7- to 8-quart pot or kettle, heat the oil over high heat. Brown the chicken parts in the hot oil, turning them frequently with long-handled tongs to ensure even browning. As the pieces brown (the smaller parts will do so more quickly), remove them to a large platter. When all the chicken is browned and removed, add the vegetables, parsley, ham, and pork to the pot. Reduce the heat to medium and cook, stirring frequently, for about 15 minutes, or until the vegetables and pieces of meat are browned. Add the sausage and seasonings and continue cooking and stirring for 5 minutes more, then add the reserved chicken parts, rice, and water. Mix gently.

Raise the heat to high and bring to a boil, then cover the pot and turn the heat to very low. Cook for 45 minutes, uncovering from time to time to stir. Uncover the pot during the last 10 minutes of cooking and raise the heat to medium. Stir gently and frequently as the rice dries out. Serve immediately.

OYSTER AND SAUSAGE JAMBALAYA

Our favorite jambalaya, with the delightful combination of oysters and smoked sausage. A variation in technique here: letting the rice brown before adding the liquid. Be sure to drain the oysters thoroughly before adding them and don't attempt to stretch this jambalaya by using more rice and water; it loses its special flavor. *(for 4)*

---

2 Tbs. salt butter
4 c. chopped onion
⅔ c. chopped green pepper
½ c. chopped shallots (scallions)
1 Tbs. finely minced garlic
2 Tbs. finely minced fresh parsley
1 c. finely chopped lean baked ham
1 lb. lean pork, cut into ½-inch cubes
6 Creole (Polish, French garlic) smoked sausages, sliced ½-inch thick (page 23)
1 Tbs. salt
½ tsp. freshly ground black pepper
⅛ tsp. cayenne
½ tsp. chili powder
2 whole bay leaves, crushed
½ tsp. dried thyme
¼ tsp. cloves
1½ c. long grain white rice
3 c. beef stock
1 pt. fresh shucked oysters (about 2 doz. medium), drained
¼ to ½ c. water, if necessary

In a heavy 7- to 8-quart pot or kettle, melt the butter over low heat. Add the vegetables, parsley, ham, and pork and brown over low heat, stirring constantly, for 15 minutes. Add the sausage and seasonings, mix thoroughly, and continue cooking over low heat, stirring frequently, for 20 minutes. Add the rice and raise the heat to medium. Cook for 5 minutes, or until the rice is lightly browned, stirring and scraping the sides and bottom of the pot. Add the beef stock and oysters and mix gently.

Raise the heat to high, bring to a boil, and cook, uncovered, for 5 minutes, then cover the pot, lower the heat to low, and cook for 50 minutes, removing the cover to stir every 5 minutes or so. If you notice the jambalaya getting too dry, add ¼ to ½ cup water after about 25 to 30 minutes. Uncover the pot during the last 10 minutes of cooking and raise the heat to medium to allow the rice to dry out. Stir very gently, so as not to break up the oysters. Serve immediately.

3

CRABS

In New Orleans we love crabs and eat them every way we can. Boiled hard shell crabs, fried soft shell crabs, sautéed buster crabs, lump crabmeat chilled in salads or sautéed and topped with rich sauces, skinny crabs in seafood gumbos, marinated crab salad, crab legs, crab claws —no part of the crab goes to waste. New Orleans restaurants are always adding new dishes to the crab canon, and when they want to crown one of their most spectacular fish or veal creations they will top it with a small buster crab or some lump crabmeat. When New Orleanians travel abroad, they are astonished and dismayed to find no soft shell crabs on menus in France, which they expect to be a kind of older New Orleans, and when they get homesick they are likely to long for nothing so much as what William H. Coleman's *Guide* in 1885 lovingly described as "those delightfully innocent, tender creatures, soft-shell crabs."

Boiled crabs are a staple of home eating. Small shacks and stands all over town attract New Orleanians on their way home from work with hand-lettered signs: "fat boiled crabs," "well seasoned crabs," "Lake Pontchartrain crabs fresh today." At modest West End seafood restaurants entire families eat boiled crabs from metal trays on tables spread with newspapers to catch the debris. Crabbing itself is an honored local pastime—setting out your crab nets at 4 a.m., then sleepily watching the sun rise over the lake, and an hour or so before noon pulling in the nets with the day's catch.

New Orleans dishes using lump crabmeat are simple to prepare, and can be duplicated anywhere in the United States. Fresh caught hard shell crabs in coastal areas, choice lump crabmeat available in the better seafood markets, or, if fresh is not available, good-quality frozen Alaska king crab (such as Wakefield's) will all work very well. If you use frozen crabmeat, defrost it thoroughly and dry it well before cooking. Check package directions to see if it is already partially precooked; if so, reduce the cooking time indicated in the recipe accordingly. And if you can get some fresh soft shell crabs, try preparing them deep fried as we do. Crisp and brown on the outside, moist and delicate on the inside, fried soft shell crabs plain or fancily sauced are among the simplest and most memorable of our local dishes.

BOILED CRABS

The secret of New Orleans boiled hard shell crabs is in the highly seasoned courtbouillon. We use locally packaged "crab and shrimp boil," a kind of Creole bouquet garni, and a great deal of salt to flavor the water in which the crabs are cooked. Where New Orleans crab boil is not available, you can make your own crab boil by combining the separate seasonings. This recipe will produce well-seasoned boiled crabs, the kind most New Orleanians prefer. Some like them even hotter than this. If you are timid about highly spiced food, try a little less cayenne the first time.

(for 4 or more)

2 doz. live hard shell crabs
6 qt. cold water
3 Tbs. liquid crab and shrimp boil (see note below)
2 c. salt
Juice of 4 large fresh lemons (about ¾ c.)
10 drops Tabasco (for Zatarain's Liquid Crab Boil; with Yogi Liquid Crab Boil use 6 drops Tabasco)

In a heavy 10- to 12-quart pot or kettle, combine the 6 quarts cold water and the seasonings. Bring to a boil and boil for 10 minutes, then add the live crabs. When the water boils up again, boil the crabs for 15 to 20 minutes, depending on the size of the crabs. Remove the crabs from the water and drain thoroughly. Allow to cool for about 10 minutes, then place in large bowls, cover with plastic wrap, and refrigerate. Serve well chilled. Or, if you prefer, serve still warm from the pot.

Note: See note on page 7 for individual seasonings if liquid crab boil is not available. Double the quantities given there for 2 dozen hard shell crabs.

FRIED SOFT SHELL CRABS

The best soft shell crabs for frying are the Atlantic blue crabs. New Orleans Lake Pontchartrain "blue claws" are the same species, and the New Orleans style of fried soft shell crabs shows them off to best advantage. The trick to that delicious crispness is careful deep frying. Many recipe writers share the belief that frying is inelegant and will tell you to sauté soft shell crabs. Sautéed crabs will never get crisp, no matter how long you cook them. Fry them at exactly 375° and you will have beautiful, crunchy soft shell crabs that taste as good as they look and are not at all oily. You will then understand the hunger of a homesick New Orleanian, quoted by William H. Coleman's *Guide* in 1885, saying, "Oh . . . if I could get back home and eat a dinner of soft shell crabs and pompano once more, I'd be willing to eat blue beef all the rest of my life."

Soft shell crabs are caught live and refrigerated or frozen as quickly as possible. They will stay fresh barely one day under refrigeration, so if you plan to keep them any longer, freeze them, which will preserve their freshness for several months. When good soft shell crabs are available, we buy them in large batches and freeze them singly or in pairs, depending on size, for later use. Soft shell crabs taste best cleaned right before cooking, since their texture and shape disintegrate rapidly after they are cleaned. Some markets will clean soft shell crabs for you; have this done only if you plan to bring them home and cook them right away. Otherwise, clean them yourself just before cooking.

(for 4)

CRABS

4 large or 8 small soft shell crabs
Cold milk for soaking
2 c. flour
1 tsp. salt
½ tsp. freshly ground black pepper
¼ tsp. cayenne
Vegetable oil for deep frying

☞ *TO CLEAN THE CRABS,* lay them, back down, on paper towels spread out on a wooden shopped surface. Remove the "apron," or loose triangular covering on the underside of the crabs, then turn them over. With a very sharp knife cut off about ⅓ inch of the front of the head. This will remove the eyes. Then reach into the opening and remove the small tan-gray sac that is behind the eye cavity. Lift up the pointed flaps on each side of the top and pull out the fibrous ("dead man") matter with your fingers. Lay the flaps down again. Be careful not to crush and mutilate the crabs when you handle them.

☞ *TO FRY,* rinse the cleaned crabs quickly under cold running water and gently pat them dry with paper towels. Put them to soak in about 1½ inches of cold milk in a pie dish or bowl for 10 to 15 minutes.

Meanwhile, combine the flour and seasonings in a large bowl, and preheat the oil for deep frying to 375°. Carefully remove the crabs from the milk, let them drain for a few seconds, then roll them gently in the seasoned flour to coat thoroughly. After coating, place the crabs on a large platter side by side, taking care not to let them overlap. Fry one or two at a time, depending on size, in the preheated oil until deep golden brown—from 6 to 12 minutes, depending on the size of the crabs and the condition of the oil. (It takes a bit longer to get the right color with oil that has not been used before. The surface is sealed as soon as the crabs are put into the oil, so you are not likely to overcook them if it takes a bit longer to achieve the right brownness.) Since soft shell crabs tend to float on the surface of the oil, turn them over frequently with tongs during frying to ensure even browning.

As each batch is done, lift the crabs out of the oil with tongs or by raising the frying basket, if you are using one. Let them drain over the pot for almost a minute, then put them on a platter lined with paper towels and place the platter in a preheated 200° oven until all the crabs are fried. Serve hot.

SOFT SHELL CRABS MEUNIÈRE

A classic New Orleans dish, fried soft shell crabs with a browned butter sauce. Superb, and simple to prepare. *(for 4)*

4 large or 8 small soft shell crabs	2 tsp. fresh lemon juice
¾ c. (1½ sticks) salt butter	½ tsp. freshly ground white pepper

Clean the crabs and fry them as for Fried Soft Shell Crabs (see page 43). Keep the cooked crabs warm in a 200° oven.

☞ *TO PREPARE THE MEUNIÈRE SAUCE,* melt the butter slowly in a heavy saucepan. Cook over low heat just until the butter begins to turn brown, then remove the pan from the heat and add the lemon juice and white pepper. Mix thoroughly. Return the pan to low heat and brown for about 1 minute more, or until the sauce is the color of hazelnuts. Serve the crabs with a generous quantity of butter sauce (about 3 tablespoons) poured over each portion.

SOFT SHELL CRABS AMANDINE

Soft shell crabs meunière with almonds. The almonds browned in butter provide a delightful taste and texture contrast, and look delectable heaped over the crisp crab. *(for 4)*

Prepare 4 large or 8 small soft shell crabs as for Soft Shell Crabs Meunière (see above). Using the same ingredients for the meunière sauce, add 1 cup of blanched, slivered almonds to the melted butter sauce just before browning. As the butter begins to brown, the almonds will turn a gold-brown color. Remove them with a slotted spoon and reserve in a small bowl until the meunière sauce is done. To serve the crabs, spread ¼ cup browned almonds over each portion before pouring the meunière sauce over.

SOFT SHELL CRABS WITH LUMP CRABMEAT

Sautéed lump crabmeat over delicately fried soft shell crabs, topped with a browned butter sauce—a very special New Orleans dish. *(for 4)*

Prepare 4 large or 8 small soft shell crabs as for Soft Shell Crabs Meunière (see above), and keep warm in a 200° oven. Using the remaining ingredients, prepare the meunière sauce as directed and set aside. In a small heavy saucepan or sauté pan, melt 2 tablespoons butter over low heat. Add ½ pound choice lump crabmeat and cook just until warmed through (about 4 to 5 minutes), stirring very gently with a spoon.

Place the fried crabs on heated plates, then divide the warmed lump crabmeat into 4 equal portions and spoon over the fried crabs. Quickly warm the meunière sauce for a few seconds over medium heat, stir to mix well, then pour in equal amounts over each portion.

BUSTER OR SOFT SHELL CRABS BÉARNAISE

At one time local crab connoisseurs made a distinction between very small soft shell crabs and busters—tiny crabs that have just molted their hard shells. Restaurants, however, continue to use the term for any very small soft shell crab. The differences if any in taste between a true buster crab and a tiny soft shell crab are slight. The small crabs used in this recipe are about the diameter of a demitasse cup, and taste best sautéed. This grand occasion dish features a sauce rarely used for seafood outside New Orleans. *(for 4)*

- 12 buster crabs or 8 very small soft shell crabs
- Cold milk for soaking
- 1½ c. flour
- 1 tsp. salt
- ¼ tsp. freshly ground white pepper
- 3 Tbs. salt butter
- 3 Tbs. vegetable oil
- 2 tsp. fresh lemon juice
- 2 tsp. finely minced fresh parsley
- 1⅓ c. Béarnaise Sauce (page 115)

Clean and rinse the crabs as directed on page 44. Handling them very gently, dry them in a soft towel, then place them in a pie dish to soak in the milk for 10 minutes.

Meanwhile, in a bowl combine the flour, salt, and white pepper. In a large heavy skillet or sauté pan, melt the butter over low heat. Add the oil, mix well, and heat for a few minutes longer. Carefully remove the crabs from the milk and allow excess liquid to drain off, then roll gently in the seasoned flour and sauté them, about 3 at a time, in the hot butter and oil until lightly browned. When cooked, place the crabs on a platter lined with paper towels and put the platter in a preheated 200° oven to keep warm.

When all the crabs are cooked, remove the skillet from the heat. With a fine mesh skimmer, remove any flour or other solids that may have settled to the bottom of the skillet, then add the lemon juice and parsley to the oil and butter mixture. Mix thoroughly, put the skillet back on the burner, and keep warm over low heat while you prepare the béarnaise sauce. (If the butter and oil mixture seems to be getting brown, cover the skillet and remove it from the heat.)

To serve, place 3 buster crabs or 2 soft shell crabs on each plate. Stir the butter and oil mixture and pour several teaspoons of it over each portion, then cover each portion with ⅓ cup béarnaise sauce.

LUMP CRABMEAT HOLLANDAISE

A delightful and easily prepared dish, the best lump crabmeat with a shimmering golden hollandaise. *(for 4)*

2 tsp. salt butter, approximately
1 lb. choice lump crabmeat
2 c. Blender Hollandaise (page 114) or Handmade Hollandaise (page 115)

Butter evenly the insides of 4 individual gratin dishes or ramekins. Place ¼ pound lump crabmeat in each dish and put the dishes in a preheated 250° oven for about 20 minutes, while you prepare the hollandaise sauce. When the crabmeat is heated through, remove the dishes from the oven and pour ½ cup hollandaise evenly over each portion. Place the dishes on dinner plates and serve.

CRABMEAT MARINIÈRE

Individual crabmeat casseroles with the local version of a classic French sauce. New Orleans shallots, chives, and plenty of pepper give this dish the characteristic Creole piquancy. *(for 4)*

¼ c. (½ stick) salt butter
¼ c. thinly sliced green shallot (scallion) tops
¼ c. shallot bottoms
1 Tbs. minced chives
3 Tbs. flour
1½ c. milk
¼ tsp. freshly ground white pepper
⅛ tsp. cayenne
⅓ c. dry white wine
1 tsp. white wine vinegar
1 lb. choice lump crabmeat

In a large, heavy skillet or sauté pan, slowly melt the butter. Set the oven temperature to 250° and put 4 ramekins in it to warm. Sauté the shallots and the chives in the melted butter until quite soft but not browned, stirring often. Remove the pan from the heat and gradually stir in the flour, keeping the mixture smooth, then put the pan back on very low heat and gradually add the milk, stirring constantly. Add the pepper, cayenne, wine, and vinegar and cook over low heat for about 10 minutes, or until the mixture has thickened to the consistency of thick heavy cream. Stir constantly and scrape the bottom and sides of the pan with a wooden spoon or spatula to prevent scorching.

Add the lump crabmeat and continue cooking over low heat until the crabmeat is heated through (about 5 to 6 minutes). Remove the heated ramekins from the oven and butter the inner surfaces by rubbing them with a stick of butter. Spoon the crabmeat and sauce mixture into the ramekins, taking care to distribute the crabmeat and sauce evenly among the portions, then put the ramekins on dinner plates and serve.

MARINATED CRAB SALAD

Marinated crab dishes are popular throughout the Gulf Coast area. Lump crabmeat is very perishable, but will keep fresh under refrigeration as long as 5 days when marinated. The three favorite regional versions of marinated crab salad are a Creole style with mustard, parsley, black pepper, and thyme; an Italian style with olive oil, vinegar, and basil; and a West Indies style with lime juice, especially popular in the Mobile area. Our favorite is a combination of all three. *(for 4)*

- ¼ c. olive oil
- 3 Tbs. white wine vinegar
- 1¼ tsp. salt
- ¾ tsp. freshly ground black pepper
- ¼ tsp. dry mustard
- 1/16 tsp. ground thyme
- ¼ tsp. dried basil
- 1 Tbs. finely minced fresh parsley
- 1¼ c. coarsely chopped onion
- ⅛ tsp. sugar
- 2 Tbs. lime juice
- 1 lb. choice lump crabmeat

Combine all the ingredients except the crabmeat in a stainless steel or porcelain bowl. (Marinades develop a metallic taste when kept in most other materials.) Mix thoroughly, then add the crabmeat and toss gently with a fork until thoroughly mixed and moistened. Pack the mixture down gently with the back of a wooden spoon, then cover the bowl with plastic wrap and refrigerate for at least 4 hours, or overnight. Stir at intervals after the initial marination period to distribute the seasonings, replacing the bowl in the refrigerator immediately after each stirring.

Serve well chilled, in coquilles or individual ramekins, with some of the marinade spooned over each serving.

CRABMEAT MANDEVILLE

Our favorite way of serving the finest backfin lump crabmeat, chilled, with a creamy, slightly tart sauce. When fresh lump crabmeat is not available, good quality frozen crabmeat will work quite well. Defrost it quickly by setting the package in a basin of cool water for about an hour and a half, then drain thoroughly and pat dry with a paper towel. Crabmeat Mandeville also makes an excellent appetizer; allow 3 ounces of lump crabmeat per portion. *(per main dish portion)*

- 3 Tbs. mayonnaise
- 1⅓ Tbs. heavy commercial sour cream
- 1 tsp. fresh lemon juice
- 6 oz. choice lump crabmeat, chilled

GARNISH

- Fresh ripe tomato wedges
- Crisp green pepper
- Cucumber slices

In a stainless steel or porcelain bowl combine the mayonnaise, sour cream, and lemon juice. Blend thoroughly with a wooden spoon until quite smooth. (Mix with an even circular motion, but don't beat. Beating will tend to thin out the sauce after a little while.)

Put the crabmeat in the middle of a dinner plate and pour the sauce over it, then surround with tomato wedges, green pepper, and cucumber slices.

CRABMEAT AU GRATIN

(for 2)

¼ c. thinly sliced green shallot (scallion) tops
1 tsp. finely minced fresh parsley
2 Tbs. plus 2 tsp. salt butter
¼ tsp. salt
⅛ tsp. freshly ground white pepper
¼ c. heavy cream
2 Tbs. milk
½ tsp. Cognac
½ lb. lump crabmeat
1 c. freshly grated sharp Cheddar cheese

Sauté the shallot tops and parsley in the 2 tablespoons butter over low heat until tender (about 6 to 8 minutes), then remove the pan from the heat. Add the salt, pepper, cream, and milk and mix well. Return the pan to very low heat and warm the mixture, stirring. Again remove the pan from the heat. Mix in the Cognac, then add the lump crabmeat and mix gently but thoroughly. Put half of the crabmeat and sauce mixture into each of two individual ramekins. Sprinkle each with ¼ cup of the grated Cheddar, then dot the top of each with 1 teaspoon butter. Bake in a preheated 375° oven for 12 to 15 minutes, then remove from the oven and sprinkle another ¼ cup grated Cheddar over each ramekin. Place the ramekins under a preheated broiler for about 2 to 3 minutes, 3½ inches from the heat, until the cheese is melted and begins to glaze. Serve immediately.

CRABMEAT RAVIGOTTE

Similar to Crabmeat Marinière, Crabmeat Ravigotte has a thicker, less tart sauce. It is equally good served hot or chilled. *(for 4)*

¼ c. (½ stick) plus 4 tsp. salt butter
¼ c. flour
½ tsp. salt
⅛ tsp. cayenne
¾ c. milk
¼ c. heavy cream
¼ c. dry white wine
1 c. thinly sliced shallots (scallions)
2 Tbs. white tarragon vinegar
1 lb. choice lump crabmeat

In a heavy saucepan, melt the butter over low heat. Gradually stir in the flour, salt, and cayenne and blend well. Slowly add the milk and cream, stirring constantly. Cook over low heat, still stirring, until the mixture begins to thicken, then add the white wine, shallots, and vinegar and blend thoroughly. Add the lump crabmeat and cook over very low heat until the crabmeat is heated through, then remove the pan from the heat and pour into individual gratin dishes or ramekins. In a separate, small saucepan melt the 4 teaspoons butter and pour over the top of each dish. Place in a preheated 325° oven for 10 to 12 minutes, then serve hot or allow to cool, refrigerate, and serve chilled.

CREOLE CRAB CAKES (OLD STYLE STUFFED CRAB)

This combination of lump crabmeat, bread, and seasonings, similar to Maryland crab cakes, was popular in nineteenth-century New Orleans. The crisp outer coating is made with local French bread crumbs. If you live elsewhere and can't get French bread, substitute cracker meal or homemade toasted bread crumbs. (Italian style bread crumbs are too highly seasoned.) We prefer this older version to the present-day New Orleans stuffed crab made with lots of garlic. *(for 4)*

---

1 lb. lump crabmeat
4 slices white bread, crust trimmed off, torn into pieces about ½ inch across
½ c. olive oil
2 large eggs, lightly beaten
1 tsp. dry mustard
½ tsp. salt
½ tsp. freshly ground white pepper
2 tsp. Worcestershire sauce
2 Tbs. mayonnaise
2 Tbs. finely minced fresh parsley
2 tsp. fresh lemon juice
1 c. French bread crumbs
Vegetable oil for deep frying

Combine all the ingredients except the French bread crumbs and oil for frying in a stainless steel or porcelain bowl. (The lemon juice will produce a metallic taste in most other materials.) Toss lightly with a fork until well blended. Preheat the oil for frying to 375°. Shape the crabmeat mixture into oval cakes about 4 inches long, 3 inches wide, and 1¼ inches thick. Put the French bread crumbs in a bowl or pie dish and roll the crab cakes gently in the crumbs to coat evenly. Fry the cakes, 2 at a time, for 7 to 8 minutes, or until crisp and golden brown. Keep the cooked cakes warm in a 200° oven while preparing the others.

4

CRAWFISH

Crawfish—often known as crayfish—grow all over the United States, although most Americans have never seen let alone eaten one. But crawfish—spelled and pronounced just that way—rank so high in Louisiana Cajun country and New Orleans that most Cajun restaurants have two menus—one for the eight months crawfish are in season and another for the rest of the year—while some simply close down when crawfish are unavailable. These delicious crustaceans look like miniature lobsters, so small early in the season that one can hold four or five in the palm of one's hand; at their largest they are generally no more than four or five inches in all, and much of that is claw. Crawfish begin to appear in November, reach their peak in May and June, and generally disappear for the year in July. Louisiana crawfish dishes range from simple, highly seasoned boiled crawfish eaten out of hand, through hearty bisques, stews, and étouffées, to haute cuisine delicacies such as Crawfish Cardinale (page 56).

Crawfish are abundant and cheap in Louisiana; at the height of the season three pounds of cooked crawfish cost about one dollar, and most local people buy crawfish already boiled from seafood stores and stands. The recipes given here require prodigious amounts of crawfish: a cupful of meat (which comes from the tail) may contain anywhere from fifty to a hundred crawfish. Fortunately, there are entire towns in the Cajun country whose principal industry is catching, cooking, and picking crawfish, so that we can purchase prepicked bagged crawfish meat for our crawfish dishes instead of having to spend hours picking them by hand. Crawfish fat (picked from the heads) is packaged frozen, eliminating the need to pound out the shells to make crawfish stock; cleaned shells ready for stuffing are sold by the bag. When we prepare crawfish dishes at home we use the packaged picked elements or start from scratch with whole crawfish, as the mood strikes us. At times it's fun to go through the elaborate rituals of readying live crawfish for cooking—and it is cheaper.

Outside Louisiana, crawfish are generally not available in the quantities needed to prepare these dishes, but the packaged picked ingredients can be ordered from the sources listed in the Shopping Guide (pages 239–40) and flown in air express. And frozen crawfish ingredients are far less perishable than live or even boiled crawfish.

BOILED CRAWFISH

Boiled crawfish cooked in a spicy, highly salted courtbouillon are generally served chilled in New Orleans; in the Cajun country they are eaten warm or hot right from the pot. The best boiled crawfish we have ever tasted are prepared by Joe Tregle, an American historian and a New Orleans connoisseur of crawfish. This is his recipe. We prefer them warm because the spices seem to come through more pungently.

(for 4)

5 lb. live crawfish
Cold salted water for purging
1¼ c. salt
8 lemons, cut into quarters
2 stalks celery, chopped
4 onions, cut into quarters
2 Irish potatoes, cut into quarters
6 whole bay leaves
3 to 4 sprigs of fresh thyme or
1 tsp. dried thyme
4 bags crab boil
1 tsp. cayenne
4 to 5 qt. plus 1½ c. cold water

Purge the crawfish by soaking them in cold salted water. Drain, rinse, and repeat the soaking process until the soaking water no longer becomes muddy. In a 10- to 12-quart pot or kettle, combine about 4 to 5 quarts of cold water with the vegetables and seasonings and bring to a boil. Boil for 10 minutes, then add the live crawfish. Also add a bit more water if necessary; the water should just cover the crawfish. Bring to a boil again and cook for 10 to 12 minutes, depending on the size of the crawfish.

At the end of cooking time, remove the pot from the heat, add 1½ cups cold water, and allow to stand at room temperature for 10 minutes. Drain the crawfish in a colander, reserving the solids (lemon, celery, onions, potatoes) to be fished out and served on plates along with the crawfish. Serve warm, Cajun style, or cool to room temperature and chill in the refrigerator.

For CRAWFISH BISQUE recipe, see page 28.

CRAWFISH ÉTOUFFÉE

This hearty, highly spiced stew makes a fine one dish meal. The best versions of crawfish étouffée are prepared at home. You can cook étouffée in advance, refrigerate it, and reheat it over a period of several days. Always cook the rice fresh. *(for 4)*

- 6 Tbs. salt butter
- ¼ c. flour
- 1 c. chopped onion
- ½ c. chopped green pepper
- ½ c. chopped celery
- 1 Tbs. finely minced garlic
- 1½ c. crawfish tails (about 30 tails)
- ½ c. crawfish fat, kept refrigerated
- 1 tsp. salt
- ¼ tsp. freshly ground black pepper
- ¼ tsp. cayenne
- 1 tsp. fresh lemon juice
- ⅓ c. thinly sliced green shallot (scallion) tops
- 1 Tbs. finely minced fresh parsley
- 1 c. cold water
- 2 c. hot water, approximately
- Boiled Rice (page 17)

In a heavy 5- to 6-quart pot or kettle, melt the butter over low heat. Gradually add the flour, stirring constantly. Cook over low heat until a medium brown roux is formed (about 15 to 20 minutes). Quickly add the onion, green pepper, celery, and garlic and continue to cook, stirring frequently, until the vegetables are glazed and tender (about 20 minutes). Add the crawfish tails, crawfish fat, salt, black pepper, cayenne, lemon juice, shallot tops, and parsley and mix well. Add the 1 cup cold water and bring to a boil, then lower the heat and simmer for 12 minutes, or until the crawfish tails are just tender, stirring frequently. Shortly before serving, heat the étouffée slowly over a low flame and gradually add 1 to 2 cups hot water to provide the gravy. Serve over boiled rice.

Note: We find crawfish étouffée an ideal dish for large groups. To prepare étouffée for 12 to 16, use the following ingredients:

- 1½ c. (3 sticks) salt butter
- 1 c. flour
- 4 c. chopped onion
- ⅓ c. chopped green pepper
- ⅓ c. chopped celery
- ⅓ c. chopped shallots (scallions), white part only
- ¼ c. finely minced garlic
- 4 lb. crawfish tails
- 1½ c. (12 oz.) crawfish fat, kept refrigerated
- 2 Tbs. salt
- 1¼ tsp. freshly ground black pepper
- 1 tsp. cayenne
- ¼ tsp. crushed red pepper pods
- 3/16 tsp. cumin
- 1 Tbs. fresh lemon juice
- ½ c. thinly sliced green shallot (scallion) tops
- ¼ c. finely minced fresh parsley
- 5 to 6 c. cold water
- Boiled Rice (page 17—triple the recipe)

Prepare as directed above, increasing simmering time to 20 minutes. At the end of cooking, let steep, loosely covered, in the pot for 1 hour.

CRAWFISH LAFAYETTE EN CRÊPE

A grand occasion dish, classic unsweetened crêpes filled with crawfish in a heady sauce and glazed just before serving. *(for 8)*

CRÊPES

7⁄8 c. flour
3 large eggs
2 Tbs. melted salt butter
2 Tbs. Cognac
1⁄4 tsp. salt
1 1⁄2 c. milk, approximately

FILLING

1⁄4 c. (1⁄2 stick) salt butter
2 c. crawfish tails (about 40 tails)
1⁄2 c. heavy cream
1⁄4 tsp. freshly ground black pepper
1⁄4 tsp. freshly ground white pepper
3⁄8 tsp. salt
1⁄8 tsp. cayenne
1⁄4 c. Cognac
1⁄8 tsp. freshly ground nutmeg
2 large egg yolks

GLAZE

1⁄4 c. (1⁄2 stick) salt butter
1 tsp. flour
1 tsp. fresh lemon juice
Scant 1⁄8 tsp. cayenne

Prepare the crêpes according to the directions on page 211. Put 8 crêpes on a warm platter and set aside while you prepare the filling. Freeze the rest of the crêpes for later use.

In a large, heavy sauté pan melt the 1⁄4 cup butter over low heat. Add all the remaining ingredients for the filling except the egg yolks and cook over very low heat for about 5 minutes, then remove the pan from the heat. Beat the yolks lightly with a fork in a small bowl and add them to the crawfish mixture. Mix thoroughly, but without beating, then return the pan to low heat for about 1 minute. Fill the 8 crêpes with the crawfish mixture and fold opposite edges over so that they overlap about 3⁄4 inch. Place the filled crêpes in a large shallow baking dish, side by side but not touching, then set in a preheated 350° oven for about 10 minutes, or until thoroughly warmed through.

Meanwhile, combine all the glaze ingredients in a small saucepan and heat, then remove the baking dish from the oven and brush the crêpes with the glaze mixture. Heat the broiler and place the baking dish under the heat at a distance of about 3 inches, just until the glaze turns light brown, about 30 to 45 seconds. Serve immediately, pouring any of the glaze sauce from the bottom of the baking dish over the crêpes.

CRAWFISH CARDINALE

Crawfish Cardinale, an haute cuisine crawfish dish, was first introduced at Antoine's several decades ago by one of the talented French-speaking Cajun waiters who constitute much of the serving staff. His name is lost to us, but his creation survives. The sauce combines a golden roux, Cognac, white wine, and aromatic spices. You must stay with this dish as it cooks to keep the texture perfectly smooth. *(for 4)*

---

5 Tbs. salt butter
⅓ c. finely chopped onion
2 Tbs. flour
¼ c. heavy cream
¾ c. milk
1 c. crawfish tails (about 20 tails)
¾ tsp. salt
¼ tsp. freshly ground white pepper
¼ tsp. cayenne
⅛ tsp. mace
⅛ tsp. allspice
⅛ tsp. cloves
1 whole bay leaf, crushed
3 Tbs. Cognac
1 Tbs. dry white wine
1 Tbs. finely minced fresh parsley
¼ tsp. finely minced garlic

In a small, heavy skillet or sauté pan, melt 2 tablespoons of the butter over low heat. Add the onion and sauté until soft and glazed but not brown. In a large heavy skillet or sauté pan, melt the remaining 3 tablespoons butter, add the flour, and cook over low heat, stirring constantly, until a light yellow roux is formed. Turn off the heat, add the contents of the small skillet to the roux, and slowly blend in the cream and milk. Turn the heat very low and cook until the mixture thickens, stirring constantly, then add the crawfish tails and mix well. Stir in the salt, pepper, cayenne, mace, allspice, cloves, and bay leaf. Add the Cognac and white wine and simmer over very low heat, stirring constantly, for about 4 minutes. Sprinkle in the minced parsley and garlic and simmer for 10 to 12 minutes more to allow the seasonings to expand. The mixture should be stirred quite frequently with a wooden spoon to prevent scorching or sticking.

Serve in heated individual ramekins or gratin dishes.

FRIED CRAWFISH TAILS

Cajun frying is heartier than Creole frying and uses hotter seasonings. A yellow corn meal batter gives these crawfish tails a delightful crisp texture. We like them this hot, but you may want to cut back on the cayenne a bit the first time you prepare them. *(for 4)*

---

2 c. large crawfish tails (about 30 tails)
Vegetable oil or pure lard for deep frying
1 c. finely ground yellow corn meal
2 tsp. salt
1 tsp. freshly ground black pepper
¼ tsp. cayenne

Rinse the crawfish tails under cold running water and place them to drain in a colander. Meanwhile, preheat the oil or lard to 375° in a deep fryer. In a wide shallow dish or pie pan, combine the corn meal, salt, black pepper, and cayenne and mix thoroughly. Roll the damp crawfish in the seasoned meal to coat thoroughly and evenly, then fry in deep fat, about ⅔ cup at a time, until golden brown. When each batch is done, drain it well and place on a platter lined with paper towels. Keep warm until served by putting the platter in a preheated 175° oven.

FRIED STUFFED CRAWFISH HEADS

Stuffed crawfish heads are crawfish shells filled with sautéed chopped crawfish meat, vegetables, and bread. Many people like to add them to crawfish bisque as lagniappe. When added to bisque, they are prepared as below but not floured and fried. You simply put them into the bisque about five minutes before removing the pot from the stove. We prefer them as a separate dish. Don't try to eat the shells—even good frying won't make them edible. *(24 to 30 stuffed heads, main dish for 4)*

STUFFING

3 Tbs. salt butter
1 c. chopped onion
¼ c. chopped green pepper
1 Tbs. chopped celery
⅓ c. chopped shallots (scallions)
2 Tbs. finely minced fresh parsley
¾ tsp. salt
¼ tsp. freshly ground black pepper
⅛ tsp. cayenne
⅛ tsp. dried thyme
Scant ⅛ tsp. allspice
1½ c. chopped crawfish meat
½ c. soaked, crumbled white bread, crust trimmed off

COATING

2 large eggs, beaten with 2 Tbs. cold water
1½ c. flour
1 tsp. salt
½ tsp. freshly ground black pepper

---

24 to 30 cleaned crawfish shells
Vegetable oil for deep frying

To prepare the stuffing, in a large heavy sauté pan or skillet, melt the butter over low heat. Add the vegetables and parsley and sauté until the vegetables are soft and just beginning to brown, then add the seasonings and blend thoroughly. Add the chopped crawfish meat and crumbled, soaked bread and toss lightly with a fork. Cook over very low heat, stirring constantly, for about 8 to 10 minutes, or until the crawfish meat is quite tender. Remove the pan from the heat.

Combine the eggs and water in a pie dish and beat lightly with a fork. Combine the flour and seasonings for the coating in a bowl. Stuff the crawfish shells with the sautéed mixture, then dip the stuffed heads in the egg and water mixture and dampen all over. Roll in the seasoned flour to coat evenly, then place them on a large platter to dry.

Meanwhile, heat oil for deep frying to 375°. When the oil is hot, fry the stuffed heads about 6 to 8 at a time until deep golden brown, about 7 to 8 minutes per batch. Drain them when you remove them from the oil and put them on a platter lined with paper towels. Keep the platter in a preheated 200° oven until all the heads are fried.

CRAWFISH STUFFED BELL PEPPERS

During the crawfish season it's fun to stuff bell (green) peppers with crawfish rather than shrimp. Parboiling the peppers briefly improves their flavor.

This dish can be prepared a day in advance and refrigerated. To reheat, put the peppers carefully (so as not to spill the stuffing) in a deep, covered casserole with about 1½ tablespoons water and set in a 375° oven for about 15 minutes.

(for 4 to 6)

Crawfish stuffing, as prepared for Fried Stuffed Crawfish Heads (page 57)

6 large or 8 small firm green peppers

Prepare the crawfish stuffing as directed on page 57. When cooked, set the pan aside.

Cut off the tops of the green peppers and remove the membrane and seeds. Set the peppers, open side up, in a heavy saucepan with about 1 inch of salted water. Bring to a boil, cover the pan, lower the heat, and cook for exactly 6 minutes, then remove the peppers from the pan and drain them thoroughly. Stuff with the crawfish mixture and set in a shallow baking dish, side by side but not touching. Bake in a preheated 350° oven for 25 minutes, or until the top of the filling turns golden brown.

CRAWFISH CROQUETTES

This dish is primarily for local cooks, who often have delightful problems peculiar to southwestern Louisiana—an enormous supply of crawfish and a need for varied ways of preparing them. *(for 4)*

Crawfish stuffing as prepared for Fried Stuffed Crawfish Heads (page 57)
1 c. additional chopped crawfish meat
½ c. Italian bread crumbs
⅛ tsp. additional cayenne
Scant ⅛ tsp. additional allspice
2 large eggs, beaten with 2 Tbs. cold water
Flour for dusting
Vegetable oil for frying

Combine all the ingredients (except the eggs and water, dusting flour, and cooking oil) and prepare as directed on page 57. After you remove the pan from the heat, allow it to cool a bit, then shape the mixture into patties about 4 inches in diameter and ¾ inches thick. Dip them in the egg and water mixture, then dust lightly but evenly with flour. Set the patties on a large platter to dry for about 8 to 10 minutes.

Meanwhile, heat oil to a depth of about 1 inch in a large skillet or sauté pan until it is very hot but not smoking. Fry the patties in the hot oil for about 4 minutes on each side, or until golden brown.

CRAWFISH PIE

We like this fine Cajun dish prepared as you would a large pie. Bring it to the table whole and serve in slices, spooning any sauce remaining in the dish over the crust. Crawfish pie can also be prepared in small individual pies about 3½ inches in diameter. Shape the top and bottom crusts by hand and seal them carefully at the edges; do not cut slits in the top. Reduce baking time by about 10 minutes. *(for 4)*

CRUST

2½ c. sifted flour
1 tsp. salt
½ c. (1 stick) salt butter
½ c. ice water

FILLING

½ c. (1 stick) salt butter
¼ c. flour
1 c. chopped onion
2 tsp. finely minced garlic
⅓ c. chopped green pepper
3 Tbs. finely minced fresh parsley
2 Tbs. chopped celery
½ c. green shallot (scallion) tops, thinly sliced
1 tsp. salt
¾ tsp. freshly ground black pepper
⅛ tsp. cayenne
¼ c. heavy cream
2 Tbs. brandy
2 lb. crawfish tails

☞ *TO PREPARE THE CRUST,* sift the flour and salt into a large mixing bowl. Cut in the butter with a spatula, knife, or pastry blender, then blend the flour and butter with your fingertips by flaking it gently in small quantities until the butter is evenly distributed through the flour. When the flour is mealy, add the ice water and work the mixture into a ball with your hands. (The pastry should stick together but not be too doughy. If it is, add a bit more ice water, sprinkling it in a few drops at a time, just enough to allow the pastry to stick together.) Roll the pastry into a ball, wrap it in waxed paper, and refrigerate it for 20 to 30 minutes while you prepare the filling.

☞ *TO PREPARE THE FILLING,* in a large heavy skillet or sauté pan, melt the butter over low heat. Gradually add the flour and cook slowly, stirring constantly, until a very light golden roux begins to form. Add the onion, garlic, green pepper, parsley, celery, and shallot tops, and continue cooking, still stirring, until the vegetables are very soft. Add the salt, black pepper, cayenne, heavy cream, and brandy. Mix gently but thoroughly and cook for about 4 minutes longer over very low heat, then add the crawfish tails and cook for 12 to 15 minutes, or until the tails are tender but not mushy. (If the crawfish tails are partially precooked, reduce cooking time to 5 to 7 minutes.) Remove from the heat.

☞ *TO COMPLETE THE PIE,* remove the chilled dough from the refrigerator. Flour a rolling pin and a board or marble pastry surface. Divide the ball of pastry in half with a sharp knife. Press down into the center of each ball with the rolling pin and roll out, always from the center, turning the pastry every few rolls so that it assumes a circular shape. Roll out to a thickness of about ⅛ inch or less. Cut 2 circles of pie crust, one 11¾ inches in diameter, the other 10½ inches. Line a 9-inch pie pan with the larger circle of crust; there will be a small amount hanging over all around. Stir the crawfish filling to mix, then fill the pie and cover with the smaller circle of crust, pressing the bottom and top crusts together where they overlap. Trim the overhang to about 1/3 inch, then pinch the edges with your fingers every inch to form a fluted edge. Cut about 8 slits in the top crust, radiating out from near the center of the pie, then bake in a preheated 350° oven for 25 to 30 minutes, or until the crust is golden brown.

CRAWFISH DRESSING (STUFFING)

In Louisiana a turkey or chicken is more likely to be stuffed with oysters or crawfish than with bread crumbs. This dressing also makes an unusual and delicious vegetable side dish.

(for 4)

Crawfish stuffing as prepared for Fried Stuffed Crawfish Heads (page 57)
3 Tbs. flour
Vegetable oil for frying

Prepare the crawfish stuffing as directed on page 57. After you have added the crawfish meat and bread, cook for 5 minutes. Add the flour and mix well, then remove the pan from the heat.

In a separate large skillet or sauté pan, heat vegetable oil to a depth of about 1/8 inch over high heat. (The oil should be quite hot, but not smoking.) Add the crawfish mixture and cook over medium heat until the bottom begins to brown slightly. (Lift near the edge with a spatula to check the color.) When the bottom is browned, break up the mixture and turn the pieces over to brown on the other side. Toss the pieces to mix the browned portions throughout. When the mixture is about one-third browned matter (which should take about 10 minutes), remove the skillet from the heat. Use to stuff poultry or fish, or serve as a side dish.

5

OYSTERS

In Louisiana, salt waters from the Gulf of Mexico mingle with the lakes and rivers to give our Plaquemines Parish oysters a special taste we call "salty." That is our way of saying they are delicious. Because we love oysters and are blessed with so many of them, we eat them year round in every way we can find. Plump and raw on the half shell at an oyster bar, perfectly fresh and cold the minute the shucker puts them on the damp marble counter. Or by the sack in the back yard, with friends to help open and eat them, washed down with plenty of beer. Or cooked–baked on the half shell Rockefeller or Bienville style, broiled with bacon en brochette, fried golden and crisp on a platter or on New Orleans French bread as an "oyster loaf," or added at the last minute to a steaming gumbo or jambalaya.

New Orleans has always had such an abundance of oysters that mid-nineteenth-century city directories listed eight or ten restaurants specializing in cooked oyster dishes and three pages of oyster houses or bars. Early in their history New Orleans French restaurants discovered that oysters were a fine substitute for snails. Oysters Rockefeller, New Orleans' best known oyster dish, grew out of *escargots bourguignons*, and gradually New World French cooking evolved an immense repertoire of cooked oyster dishes. Arnaud's menu gives some idea of how many elaborate oyster dishes New Orleans has produced, and still others are being added all the time by inventive chefs. Older New Orleanians remember fondly a pastime they enjoyed in the 1920s—making the rounds of the grand restaurants on a Saturday evening eating cooked oyster dishes until they could eat no more. Many of us still delight in what might be called an oyster orgy, a meal consisting of a dozen or two on the half shell, followed by a plate of fried, then some Rockefellers and some Bienvilles, and perhaps a few en brochette for dessert.

We have included here some of our favorite local oyster dishes. The principal ingredient in each case is the freshest possible batch of local oysters you can obtain wherever you live. If you buy them freshly shucked in jars, be sure to save the oyster liquor; it is an important ingredient in many of the recipes, and also makes an excellent flavoring stock in other seafood dishes. If the oysters are fat (milky), as they can be late in the season, you may have a little difficulty frying them properly. Just be sure to dry them as well as possible and problems will be minimal. The classic New Orleans baked and broiled oyster dishes are simple to prepare and a joy to eat.

OYSTERS ROCKEFELLER

Oysters Rockefeller have become symbolic of New Orleans cuisine—plump, fresh oysters on well-scrubbed shells under a thick pungent sauce made with chopped greens and a rich mixture of aromatic seasonings. The dish was invented at Antoine's around the turn of the century and named for Rockefeller because it was incredibly rich. It is simple to prepare oysters Rockefeller at home, and any extra sauce can be shaped and refrigerated. Use the freshest shucked oysters you can obtain, and ask for the deeper half of the shell—oysters on half shells on rock salt is the classic presentation. You can also use small scallop shells or ramekins. *(for 4)*

---

2 doz. oysters on the half shell, drained
4 pans rock salt

ROCKEFELLER SAUCE

1 c. (2 sticks) salt butter, softened
¾ c. very finely chopped cooked spinach
6 Tbs. very finely chopped watercress leaves
¼ c. very finely chopped fresh parsley
½ c. very finely chopped green shallot (scallion) tops
2 Tbs. very finely chopped celery
¾ tsp. salt
½ tsp. freshly ground white pepper
½ tsp. dried marjoram
½ tsp. dried basil
½ tsp. cayenne
½ tsp. freshly ground anise seed
¼ c. Pernod (or Herbsaint)

Combine all ingredients in a stainless steel or porcelain bowl and cream with a wooden spoon or pastry blender. Complete mixing with a whisk or electric beater at medium speed. Shape the sauce into oval patties about 2½ by 2 inches and ½ inch thick by scooping 2 tablespoons of sauce from the bowl with your fingers, and pressing into the palm of your other hand. Set the patties on a platter and refrigerate while preparing the oysters for baking. Preheat the oven to 500°. Wash the oyster shells thoroughly and dry. Place a drained oyster on each shell and set them 6 to a pan on rock salt. Cover each oyster with a patty of sauce and bake 14 to 16 minutes, until the sauce bubbles and becomes lightly browned on top. Set the pans on dinner plates and allow to cool down for about 3 to 6 minutes before serving.

Variation: Use 1⅛ cups spinach in place of the spinach and watercress in preceding recipe.

OYSTERS BIENVILLE

New Orleans honored its founder, Jean Baptiste le Moyne, Sieur de Bienville, with one of its finest oyster dishes. These fresh oysters baked on the half shell with a rich roux-based sauce are far less complicated to prepare than you might expect. One of the secrets of successful oysters Bienville is to use well-seasoned boiled shrimp in the sauce.

(for 4)

BIENVILLE SAUCE

½ c. (1 stick) salt butter
1 c. finely chopped shallots (scallions)
¼ c. finely minced parsley
1½ tsp. finely minced garlic
½ c. flour
½ c. heavy cream
1½ c. milk
4 large egg yolks, well beaten
¼ c. dry sherry
1 tsp. salt
1 tsp. freshly ground white pepper
½ tsp. cayenne
⅔ c. finely chopped mushrooms
½ lb. shrimp, boiled and diced fine (page 75)

2 doz. oysters on the half shell, drained
4 pans rock salt

TOPPING (OPTIONAL)

6 Tbs. freshly grated Romano cheese
4 Tbs. dried bread crumbs
⅜ tsp. paprika
½ tsp. salt

To prepare the sauce, in a large heavy saucepan melt the butter over low heat. Add the shallots, parsley, and garlic and cook, stirring frequently, until quite soft, about 10 minutes. Gradually stir in the flour and mix with a wooden spoon until smooth. Add the cream and milk slowly, stirring constantly until the mixture is quite smooth, then add the egg yolks, sherry, salt, pepper, and cayenne; blend thoroughly, then continue cooking over low heat until the mixture begins to thicken. Stir in the mushrooms and cook for 2 minutes, then add the shrimp and continue to cook over low heat for about 3 to 4 minutes, until the sauce is quite thick. Spoon the sauce into a large, shallow porcelain or glass dish, to a depth of 1½ to 2 inches. Let cool for a few minutes at room temperature, then cover with plastic wrap and refrigerate for at least 1½ hours.

Half an hour before you plan to bake the oysters, place the pans of rock salt in the oven preheated to 500°.

To prepare the oysters for baking, wash the shells well and dry them. Put an oyster on each shell and set them 6 to a pan on the rock salt, spooning 1 heaping tablespoon of sauce evenly over each oyster. Prepare optional topping by spinning all ingredients in an electric blender at high speed for a few seconds, then turning the blender off; repeat several times. Sprinkle 1 level teaspoon of topping evenly over each sauced oyster. Bake for 15 to 18 minutes or until well browned on top.

OYSTERS SUZETTE

This old favorite combining bacon, green pepper, and pimiento is dramatic, delicious, and one of the easiest of our baked oyster dishes to prepare. *(for 4)*

- 2 doz. oysters on the half shell, drained
- 4 pans rock salt
- 2 slices lean bacon, chopped
- 2 Tbs. salt butter
- ⅔ c. chopped green pepper
- 2 tsp. finely chopped pimiento
- ½ tsp. salt
- ¼ tsp. freshly ground black pepper

Prepare the pans and oysters as directed on page 64. In a small heavy skillet or sauté pan, fry the bacon until not quite crisp, then add the butter and cook over low heat until melted. Add the green pepper, pimiento, salt, and pepper and sauté for 7 to 10 minutes, or until the green pepper is soft but not browned.

While the broiler is preheating, arrange 6 oysters on the half shell on each pan of rock salt. Place the pans 3½ to 4 inches from the heat and broil for 5 to 6 minutes, or until the topping bubbles and begins to brown. Serve immediately.

OYSTERS EN BROCHETTE

Our favorite version of a popular New Orleans dish. Be sure to preheat your broiler and place the oysters about 3½ inches from the heat to get a lovely, crisp crust. *(per portion)*

- 2 slices lean bacon, cut into 1-inch squares
- 12 medium-sized or 10 large fresh shucked oysters, drained
- Salt and freshly ground black pepper
- Cayenne
- Flour for dusting
- ½ c. (1 stick) melted salt butter
- ¼ c. fresh lemon juice

Preheat the broiler. In a heavy skillet fry the bacon squares for about 3 to 4 minutes, to cook only partially, then drain on paper towels for several minutes. Starting and ending with a piece of bacon, place alternating pieces of bacon and oysters on a long flat skewer. Sprinkle generously on all sides with salt and black pepper; also sprinkle on a very small amount of cayenne. Dust evenly with a light coating of flour, using a shaker or your fingers.

In a small saucepan combine the melted butter and lemon juice and warm for a minute. Drizzle about one-third of the lemon-butter sauce over the skewered oysters, then place the skewer across a broiling pan so that the ends of the skewer rest on the raised edges of the pan and the oysters do not touch the bottom. Broil 3½ to 4 inches from the heat for about 3 minutes on each side, or until a light brown crust forms on the oysters. Place on a preheated dinner plate and then, at the table, slide the oysters and bacon onto the plate by holding the ring end of the skewer with a potholder and pushing down with a fork. Pour the remaining sauce over the portion.

FRIED OYSTERS IN CORN MEAL

Fresh plump oysters with a crisp well-seasoned crust is the way we like to prepare this old New Orleans favorite at home. Be sure the oil is just the right temperature and watch the color: when the oysters turn a light golden brown, they're ready.

(for 4)

1½ pt. fresh shucked oysters (about 2½ doz. medium-sized oysters)
Vegetable oil for deep frying
1 c. finely ground yellow corn meal
2 tsp. salt
¾ tsp. fresh, finely ground black pepper
⅛ tsp. cayenne

Drain the oysters thoroughly in a colander. Meanwhile, heat the oil to 375° in a deep fryer.

In a bowl combine the corn meal, salt, black pepper, and cayenne and mix thoroughly. Roll the drained oysters about 6 to 8 at a time in the seasoned corn meal, taking care to coat each one evenly and thoroughly. Fry the oysters in batches of 6 to 8, taking care to keep the frying temperature between 360° and 375°; wait a few minutes after frying a batch for the oil temperature to rise again to the desired level. (If you use a heavy kettle or saucepan, be sure to clip a deep frying thermometer to the side of it and to adjust the burner heat to keep the oil temperature constant.) Fry each batch of oysters for about 2 minutes, or until golden brown. When done, drain thoroughly by raising the frying basket out of the oil or by using a long-handled skimmer. Place each cooked batch on a large platter lined with paper towels, then set in a preheated 200° oven to keep warm until all the oysters are fried.

BATTER FRIED OYSTERS

Another style of frying oysters, with a batter crust. These are delicious served plain, or inside a freshly prepared oyster loaf, or with a hearty brown meunière sauce.

(for 4)

1½ pt. fresh shucked oysters (about 2½ doz. medium-sized oysters)
Vegetable oil for deep frying
2 large eggs, lightly beaten with 2 Tbs. cold water
1½ c. flour
1½ tsp. salt
½ tsp. freshly ground black pepper
⅛ tsp. cayenne

Drain the oysters in a colander. Meanwhile, preheat oil in a deep fryer to 375°.

Put the eggs and water in a pie dish. Combine the flour, salt, pepper, and cayenne in a bowl, mixing very thoroughly with a large spoon or a wire whisk. Dip the oysters first in the egg and water mixture, then in the seasoned flour to coat thoroughly. Place them side by side but not touching on a large platter to dry for a few minutes.

When you are ready to fry the oysters, dip them once more lightly in seasoned flour to cover any moisture that may have collected on their surface, then fry in batches of 6 to 8 until golden brown (about 3 minutes). Drain the oysters, then place on a platter lined with paper towels. Set the platter in a preheated 200° oven to keep warm until all the oysters are fried.

OYSTER LOAF

The oyster loaf was the father of the New Orleans poor boy sandwich. It was called the Creole "peacemaker": the man of the house brought one home to placate an angry wife, certain that such a treat would settle any quarrel. The classic New Orleans oyster loaf consists of a sliced loaf of warm fresh French bread buttered and filled with freshly fried oysters. *(1 loaf or sandwich)*

1 doz. fresh fried oysters
1 small loaf French bread (about 1 ft. long; see page 202 for directions if you want to bake it yourself)
¼ c. (½ stick) salt butter
Mayonnaise (optional)
Tabasco (optional)
Salt (optional)

Prepare the fried oysters according to the directions for one of the two preceding recipes—Fried Oysters in Corn Meal or Batter Fried Oysters. Slice the French bread in half across and then in half lengthwise. Place in a 300° oven to warm for about 6 minutes. Spread butter generously over the inner surfaces of the bread and heap the fried oysters on the bottom pieces. Add mayonnaise and Tabasco, or just a bit of salt if you prefer, and cover with the top pieces of bread. Serve hot.

BAKED OYSTERS

A delicious Italian addition to the Creole cuisine. *(for 4)*

¼ c. (½ stick) salt butter
¼ c. olive oil
⅔ c. Italian bread crumbs
½ tsp. salt
½ tsp. freshly ground black pepper
⅛ tsp. cayenne
½ tsp. dried tarragon
½ tsp. oregano
2 Tbs. finely minced fresh parsley
2 tsp. finely minced garlic
2 Tbs. finely chopped green shallot (scallion) tops
1½ pt. fresh shucked oysters (about 2½ doz. medium-sized oysters), drained

In a heavy saucepan, melt the butter over low heat. Mix in the olive oil and heat a few minutes longer. Add all the other ingredients except the oysters and mix well, then remove the pan from the heat. Place the well-drained oysters in individual ramekins or gratin dishes and pour equal portions of the sauce over each. Bake in a preheated 450° oven until the topping is well browned, about 18 minutes. Set on dinner plates and serve immediately.

OYSTER AND EGGPLANT CASSEROLE

This delightful combination can be served as a main-dish casserole, a "dressing" (stuffing) for roast turkey, or a substantial vegetable side dish. *(for 4)*

---

1 medium eggplant
¼ c. (½ stick) salt butter
¾ c. chopped onion
½ c. Italian bread crumbs
½ tsp. salt
⅛ tsp. freshly ground black pepper
1½ pt. fresh shucked oysters (about 2½ doz. medium-sized oysters)in their own liquor
½ c. light cream
¼ c. grated sharp Cheddar cheese

Bake the eggplant in a preheated 350° oven for 50 minutes, or until a fork pierces it easily. Peel and cut into 1-inch cubes, then set aside.

In a medium-sized heavy skillet or sauté pan, melt the butter over low heat and sauté the onion in butter until yellow and glazed (transparent) but not brown. Add the bread crumbs, salt, and pepper and mix well, then remove the pan from the heat. In a heavy saucepan heat the oysters in their own liquor just until the edges begin to curl (about 4 to 5 minutes), then remove the pan from the heat.

Butter the inside of a 2- to 3-quart casserole. Place a layer of half the eggplant at the bottom of the casserole and sprinkle with one-fourth of the onion and bread crumb mixture. Next make a layer of half the oysters and sprinkle with another fourth of the onion and bread crumb mixture. Repeat the layers of eggplant, crumb mixture, oysters, crumb mixture. Sprinkle the cream evenly over the top, then cover evenly with the grated cheese. Bake uncovered in a preheated 350° oven for about 15 minutes, or until brown on top.

BAKED OYSTERS AND EGGPLANT

A main dish served in individual ramekins. *(for 4)*

---

2 firm medium eggplants (about 1¼ lb. each)
4 c. chopped onion
⅝ c. (1¼ sticks) salt butter
½ lb. thinly sliced bacon
½ c. plus 4 heaping tsp. Italian bread crumbs
1 tsp. salt
½ tsp. freshly ground black pepper
1½ pt. fresh shucked oysters (about 2½ doz. medium-sized oysters), drained

In an open shallow baking dish, bake the eggplants for 40 minutes in a preheated 425° oven. Remove from the oven and allow to cool. In a small skillet sauté the onion in ¼ cup of the butter until glazed but not brown. In another small skillet, fry the bacon until crisp, then drain on several layers of paper towels.

With a sharp knife, cut off the stem ends of the eggplants and peel them carefully. Discard the skin and place the meat of the eggplants in a colander to drain. After the eggplant is well drained, chop into ¾-inch cubes and combine with the sautéed onion in a large china or stainless steel mixing bowl. Crumble the bacon into the mixture, then add ½ cup Italian bread crumbs, salt, pepper, and drained oysters.

Melt the remaining butter in a small saucepan. Divide the eggplant and oyster mixture into four equal portions and place in individual ramekins or baking dishes. Pour one-fourth of the melted butter over each portion, then sprinkle each evenly with a heaping teaspoon of Italian bread crumbs. Place the ramekins on a baking sheet and bake in a preheated 425° oven for 20 minutes, or until the mixture bubbles vigorously around the edges and the top is well browned.

CREOLE OYSTER PIE

An old New Orleans favorite that has disappeared from restaurant menus but not from home kitchens. The rich biscuit dough covers only the top of the pie. When you serve it, spoon some of the liquid from the pie pan over each portion. *(for 4)*

BISCUIT DOUGH

½ c. flour
¾ tsp. double-acting baking powder
¼ tsp. salt
1 Tbs. vegetable shortening
¼ c. milk

FILLING

⅔ c. chopped onion
4 slices bacon, cut into ½-inch squares
1 pt. fresh shucked oysters (about 2 doz. medium-sized oysters), drained
1¼ Tbs. finely minced fresh parsley
¾ tsp. salt
⅛ tsp. freshly ground black pepper
1½ Tbs. fresh lemon juice
Scant ⅛ tsp. cayenne
1 Tbs. melted salt butter

To prepare the crust, sift the dry ingredients together twice. Combine them in a mixing bowl with the shortening and milk, and mix thoroughly with a wooden spoon. Flour a board or marble pastry surface and a rolling pin. Knead the dough by hand for 4 to 5 minutes, then roll it out to a thickness of ½ inch. Invert the pie pan you will be using and press it into the dough to mark a circle. Cut out the circle of dough with a sharp knife. If it appears a bit damp, flour it lightly. Set aside while preparing the filling.

Fry the chopped onion and the bacon squares together in a small heavy skillet or sauté pan until the bacon is moderately crisp and the onions are soft. Grease a 9-inch pie pan with butter. Place half the drained oysters on the bottom and sprinkle with half the onion, bacon, parsley, salt, black pepper, and cayenne. Add ¾ teaspoon of the lemon juice. Make a second layer with the remaining oysters and cover with the remaining seasonings. Pour the melted butter over the top, then cover with the ½-inch-thick round of biscuit dough. Rub the crust with butter. Cut six 1½-inch slits in the crust, radiating from an uncut circle 2 inches wide at the center, then bake for 15 minutes in a preheated 450° oven.

Serve in wedges, spooning about 2 teaspoons of the liquid over the crust of each piece.

BROILED SKEWERED OYSTERS AND BACON

A variation on the more familiar oysters en brochette, without a crust. *(for 4)*

1½ pt. fresh shucked oysters (about 2½ doz. medium-sized oysters)
½ lb. lean breakfast bacon, sliced
¼ tsp. freshly ground white pepper
2 Tbs. finely minced fresh parsley
1½ Tbs. fresh lemon juice

GARNISH
lemon wedges

Drain the oysters thoroughly in a colander, then place on several layers of paper towels to absorb the remaining liquid. Cut the slices of bacon into thirds. Wrap a piece of bacon around each oyster, overlapping the ends, then spear on long skewers so that each oyster is firmly wrapped in a bacon slice. Divide the oysters and bacon evenly among the four skewers.

Preheat the broiler and broiling pan. Sprinkle the oysters and bacon with white pepper and parsley on all sides, then place the skewers on a rack in the broiling pan and place the pan about 3½ inches from the heat. Broil, turning the skewers a quarter turn every 4 or 5 minutes, so that the bacon cooks evenly on all sides. When the bacon appears almost cooked, remove the broiling pan from the broiler. Sprinkle the skewered oysters and bacon with the lemon juice and return to the broiler, placing the pan close to the flame (about 1 inch away). Broil for 2 minutes more, turning over once. Slip the bacon-wrapped oysters carefully onto heated dinner plates by pushing down with a fork from the ring end of each skewer. Serve with lemon wedges.

OYSTERS AND SPAGHETTI

The New Orleans equivalent of spaghetti with clams. Take care to cook the garlic only until it begins to brown; after a point garlic gets milder the longer you cook it. Let the finished dish stand in the pot for a few minutes before serving. *(for 2; for 4 see note)*

¼ c. (½ stick) salt butter
¼ c. plus 1½ tsp. olive oil
3 large cloves garlic, peeled and cut into pieces about ⅓ inch thick
½ tsp. dried basil
1 Tbs. finely minced fresh parsley
½ tsp. freshly ground black pepper
1 Tbs. plus ¼ tsp. salt
1 pt. fresh shucked oysters (about 2 doz. medium-sized oysters), drained
4 qt. cold water
10 to 12 oz. spaghetti

In a heavy 2-quart sauté pan or saucepan melt the butter over low heat. Add ¼ cup olive oil, mix thoroughly, and continue to heat for about 3 minutes. Add the pieces of garlic and cook over medium heat for about 4 minutes, or just until the garlic begins to brown. Quickly remove the garlic with a slotted spoon, then add the basil, parsley, pepper, and ¼ teaspoon salt to the butter and oil mixture; simmer for about 3 to 4 minutes. Add the drained oysters and warm over low heat for 5 minutes, then remove the pan from the heat, cover, and set aside while cooking the spaghetti.

In a heavy 6- to 8-quart saucepan, combine the water, 1 tablespoon salt, and

1½ teaspoons olive oil. Bring to a rolling boil, then add the spaghetti. When the water comes to a boil again, cook for 7 minutes, then immediately pour the contents of the saucepan into a large colander placed in the sink and allow the spaghetti to drain thoroughly. Return the drained spaghetti to the saucepan, add the oil and oyster mixture, and mix gently but thoroughly with a fork. Cover the saucepan and allow to stand on a warming tray or in a 175° preheated oven for about 8 minutes before serving.

When you are ready to serve, toss the oysters and spaghetti thoroughly with a large spoon, making sure to redistribute the sauce, which will have settled to the bottom of the pan. Serve portions with plenty of sauce and oysters on top of the spaghetti.

Note: If you wish to prepare this dish for 4, double everything but the water for boiling the spaghetti. For 24 ounces of spaghetti you will need about 6 quarts of water.

OYSTERS IN CHAMPAGNE

This dish is based on one we tasted in France, where oysters are too expensive to be used as freely as they are in New Orleans. It makes a delicate and unusual first course.

(for 4)

1½ pt. fresh shucked oysters (about 2½ doz. medium-sized oysters)
½ c. (1 stick) salt butter
1 c. heavy cream
1 tsp. freshly ground white pepper
¼ tsp. freshly ground black pepper
1 tsp. coriander
½ tsp. allspice
½ tsp. salt
2½ tsp. freshly ground nutmeg
½ c. extra dry champagne
½ tsp. flour

Drain the oysters thoroughly in a colander. In a heavy 3- to 4-quart saucepan melt the butter over low heat. Add the cream, white and black pepper, coriander, allspice, salt, and ½ teaspoon of the nutmeg. Cook over low heat until the mixture is thoroughly warmed but not boiling, then add the champagne. Sprinkle in the flour gradually, stirring constantly, until the mixture thickens to the consistency of light sour cream. Remove the pan from the heat.

Place the oysters in individual ramekins or gratin dishes and cover each portion evenly with one-fourth of the mixture from the saucepan. Sprinkle the remaining nutmeg evenly over the portions, then place the ramekins in a preheated broiler 3½ inches from the heat, and broil for 10 to 12 minutes, or until the oysters are heated through and the sauce begins to brown on top. Remove from the broiler and serve immediately.

SCALLOPED OYSTERS

(for 4)

1½ pt. fresh shucked oysters (about 2½ doz. medium-sized oysters) and their liquor
¾ c. coarsely crumbled plain crackers
⅛ tsp. freshly ground black pepper
1 c. (2 sticks) melted salt butter
⅛ tsp. coriander
⅛ tsp. paprika
1 tsp. Worcestershire sauce
1 c. milk

Drain the oysters and reserve the liquor. Combine the cracker crumbs, pepper, and melted butter. Butter a round baking dish about 8 inches in diameter and 2 inches deep, then sprinkle one-third of the buttered crumb mixture over the bottom of the baking dish. Cover with half the oysters, then sprinkle half the coriander and paprika evenly over the oysters. Repeat the layers of buttered crumb mixture, oysters, coriander, and paprika.

In a small bowl combine the Worcestershire, milk, and 2 tablespoons of the reserved oyster liquor. Pour over the top layer of oysters and sprinkle with the remaining third of buttered crumbs. Bake in a preheated 400° oven for 20 to 25 minutes, or until brown on top.

OYSTERS GREEN MANSIONS

A combination of fresh oysters, French shallots, and Pickapeppa Sauce (a Jamaican version of Worcestershire prepared with mangos, tamarinds, raisins, pepper, and cane vinegar). Be sure to drain the oysters well before cooking. *(for 4)*

1½ pt. fresh shucked oysters (about 2½ doz. medium-sized oysters), drained
5 to 6 slices lean bacon
½ c. finely minced French shallots
½ c. freshly grated sharp Cheddar cheese
¼ c. dry white wine
½ tsp. freshly ground black pepper
½ tsp. salt
2 Tbs. salt butter, softened
½ c. Pickapeppa Sauce

Drain the oysters in a colander and dry them thoroughly between several layers of paper towels. Place them, widely spaced, in the bottom of a heavy shallow baking or gratin dish about 10 inches long and 5 inches wide. Cut the bacon into 1-inch squares and place a square on top of each oyster. Distribute the minced shallots evenly between the oysters on the bottom of the baking dish, then cover the whole surface with the grated sharp Cheddar cheese. Sprinkle evenly with the white wine, pepper, and salt, then cut the softened butter into about 10 small pieces and distribute evenly over the dish. Spoon on the Pickapeppa Sauce in widening concentric circles from the center.

Preheat the broiler. Place the baking dish 3½ inches below the heat and broil for about 8 to 10 minutes, or until the sauce begins to glaze and turn dark brown in color. Remove the dish from the oven and carefully spoon the portions onto heated plates so that some of the browned cheese crust covers each one. Also, spoon any sauce remaining in the baking dish around the individual portions.

6

SHRIMP

"S'rimp," as they're often called locally, come in many sizes and forms, most of them highly seasoned. For someone who has never seen a whole shrimp, a trip to Manale's for an order of barbecue shrimp will reveal what shrimp cocktails politely conceal—that a shrimp has a huge head and a long tail. In New Orleans we boil whole shrimp in a spicy courtbouillon seasoned with "shrimp boil" and shell them by hand at the table, or eat them peeled and chilled with a heady remoulade sauce. Mountains of fried shrimp are eaten in homes and in modest restaurants all over the city. Well-seasoned boiled shrimp are essential to such sauces as Marguery and Bienville, and hearty shrimp stew is to New Orleans workingmen's restaurants what beef stew is elsewhere. In the Cajun country French-speaking Louisianians prepare shrimp sauce piquante, a dish hot enough to bring tears to your eyes.

Because shrimp are available all over the country fresh or frozen, New Orleans shrimp dishes are accessible to anyone who likes to cook and to eat well. If you use frozen shrimp, defrost them thoroughly and dry them well before cooking. If package directions indicate they are partially precooked, reduce cooking time accordingly. Fresh or frozen, shrimp fare best when they are not overcooked; a whole fresh shrimp takes only 5 to

7 minutes to cook, depending on its size. Preboiling the seasoned courtbouillon ensures spicy shrimp without overcooking. Shelled shrimp fry in a couple of minutes, and in dishes whose preparation includes shrimp, it is generally best to add them toward the end of the cooking.

BOILED SHRIMP

New Orleanians like their shrimp very well seasoned. But because of the mistaken notion that shrimp must cook a long time to absorb flavor, many local boiled shrimp are soggy. The best way to ensure firm and spicy shrimp is to boil the court-bouillon for 10 minutes *before* adding the shrimp, then boil no more than the prescribed 5 to 7 minutes and remove at once from the water. *(for 4)*

---

2 lb. whole fresh shrimp
1½ Tbs. liquid shrimp and crab boil (see page 7 for substitute)
1 c. salt
Juice of 2 large, fresh lemons (about 6 Tbs.)
5 drops Tabasco (if Zatarain's Liquid Crab Boil is used; use 3 drops Tabasco with Yogi Liquid Crab Boil)
4 qt. cold water

Put all the ingredients except the shrimp into a heavy 8- to 10-quart pot or kettle. Bring to a boil and boil for 10 minutes, then add the whole fresh shrimp to the boiling water. When the water boils up again, boil the shrimp for 5 to 7 minutes. (Small shrimp will take 5 minutes, very large 7.) Remove the shrimp immediately from the boiling water by dumping them into a colander. Allow to drain thoroughly, then let them cool at room temperature for 5 minutes.

Place the shrimp in a large bowl, cover with several layers of plastic wrap, and refrigerate. Serve well chilled. Many people like an accompanying dipping sauce made of ketchup, hot prepared horseradish, fresh lemon juice, and a few drops of Tabasco.

FRIED SHRIMP

Whole shrimp fried with a crisp, well-seasoned corn flour crust. Corn flour is widely used for frying in New Orleans and is sold locally as "Fish-Fri"; any finely milled yellow corn flour can be used. Fried this way, even the tails on smaller shrimp are delicious. *(for 4)*

---

1 lb. whole fresh shrimp, peeled and deveined, tails left on
1½ c. yellow corn flour (Fish-Fri)
3 tsp. salt
1 tsp. freshly ground black pepper
⅜ tsp. cayenne
Vegetable oil for deep frying

Wash the peeled shrimp and place them on several layers of paper towels to drain. Combine the corn flour and seasonings in a large mixing bowl and mix thoroughly.

Preheat the oil in a deep fryer to 375°. Roll the slightly damp shrimp in seasoned corn flour to coat thoroughly, then fry in batches of 10 to 14, depending on the size of the shrimp, until golden brown (about 4 to 5 minutes). (It is essential both not to overcrowd the fryer and not to overcook the shrimp.) When each batch is done, drain and place on a platter lined with paper towels. Put the platter in a preheated 175° oven to keep warm until all the shrimp are fried.

SHRIMP REMOULADE

New Orleans remoulade sauce is highly seasoned and reddish in color. Our favorite version of shrimp remoulade closely resembles the one served at Galatoire's and contains both pureed and minced fresh vegetables. The sauce can be prepared in advance and refrigerated, but don't sauce the shrimp until a few minutes before serving or they will get soggy. *(for 4)*

REMOULADE SAUCE

1 bunch shallots (scallions), cut up
2 small stalks celery, cut up
2 sprigs fresh parsley, cut up
3 Tbs. Creole mustard
5 tsp. paprika
1¼ tsp. salt
½ tsp. freshly ground black pepper
¼ tsp. cayenne
6 Tbs. white wine vinegar
5 tsp. fresh lemon juice
½ tsp. dried basil
¾ c. olive oil

1 shallot (scallion), chopped
1 Tbs. chopped celery
2 tsp. finely minced fresh parsley
1 c. coarsely chopped Romaine lettuce
1 lb. whole fresh shrimp, boiled (page 75), peeled and deveined, and chilled

Grind the bunch of shallots, celery stalks, and parsley sprigs in a food mill or reduce almost to a puree in an electric blender. Place the vegetable puree in a china or stainless steel bowl, then add the mustard, paprika, salt, pepper, and cayenne and blend with a wooden spoon. Add the vinegar, lemon juice, and basil and blend again. Gradually add the olive oil, stirring constantly. When well blended, add the chopped shallot, chopped celery, and finely minced parsley and stir to mix thoroughly. Cover the bowl with plastic wrap and refrigerate for at least 3 hours.

At serving time, chop the lettuce and put ¼ cup on each salad plate. Place the boiled shrimp on top of the lettuce, and after stirring it well pour about ¼ cup remoulade sauce over each portion; the sauce should completely cover the shrimp. Serve well chilled.

SHRIMP ÉTOUFFÉE

(for 4)

Prepare as for Crawfish Étouffée (see page 54), substituting 1½ cups small or medium-sized peeled and deveined raw shrimp for the crawfish.

SHRIMP SAUCE PIQUANTE (SHRIMP CREOLE)

Shrimp sauce piquante was the original version of shrimp Creole. Firm shrimp, plenty of whole tomatoes, and lots of pepper—a far cry from the bland, soggy restaurant dish served all over America. This is a really spicy Cajun dish. You may want to reduce the cayenne a bit the first time you try it, then work your way toward the degree of hotness we prefer in southwestern Louisiana. If you double the recipe, do *not* increase the cooking time. *(for 4)*

SAUCE PIQUANTE

- ⅔ c. vegetable oil
- ½ c. flour
- 1¾ c. thinly sliced shallots (scallions)
- ⅓ c. chopped celery
- 1 c. chopped onion
- ½ c. chopped green pepper
- 4 tsp. finely minced garlic
- 3 Tbs. finely minced fresh parsley
- 1 one-lb. can Italian style whole peeled tomatoes, drained
- 1 eight-oz. can tomato sauce
- 1 Tbs. minced chives
- 4 Tbs. dry red wine
- 4 whole bay leaves, crushed
- 6 whole allspice
- 2 whole cloves
- 2 tsp. salt
- ¾ tsp. freshly ground black pepper
- ½ tsp. cayenne
- ¼ tsp. chili powder
- ¼ tsp. mace
- ¼ tsp. dried basil
- ½ tsp. dried thyme
- 4 tsp. fresh lemon juice
- 2 c. water

- 2 lb. whole fresh shrimp, peeled and deveined
- Boiled Rice (page 17)

In a heavy 6- to 8-quart pot or kettle, heat the oil and gradually add the flour, stirring constantly. Cook over low heat, stirring constantly, until a medium brown roux (the color of rich peanut butter) is formed. Remove from the heat and add the fresh vegetables and parsley. Mix well with the roux, then return to low heat and cook, stirring constantly, until the vegetables begin to brown. Mix in the canned tomatoes and tomato sauce, then add the chives, wine, seasonings, and lemon juice and mix again.

Raise the heat under the pan and bring to a low boil. Add the water and mix thoroughly. When the mixture boils up again, reduce the heat and simmer for 45 minutes. Add the shrimp and allow to come to a low boil again, then cover, reduce the heat slightly, and simmer for 20 minutes. Remove the pot from the burner and allow to stand, covered, at room temperature for about 10 minutes before serving. Serve over boiled rice.

BARBECUE SHRIMP

Our version of a local favorite, whole shrimp in the shell cooked in a peppery butter sauce. Serve this dish in gumbo or soup bowls and be sure to stir the sauce well when you ladle it out; the solids that settle to the bottom of the pan should be poured over the shrimp along with the sauce. Some people like knives and forks, but it's perfectly good form to eat this gloriously messy dish with your hands and a soup spoon (for any sauce left in the bowl). Headless whole shrimp work perfectly; shrimp with the heads on are more dramatic. *(for 4)*

---

1 c. (2 sticks) salt butter
1 c. vegetable oil
2 tsp. finely minced garlic
4 whole bay leaves, crushed fine
2 tsp. crushed dried rosemary leaves
½ tsp. dried basil
½ tsp. oregano
½ tsp. salt
½ tsp. cayenne
1 Tbs. paprika
¾ tsp. freshly ground black pepper
1 tsp. fresh lemon juice
2 lb. whole fresh shrimp in the shell

In a heavy sauté pan or saucepan melt the butter, then add the oil and mix well. Add all the other ingredients except the shrimp and cook over medium heat, stirring constantly, until the sauce begins to boil. Reduce the heat to low and simmer for 7 to 8 minutes, stirring frequently, then remove the pan from the heat and let it stand, uncovered, at room temperature for at least 30 minutes. Add the shrimp to the sauce, mix thoroughly, and put the pan back on the burner. Cook over medium heat for 6 to 8 minutes, or just until the shrimp turn pink, then put the pan in a preheated 450° oven and bake for 10 minutes. Serve equal portions of shrimp with about ½ cup of sauce ladled over each one.

SHRIMP SAKI

Shrimp butterflied, covered with a seasoned butter sauce, baked, and then browned under the broiler—this Pontchartrain Hotel specialty makes a good main course or an excellent appetizer. Large shrimp are most attractive; leave the tails on when you peel them—some of us think they are the best part—and serve with lemon butter sauce for dipping. *(for 4 as a main dish; for 8 as an appetizer)*

---

2 lb. whole fresh shrimp
1 c. (2 sticks) salt butter
1 tsp. freshly ground white pepper
½ tsp. salt
¼ tsp. cayenne
½ tsp. paprika

DIPPING SAUCE

½ c. (1 stick) salt butter
3 Tbs. fresh lemon juice

Remove the shrimp heads, then peel and devein the shrimp, leaving the tails on. To butterfly, split the shrimp down the back two-thirds of the way through and flatten. Rinse the shrimp under cold running water and pat dry gently with paper towels. Put them, split backs down, in a large shallow baking dish.

In a saucepan melt 1 cup of the butter and add the pepper, salt, cayenne, and paprika. Mix thoroughly and pour evenly over the shrimp. Bake in a preheated 400° oven for 6 minutes, then remove the baking pan from the oven. Heat the broiler, and when it is quite hot, place the baking pan about 4 inches from the heat for 2 to 3 minutes, or until the shrimp are lightly browned and slightly crisp at the edges. Meanwhile, melt the ½ cup butter in a saucepan, then add the lemon juice and mix well.

Serve the shrimp on heated plates, fanning out from a small ramekin or glass bowl placed in the center and filled with the lemon-butter sauce for dipping.

SHRIMP STEW

A hearty "back-of-town" dish, one of the few that uses potatoes rather than rice. If you double the recipe, increase the total cooking time by about 10 minutes, but do not add the shrimp until 25 minutes before the end. *(for 4)*

½ c. vegetable oil
½ c. flour
1¾ c. chopped onion
¾ c. thinly sliced shallots (scallions)
⅓ c. chopped celery
4 tsp. finely minced garlic
2½ tsp. salt
1 tsp. freshly ground black pepper
⅛ tsp. cayenne
3 whole bay leaves, crushed
1 tsp. dried thyme
2 lb. ripe Creole (beefsteak, Jersey) tomatoes, coarsely chopped (about 2½ to 3 c.)
3 c. water
1 tsp. fresh lemon juice
2 lb. white potatoes, peeled and cut into 1½-inch cubes
2 lb. whole fresh shrimp, peeled and deveined

In a heavy 6- to 8-quart pot or kettle, heat the oil and gradually stir in the flour. Cook over low heat, stirring constantly, until a medium brown roux (the color of rich peanut butter) is formed (about 20 to 30 minutes). When the desired color is reached, lower the heat immediately and add the chopped onion, shallots, celery, and garlic. Stir thoroughly and cook over low heat for 10 minutes more, stirring constantly. Add the salt, black pepper, cayenne, bay leaves, and thyme and mix well. Add the chopped tomatoes, water, and lemon juice, then simmer for 1 hour, stirring frequently. Add the cubed potatoes and simmer for 10 minutes longer. Add the shrimp, cover the pot, and simmer over low heat for 25 minutes more.

BROILED SHRIMP HOLLANDAISE

A delicious and simple-to-prepare dish. *(for 4)*

1 c. Blender Hollandaise (page 114) or Handmade Hollandaise (page 115)
1 lb. whole large fresh shrimp, peeled and deveined
1½ Tbs. lemon juice
1 Tbs. olive oil
½ tsp. salt
⅛ tsp. freshly ground black pepper (grind as fine as you can)
⅛ tsp. cayenne

Prepare the hollandaise sauce, then set the container in warm water in a bowl or basin to keep warm while you prepare the shrimp. Dry them thoroughly with paper towels, then arrange in a large shallow baking dish. Sprinkle with the lemon juice, olive oil, salt, black pepper, and cayenne.

Preheat the broiler. Place the baking dish 3½ to 4 inches from the heat and broil for 3 minutes, then turn the shrimp over and broil for 3 minutes on the other side. Remove the baking dish from the oven and spoon 1 cup of the warm hollandaise sauce evenly over the shrimp, then put the dish under the broiler for 30 seconds to 1 minute, just until the hollandaise begins to develop a light brown glaze. Remove the dish quickly from the broiler and, using a large spoon, carefully put the portions on heated plates, picking up a spoonful at a time from underneath so that the shrimp remain under the glazed hollandaise. Serve immediately.

SHRIMP AND ARTICHOKE HEARTS

(for 4)

½ c. (1 stick) salt butter
10 oz. cooked artichoke hearts (see note below)
2 Tbs. water
½ tsp. fresh, coarsely ground black pepper
2 Tbs. fresh lemon juice
1 Tbs. very finely chopped green pepper
1 lb. large fresh shrimp, peeled and deveined
⅛ tsp. paprika

In a large heavy skillet or sauté pan melt the butter slowly over low heat. Add the artichoke hearts and water and cook over low heat, stirring frequently with a wooden spoon. When the artichoke hearts are warmed through, add the black pepper, lemon juice, and green pepper and mix gently. Add the shrimp and continue to cook slowly, stirring. When the mixture begins to boil, quickly sprinkle the paprika over the shrimp, cover the skillet, reduce the heat still further, and cook for exactly 4½ minutes. Remove the skillet from the burner and serve immediately.

Note: If fresh artichokes are out of season, frozen artichoke hearts may be substituted. In that case, eliminate the 2 tablespoons water called for in the recipe.

For other shrimp recipes, see also: STUFFED MIRLITONS (page 168), STUFFED PEPPERS (page 172).

7

FISH

"There is an incredible quantity of fishes in this country," Le Page Du Pratz noted in his 1774 *History of Louisiana.* With its vast areas of salt and fresh water, Louisiana has been a haven for fishermen for several hundred years, and as a result of always having had more fish and shellfish than good beef, French Louisiana has developed an enormous repertoire of fish dishes. Obviously, to prepare most of these recipes so that they taste precisely like the dishes we eat, one should use the native fish called for. However, you can substitute regional varieties of fish to prepare excellent New Orleans style dishes. The *manner* of cooking the fish is more important than the exact ingredients, so we have experimented with different regional fish from all over the country and drawn up a chart to show which species will produce results similar to the actual dishes eaten here.

New Orleans' most popular fish is speckled trout, our all-purpose fish. We fry it, broil it, poach and sauce it, and often use it in place of other scarcer, more expensive fish in a number of dishes. One collection of New Orleans restaurant recipes inadvertently revealed what many of us have suspected all along: the recipe for pompano en papillote began, "Take a nice trout . . ." No one in New Orleans seems to mind that our local trout is technically not a trout at all but a weakfish; it's good to eat, and we have lots of it. Redfish, a member of the bass family and another great local favorite, is broiled, baked, poached and sauced, and used in redfish courtbouillon. Although it is now closely identified with the procedure, redfish should not be used for blackening (see page 106). Red snapper, available in many parts of the country, is widely eaten in New Orleans, and river catfish, America's most popular fish, is the staple of Cajun fish cooking. Fishermen's favorites include croaker, sheepshead, mullet, and drum. Mackerel is an important commercially caught fish, and from the Gulf of Mexico we get pompano, considered by many of us to be our finest local fish. William H. Coleman's *Guide* in 1885 said of pompano that "like the Lilly of the valley, he needs no adornment to enhance his merits."

Once you become familiar with the few basic principles of New Orleans fish cooking, you will easily be able to prepare the fish dishes we love, from crisp Fried Trout and classically simple Broiled Pompano Meunière to Trout Marguery, Pompano en Papillote, and Redfish Courtbouillon.

FISH

RECOMMENDED SUBSTITUTIONS WHERE NEW ORLEANS FISH ARE UNAVAILABLE

speckled trout	freshwater bass* brook trout* weakfish perch pike perch* whiting scamp whitefish* pike* haddock grouper scrod pollock yellow perch
redfish	*For broiled dishes:* sea bass striped bass sole scamp rockfish whiting whitefish* brook trout *For baked dishes and courtbouillon:* haddock large cod swordfish turbot yellowtail red snapper pickerel
red snapper	yellowtail gray snapper schoolmaster
pompano	*Broiled:* NO SUBSTITUTE *En papillote:* red snapper redfish bluefish mackerel (Spanish, Boston, or king) halibut kingfish turbot pickerel
flounder	sole yellowtail dab gray sole lemon sole turbot
drum	small striped bass sea bass redfish speckled trout brook trout
catfish*	NO SUBSTITUTE
sheepshead (gaspergou)	swordfish red snapper
croaker	*See* speckled trout
grouper	*See* redfish
scamp	*See* redfish

*Indicates freshwater fish.

FISH

A NOTE ON THE CLEANING AND PREPARATION OF FISH FOR COOKING

The following terms are used in the recipes:

Whole (the fish is split, cleaned, head removed if desired, tail left on)

Filleted (the fish is split, cleaned, head and tail removed, center bone removed, skin left on)

Tenderloined (a New Orleans term; same as filleted, with skin also removed).

A NOTE ON SIZE

It is best to prepare the recipes with fish of the same general size as the ones indicated. Up to 1½ pounds is a small fish, 1½ to 2½ pounds is medium, and over 2½ pounds is large. Cooking times are given for the size category indicated in the recipe. If you must substitute a medium-sized fish for a small one, or the reverse, you will have to adjust the cooking time a little, by about 1 to 2 minutes more or less for broiling or poaching, by about 4 to 5 minutes more or less for baking. It is not recommended that you substitute a large fish for a small or medium one. The manner of cutting up the fish and the suitable ways of preparing it will differ greatly. If you can find only a large fish, select a recipe that calls for one.

FRIED TROUT

The secret of some of New Orleans' most famous trout dishes is simple—the trout is deep fried rather than sautéed. As discussed earlier, many books on New Orleans food have tended to confuse the two methods of cooking, leading many good cooks here and elsewhere to despair of ever getting some of our fish dishes to taste right.

This simple fried trout is a great favorite in New Orleans as a home meal—a heaping platter of fish at the center of the table and plenty of cold beer, iced tea, or Barq's root beer to wash it down—and as the base for more elegant dishes such as trout meunière and trout amandine. Once you learn to prepare it properly, you can do the fancier ones as a matter of course. The oil temperature for deep fried fish is crucial—375°. We prefer to use an electric deep fryer or an electric deep skillet (also called an electric Dutch skillet) with a thermostatic control. You can also use a heavy pot, but be sure to keep a deep fat thermometer clipped to the side and watch the temperature carefully. Oil that is not hot enough will give you greasy fish; oil that is too hot will tend to turn dark and to discolor the fish before it cooks through.

(for 4)

---

2 small to medium-sized speckled trout,* tenderloined
1 c. flour
2 tsp. salt
½ tsp. freshly ground black pepper
¼ tsp. cayenne
Vegetable oil for deep frying

Prepare the fish fillets for coating by rinsing them under cold running water and then shaking them over the sink to remove excess water. Do not dry them; the dampness that remains will permit the flour to adhere to the fish.

Prepare the coating by combining the flour, salt, pepper, and cayenne in a bowl. Mix thoroughly with a wire whisk or a spoon.

In a deep fryer or deep skillet, preheat the oil for frying to 375°. (Some large electric deep skillets require a 400° temperature because they have a larger than average top surface area in proportion to their depth. Check the recommended temperatures indicated on the appliance; if 400° is the indicated deep frying temperature, use it instead of 375°.) The oil should be from 1¾ to 3 inches deep in the fryer—that is, just a bit over half the depth of the container—which allows for the bubbling up that takes place when you first lower the food into the oil, caused by the moisture in the food coming into contact with the hot oil; this normally stops after a minute or two. (If it continues for much longer, it is an indication that there are too many solid particles in the oil. The bubbling will not affect the food, but may cause the oil to spatter; see note below.)

Note: Always skim the oil after you use it and strain carefully before storing it in the refrigerator. A useful trick we have found for extending the life of frying oil is to use all but the bottom ½ inch from the storage container when you pour it into the fryer; most of the solids that escape straining settle to the bottom. Discard the bottom layer and add about ⅓ cup fresh oil each time you fry. A good rule of thumb is to use the oil no more than 12 times. You will know when to discard the oil by color

*For suggested substitutes in other areas, see the chart on page 83.

and smell; it will get very dark and have a slightly scorched, rancid odor. If for some reason the oil reaches its limit sooner, discard it.

Coat the fillets by dipping them in the seasoned flour and turn them over in the flour several times to get an even coating; pat some flour over any damp spots with your fingers. Put the coated fillets on a platter, not touching one another, to let them dry for a few minutes.

To fry, lower one to two fillets at a time into the hot oil. Fry until golden brown, which should take about 8 minutes per batch. (Do not try to fry too many pieces at once; this will lower the oil temperature radically and the fish will be greasy.) When the fillets are cooked, lift them out of the oil with tongs, or by raising the frying basket if you are using one. Hold the fillets over the fryer for about 30 seconds to let the oil drain off, then place on a large platter lined with several layers of paper towels.

To keep warm, set the platter in a preheated 200° oven while you fry the rest of the fillets; you can keep fried fish warm in the oven for 30 to 40 minutes without any deterioration in taste or texture. As you add fillets to the platter—if necessary using a second platter—place them side by side rather than one on top of the other. (It's all right for the pieces to overlap a bit at the edges, but stacking them may make them a bit soggy because the warm air will not circulate properly.)

TROUT MEUNIÈRE GALATOIRE STYLE

Crisp deep fried trout with New Orleans meunière sauce—delicious and surprisingly simple to prepare. *(for 4)*

Fried Trout (page 85)   Meunière Sauce (page 113)

After frying the fish, keep warm in the oven as directed while preparing the meunière sauce. To serve, place each fillet on a heated plate and pour about 3/8 cup meunière sauce over it. Stir well each time you spoon out the sauce to distribute the browned solids at the bottom of the pan. These should be poured over the fish along with the sauce—they are part of it.

TROUT MEUNIÈRE ARNAUD STYLE

The other New Orleans trout meunière, served at Arnaud's, is a different dish. Fried trout with an unseasoned batter crust and a rich beef stock sauce, this old favorite has partisans who say it's the *real* one. We like them both. The brown meunière sauce is best prepared in advance in large quantities and refrigerated. To reheat it for saucing the fish, you may have to add a few teaspoons of water to thin it out a bit; it should have the consistency of very heavy cream. *(for 4)*

---

2 small to medium-sized speckled trout,* tenderloined
2 large eggs
2 Tbs. cold water
1½ c. flour
Vegetable oil for deep frying
2 c. Brown Meunière Sauce (page 113)

*For suggested substitutes in other areas, see the chart on page 83.

Rinse the fillets under cold running water and pat dry with paper towels. Combine the eggs and water in a pie dish and beat lightly with a fork to mix; put the flour in a bowl. Dip the fillets in the egg and water mixture, then in flour to coat, rolling them over several times to get as even a coating as possible. Place the coated fillets on a large platter to dry for a few minutes before frying; don't let the pieces touch.

Preheat the oil in the deep fryer at 375°, then fry the fish according to the directions on page 85. (This style of fried trout takes about 6 to 7 minutes to get golden brown.) Keep warm in the oven as directed while preparing the brown meunière sauce or reheating some you already have prepared. To serve, place each fillet on a heated dinner plate and pour ½ cup brown meunière sauce over it.

TROUT AMANDINE

Add almonds to trout meunière Galatoire style and you have a brand new dish. Many New Orleanians consider this their finest fish dish. We find that a slightly stiffer crust is more successful with amandine sauce, so we soak the fillets in milk before coating them. You can do that with any fried fish if you prefer a little more crunch to the crust. *(for 4)*

2 small to medium-sized speckled trout,* tenderloined
Cold milk for soaking
1 c. flour
1½ tsp. salt
¼ tsp. freshly ground black pepper
⅛ tsp. cayenne
Vegetable oil for deep frying

AMANDINE SAUCE

1½ c. (3 sticks) salt butter
1⅓ c. blanched slivered almonds
2 Tbs. fresh lemon juice
1 tsp. freshly ground black pepper

Rinse the fillets and dry them thoroughly with paper towels. Place them in a pie dish or bowl and add cold milk just to cover; combine the flour and seasonings in a bowl. Meanwhile, preheat the oil in a deep fryer to 375°.

Coat the fillets by lifting them one at a time out of the milk, letting the excess drain off over the bowl for about 30 seconds, then dipping them in the seasoned flour to cover evenly. Fry according to the directions on page 85 and keep warm in the oven as directed while preparing the amandine sauce.

In a heavy saucepan, melt the butter over low heat, then add the almonds and cook over low heat until the butter begins to turn brown (the color of hazelnuts). Remove the pan from the heat immediately and add the lemon juice and black pepper. Mix well, then return the pan to low heat for 1 minute. Remove from the heat again and mix the sauce thoroughly with a spoon.

To serve, place the fried fillets on heated plates and spoon about ½ cup sauce over each. Half the almonds in each portion should be on top of the fish; the other half should surround the fish.

*For suggested substitutes in other areas, see the chart on page 83.

FRIED TROUT IN PEARLY MEAL

"Pearly meal" is the local name for a half-and-half mixture of yellow corn meal and corn flour. We like the crust this mixture makes on fried fish; it's crunchier than white flour, but not as hard as pure corn flour. Try this coating for any small fried fish or for a mixed catch from a good day's fishing. *(for 4)*

- 2 small to medium-sized speckled trout,* tenderloined
- Cold milk for soaking
- 1 c. yellow corn flour (Fish-Fri)
- 1 c. yellow corn meal
- 1½ tsp. salt
- ¼ tsp. freshly ground black pepper
- 1/16 tsp. cayenne
- Vegetable oil for deep frying

Rinse the fillets and dry them thoroughly with paper towels. Place them in a pie dish or bowl and add cold milk just to cover; combine the flour and seasonings in a bowl. Meanwhile, preheat the oil in a deep fryer to 375°.

Coat the fillets by lifting them, one at a time, out of the milk, letting the excess drain off over the bowl for about 30 seconds, then dipping them in the seasoned flour to cover evenly. Fry as directed on page 85.

Serve in a large wide bowl or on a large platter placed at the center of the table, and let everyone help himself.

PAN FRIED GROUPER

Another style of fried fish, prepared in a skillet with a mixture of butter and olive oil. We like to add some sliced shallots and a few extra seasonings, and then use the frying oil as a sauce. The fish will not be quite as crisp as deep fried, but you should be able to get an attractive brown crust if the oil is hot enough. *(for 4)*

- 2 medium-sized groupers,* filleted or tenderloined
- 2 large eggs
- 2 Tbs. cold water
- 1½ c. flour
- 1¼ tsp. salt
- ¼ tsp. freshly ground white pepper
- Scant ⅛ tsp. cayenne
- ¼ c. (½ stick) salt butter
- ¼ c. olive oil
- ⅓ c. finely minced shallots (scallions)
- 1 whole bay leaf, crumbled
- ¾ tsp. dried marjoram

Rinse the fillets and place them on paper towels to drain. Combine the eggs and water in a pie dish and beat lightly with a fork to mix; combine the flour, salt, pepper, and cayenne in a bowl and mix well. Dip the fillets in the egg and water mixture, then roll them in the seasoned flour to coat thoroughly. Place them on a platter, not touching, to dry for about 5 minutes.

In a large heavy skillet melt the butter over medium heat, then mix in the olive oil with a spoon and continue cooking until the oil is quite hot. (You can test the temperature by wetting the tip of your finger under the faucet and shaking a drop or two of water into the skillet. If the drops dance quickly in the oil and make a little sizzling noise, the oil is hot enough.) Fry the fillets in hot oil until browned (about

*For suggested substitutes in other areas, see the chart on page 83.

3 to 4 minutes on each side), adding the shallots, bay leaf, and marjoram to the oil in the spaces around the sides of the skillet after the fish begins to brown on the first side. When the fish is fried on both sides, remove it to a paper towel-lined platter and simmer the sauce in the skillet for about 3 more minutes. Serve the fillets with about 2 tablespoons of sauce from the skillet over each one.

FRIED CROAKER

Croaker is a small, slightly sweet fish widely caught by local fishermen. A huge platter of fried croaker, or croaker and small speckled trout mixed, makes a fine informal feast. Some of us consider the center bones with the tail attached and some meat still on them a delicacy; we save them when we clean the fish or have the fish market save them, then coat and fry them along with the fillets. The tails on small fried fish are crunchy and delicious. For a fish fry dinner, figure at least 2 small fish per person.

(for 4 to 6)

8 to 12 small croakers,* tenderloined, center bones with tails attached reserved
Cold milk for soaking
2 c. yellow corn flour (Fish-Fri)
2 c. yellow corn meal
1 Tbs. salt
1/2 tsp. freshly ground black pepper
1/16 tsp. cayenne
Vegetable oil for deep frying

Rinse the fillets and dry them thoroughly with paper towels. Place them, along with the center bones, in a pie dish or bowl and add cold milk just to cover; combine the flour and seasonings in a bowl. Meanwhile, preheat the oil in a deep fryer to 375°

Coat the fillets and bones by lifting them, one at a time, out of the milk, letting the excess drain off over the bowl for about 30 seconds, then dipping them in the seasoned flour to cover evenly. Fry as directed on page 85.

Serve in a large bowl or platter, and let everyone help himself.

*For suggested substitutes in other areas, see the chart on page 83.

FRIED CATFISH

The best fried catfish we have tasted are prepared in the Cajun country, where they are caught and cooked absolutely fresh. Most catfish are medium-sized or large-sized; the best way to prepare them for frying is to tenderloin them, then slice the fillets across as thin as you can, about ⅛ to ¼ inch thick. Use a very sharp knife.

We like a *very hot* corn meal crust for fresh catfish; it seems to set off the sweet taste of the fish perfectly. If you are a bit shy about pepper, reduce the cayenne by half the first time you prepare catfish this way. *(for 4)*

---

1 medium-sized to large freshwater catfish, tenderloined and the fillets then sliced across about ⅛ inch thick
Cold milk for soaking
1½ c. finely ground yellow corn meal
2¼ tsp. salt
1 tsp. freshly ground black pepper
1½ tsp. cayenne
Vegetable oil for deep frying

Rinse the catfish fillets quickly under cold running water and dry very thoroughly with paper towels. Put them in a pie dish or bowl and add cold milk to cover; combine the corn meal and seasonings in another bowl. Preheat the oil in a deep fryer to 375°. When the oil is hot, quickly lift the pieces of fish out of the milk, roll them in the seasoned meal, and lay them flat and not touching on a platter to dry for a few minutes before frying. (This should be done in batches of 4 to 6 pieces at a time. You can prepare the next batch while the first one is frying.) Fry until golden brown, about 5 to 7 minutes per batch, according to the directions on page 85. Drain, then place on a paper towel-lined platter in a preheated 200° oven to keep warm until served.

BROILED FLOUNDER

A delicate fish seasoned with a simple lemon-butter sauce and broiled whole. This is the classic way to prepare any fine-textured small to medium fish with a thin skin. Broiled flounder looks most attractive with the tail left on and the skin scored. Watch the timing: overcooking the fish destroys its texture—and even one minute is crucial.

(per portion)

- 6 Tbs. (¾ stick) salt butter
- 2 tsp. finely minced fresh parsley
- 4 tsp. fresh lemon juice
- ⅛ tsp. salt
- 1 small to medium-sized flounder, cleaned and left whole
- Salt and freshly ground pepper

GARNISH

Lemon wedge

Preheat the broiler and broiling pan for 10 minutes. (The concentrated heat will cook the bottom side of the fish; it will not be necessary to turn it over.) Meanwhile, melt the butter in a small heavy saucepan over low heat. Turn the heat off, then add the parsley, lemon juice, and ⅛ teaspoon salt and mix well. Remove the broiling pan and rack from the oven after preheating and brush the rack with some of the butter sauce.

Rinse the cleaned whole flounder and dry it thoroughly with paper towels. To season the fish, score the thick top side of the flounder with about 4 X-shaped slits, then sprinkle on both sides with salt and pepper. (Many restaurants use paprika to disguise a poorly broiled fish. This is not recommended. Proper heat and distance will give you the attractive color and unmistakable flavor of good broiling.) Place the fish on the broiling rack and pour about 2 tablespoons of the butter sauce over it.

Broil the fish (5 minutes for a small flounder, 6 minutes for a medium flounder) at a distance of 3½ to 4 inches from the heat. The distance is crucial: placed too close to the heat, the fish will burn; placed too far, it will not cook quickly enough to get crisp and brown—and slow broiling at a greater distance gives the fish a baked, overcooked quality. Watch the timing carefully; it takes only a minute or two to overcook broiled fish.

Remove the broiling pan from the oven as soon as the recommended time has elapsed. (If you want to check for doneness, prick the fish lightly with a toothpick or fork: if it flakes easily it's done. If not, put the broiling pan back in the oven for one minute more.) Put the flounder on a heated dinner plate the pour the remaining butter sauce over it. Serve with a wedge of lemon.

BROILED SPECKLED TROUT

New Orleans' basic fish, filleted with the skin left on, and broiled simply. A bit of dry white wine in the butter sauce provides additional flavor. The skin side is placed down to help the fillets of a loose-textured fish keep their shape during broiling. You can remove the skin before saucing and serving or leave it on. *(for 4)*

1½ c. (3 sticks) salt butter
¼ c. dry white wine
1½ Tbs. finely minced fresh parsley
¼ tsp. salt
⅛ tsp. freshly ground black pepper
2 small to medium-sized speckled trout,* filleted
Salt and freshly ground pepper for sprinkling

GARNISH

Lemon wedges

Prepare the broiler and broiling pan and rack as directed on page 91. Meanwhile, prepare the sauce as directed on page 91, adding the parsley, ¼ teaspoon salt, and ⅛ teaspoon pepper. Set aside.

Rinse the fillets and dry them thoroughly, then sprinkle the fillets with salt and pepper on the top side (no skin) only. Place them on the preheated broiling rack, pour half the sauce over, and broil for 6 minutes as directed on page 91. Remove from the broiler promptly.

Stir the remaining sauce to mix thoroughly, then place the fillets on heated dinner plates, cover with the sauce, and serve with lemon wedges.

BROILED POMPANO

A majestic Gulf fish simply prepared. If you leave the skin on, place the fillets skin side down during broiling. *(for 4)*

---

1 c. (2 sticks) salt butter
2 Tbs. finely minced fresh parsley
2½ Tbs. fresh lemon juice
½ tsp. salt
2 small to medium-sized pompano, filleted or tenderloined
Salt and freshly ground pepper

Prepare according to the directions on page 91. Broil 6 minutes for a small pompano, 7 minutes for a medium-sized pompano. Sauce and serve as directed.

*For suggested substitutes in other areas, see the chart on page 83.

BROILED POMPANO MEUNIÈRE

Carefully broiled pompano with a browned butter sauce poured over it just before serving—our favorite way of serving this delicious fish. The meunière sauce is prepared separately from the small amount of lemon-butter sauce needed for proper broiling.

Broiled fish should be served as soon as it is cooked, so prepare the meunière first, set it aside, then reheat it quickly at the last minute. *(for 4)*

- 1¼ c. Meunière Sauce (page 113)
- 2 small to medium-sized pompano, filleted or tenderloined
- ½ c. (1 stick) salt butter
- 1 Tbs. finely minced fresh parsley
- 1 Tbs. fresh lemon juice
- ¼ tsp. salt
- Salt and freshly ground pepper

Prepare the meunière sauce and set aside. Broil the pompano according to the directions on page 91 and put all the butter sauce on the fish before broiling. After the pompano is in the oven, set the pan of meunière sauce on the burner over medium heat for about 1 minute, then turn off the heat; it should stay warm enough if you use a heavy saucepan. Otherwise, reheat the meunière after you have put the pompano on heated dinner plates: use high heat and warm the meunière for 30 seconds. Pour about ¼ cup meunière sauce over each fish before serving.

POMPANO AMANDINE

Broiled pompano meunière with almonds, a delightful combination of tastes and textures. *(for 4)*

Prepare 2 small to medium-sized pompano, filleted or tenderloined, as for Broiled Pompano Meunière (see above). Prepare 1¼ cups Meunière Sauce (see page 113), adding 1 cup of blanched slivered almonds to the sauce just before browning. As the butter begins to brown, the almonds will turn a gold-brown color. Remove them with a slotted spoon and reserve in a small bowl until the meunière sauce is done.

To serve, place the pompano on heated dinner plates, cover each one with ¼ cup browned almonds, then pour about ¼ cup meunière sauce over the almonds and the fish.

BROILED REDFISH

Redfish is a firm fish with a medium to large flake, depending on its size. We like it best broiled without the skin. *(for 4)*

1 c. (2 sticks) salt butter
2 Tbs. finely minced fresh parsley
3 Tbs. fresh lemon juice
½ tsp. salt
2 small to medium-sized redfish,* tenderloined
Salt and freshly ground pepper

Prepare according to the directions on page 91, omitting the details dealing with the skin. Broil 6 minutes for most redfish fillets, 7 minutes for very thick ones (over ¾ inch thick). Sauce and serve as directed.

BROILED REDFISH MEUNIÈRE

(for 4)

1¼ c. Meunière Sauce (page 113)
2 small to medium-sized redfish,* tenderloined
½ c. (1 stick) salt butter
1 Tbs. finely minced fresh parsley
1 Tbs. fresh lemon juice
¼ tsp. salt
Salt and freshly ground pepper

Prepare the meunière sauce and set aside. Broil the redfish fillets according to the directions on page 91 and put all the sauce on the fillets before broiling. After the redfish is broiled, place the fillets on heated dinner plates. Quickly reheat the meunière sauce over high heat for about 30 seconds, then pour about ¼ cup of the sauce over each fillet before serving.

REDFISH AMANDINE

Prepare according to the directions for Pompano Amandine, page 93.

BROILED REDFISH HOLLANDAISE

(for 4)

Prepare 2 cups Blender Hollandaise (see page 114) or Handmade Hollandaise (see page 115), then set the container in a basin or bowl of warm water to keep the sauce warm while broiling the fish. Prepare 2 small to medium-sized redfish,* tenderloined, as for Broiled Redfish Meunière (see above). To serve, place the fillets on heated dinner plates and cover each one with ½ cup hollandaise sauce.

RED SNAPPER HOLLANDAISE

Prepare according to the directions for the preceding recipe.

*For suggested substitutes in other areas, see the chart on page 83.

REDFISH WITH LUMP CRABMEAT HOLLANDAISE

This fish dish for special occasions was created by Arnaud's. In order to have everything ready when you need it, prepare the sautéed crabmeat first and set it in a warm oven. Then make the hollandaise. Broil the fish last, cover it with the crabmeat, then top each serving with a sea of golden hollandaise. *(for 4)*

---

1 lb. choice lump crabmeat
6 Tbs. (¾ stick) salt butter
2 c. Blender Hollandaise (page 114) or Handmade Hollandaise (page 115)
1½ Tbs. fresh lemon juice
½ tsp. salt
½ tsp. freshly ground white pepper
2 small to medium-sized redfish,* tenderloined

In a skillet or sauté pan melt 2 tablespoons of the butter over low heat, add the crabmeat, and cook for about 5 minutes, just to warm through. Stir gently with a wooden spoon as you heat, taking care not to break up the lumps too much. When the crabmeat is warm, set the skillet in a preheated 175° oven to keep warm until needed.

Prepare the hollandaise sauce and set the container in warm water until needed. Melt the remaining butter in a saucepan and mix in the lemon juice, salt, and white pepper, then broil the redfish fillets according to the directions on page 91, omitting the details dealing with the skin.

To serve, put the fillets on heated dinner plates. Place one-quarter of the sautéed lump crabmeat on top of each fillet and cover each portion evenly with ½ cup hollandaise sauce.

REDFISH WITH LUMP CRABMEAT MEUNIÈRE

(for 4)

Prepare as for Redfish with Lump Crabmeat Hollandaise (see above), substituting 1¼ cups Meunière Sauce (see page 113) for the 2 cups hollandaise. Sauté the crabmeat first and set in a warm oven as directed. Then prepare the meunière sauce and set the pan aside. Broil the redfish as directed. Place the fillets on heated dinner plates, cover each with one-quarter of the sautéed lump crabmeat, then pour about ¼ cup meunière sauce over each portion.

*For suggested substitutes in other areas, see the chart on page 83.

REDFISH PONTCHARTRAIN

Broiled redfish topped with one or two buster or soft shell crabs, a favorite New Orleans combination. *(for 4)*

- 1 c. Meunière Sauce (page 113)
- ½ c. (1 stick) salt butter
- 2 Tbs. fresh lemon juice
- ¼ tsp. freshly ground white pepper
- 2 small to medium-sized redfish,* tenderloined
- 8 buster crabs or very small soft shell crabs, cleaned (page 44)

Prepare the meunière sauce and set the pan aside. Preheat the broiler, including broiling pan and rack, for 10 minutes. Meanwhile, melt the butter over low heat in a saucepan and mix in the lemon juice and white pepper. When the broiler is hot, brush the rack with some of the lemon-butter sauce, then place the fillets and the crabs on the rack and pour the remaining sauce over them. Broil according to the directions on page 91, omitting the details dealing with the skin.

To serve, place the redfish fillets on heated dinner plates and top each one with 2 crabs, placed side by side. Reheat the meunière sauce over high heat for about 30 seconds, stir to mix, then pour ¼ cup of the sauce over each portion.

STUFFED FLOUNDER WITH CRAWFISH

In New Orleans flounder is frequently "stuffed" (topped) with crabmeat and baked. We prefer this version: the flounder is broiled and topped with a puree of crawfish. *(for 4)*

- 1 c. Crawfish Dressing (page 118)
- 3 Tbs. boiling water
- 2 Tbs. dry white wine
- ⅓ lb. crawfish tails, parboiled for 3 minutes
- ½ c. (1 stick) salt butter
- 2 tsp. lemon juice
- 2 Tbs. finely minced fresh parsley
- ¼ tsp. freshly ground white pepper
- ¼ tsp. salt
- 4 small to medium-sized flounder,* cleaned and left whole

To prepare the crawfish stuffing, put the crawfish dressing in a heavy saucepan. Add the water, white wine, and parboiled crawfish tails and cook over low heat for 10 to 12 minutes, or until the crawfish tails are warmed through. Remove the pan from the heat and set it in a 175° oven to keep warm while preparing the flounder.

Melt the butter over low heat and mix in the lemon juice, parsley, pepper, and salt. Broil the flounder according to the directions on page 91, using all the butter sauce.

To serve, place the fish on heated dinner plates. Heap the crawfish mixture over the fish, then pour the liquid that has collected at the bottom of the pan around the fish.

*For suggested substitutes in other areas, see the chart on page 83.

BROILED DRUM BEURRE BLANC

Drum is a small freshwater bass. The delicate taste of this small fish is set off well by broiling the fillets for just 5 minutes and saucing them with beurre blanc, a classic, slightly tart French butter sauce. We also like to prepare small redfish this way. *(for 4)*

1½ c. Beurre Blanc (page 118)
½ c. (1 stick) salt butter
1½ Tbs. fresh lemon juice
½ tsp. freshly ground white pepper
¼ tsp. salt
2 small drum,* tenderloined

Prepare the beurre blanc, then set the pan in a basin or bowl of water while broiling the fish. Melt the butter and mix in the lemon juice, pepper, and salt. Broil the drum fillets according to the directions on page 91, omitting the details dealing with the skin, using all the butter sauce, and broiling for exactly 5 minutes.

To serve, place the fillets on heated dinner plates and cover each one with about ⅓ cup beurre blanc.

SCAMP AMANDINE

Scamp is caught along the Gulf Coast and is an excellent fish for broiling. In the Mobile area the term "amandine" means a carefully broiled fish sauced with lemon butter and toasted almonds. *(for 4)*

2 small to medium-sized scamp,* tenderloined
1 c. (2 sticks) salt butter
2 Tbs. finely minced fresh parsley
3 Tbs. fresh lemon juice
½ tsp. salt
Salt and freshly ground pepper
¾ c. blanched, slivered almonds, toasted in a hot oven for 8 minutes

Broil the fillets according to the directions on page 91. To serve, place the fillets on heated dinner plates, sprinkle each one with 3 tablespoons toasted almonds, then pour one-quarter of the remaining butter sauce over each portion of almonds.

*For suggested substitutes in other areas, see the chart on page 83.

BROILED SPANISH MACKEREL

Mackerel is an oily fish, and is particularly good broiled if you marinate the fillets for several hours before cooking. If you find it more convenient, set the fillets to marinate in the morning and take them out when you are ready to prepare dinner; the extra marinating time won't affect the fish. *(for 4)*

---

2 medium-sized Spanish mackerel, tenderloined

MARINADE

3 Tbs. fresh lemon juice
¾ tsp. freshly ground black pepper
½ tsp. salt
½ tsp. ground marjoram
¼ tsp. dried basil

½ c. (1 stick) salt butter
2 Tbs. fresh lemon juice
1 Tbs. finely minced fresh parsley
¼ tsp. freshly ground white pepper
¼ tsp. salt

Place the mackerel fillets in a stainless steel or porcelain bowl. (Marinades tend to produce a faint metallic taste in most containers made of other materials.) In a small bowl or a cup, combine the ingredients for the marinade and mix well with a fork. Pour the marinade over the fish fillets, then turn the fillets over several times to dampen all surfaces. Cover the bowl with plastic wrap and refrigerate for at least 2½ hours.

When you are ready to cook the fish, remove the fillets from the marinade with a fork and place them on a large platter to let some of the marinade drain off. Meanwhile, melt the butter over low heat and add the lemon juice, parsley, white pepper, and salt. Broil the fillets according to the directions on page 91 for 7 minutes, omitting the details dealing with the skin, and using all the butter sauce. To serve, place the fillets on heated dinner plates and spoon the pan drippings over the fish.

KING MACKEREL MARTINIQUE

King mackerel is a favorite Gulf sport fish. Marinating slices of this large, oily fish in lime juice before broiling is a technique used in French Martinique. If you can't get fresh limes, frozen or bottled lime juice is acceptable, as long as it is unsweetened. Use about half again as much as you would fresh, since it tends to be a bit less tart.

(for 4)

A 2 lb. steak of king mackerel, skin left on

MARINADE

- Juice of 3 fresh limes
- ½ tsp. freshly ground black pepper
- ¾ tsp. ground marjoram

- ½ c. (1 stick) salt butter
- ¼ tsp. salt
- ½ tsp. freshly ground black pepper
- 1 Tbs. finely minced fresh parsley
- 2 Tbs. fresh lemon juice

Place the piece of mackerel in a stainless steel or porcelain bowl. In a small bowl or cup, combine the ingredients for the marinade and mix well with a fork. Pour the marinade over the fish, then turn the steak several times to coat thoroughly. Cover the bowl with plastic wrap and refrigerate for 3 to 4 hours.

When you are ready to broil the fish, remove the fish from the marinade and place it on a plate. Score the skin on the top side with X-shaped slits at 1½-inch intervals, then set the fish aside while you preheat the broiler, broiling pan, and rack for 10 minutes. Meanwhile, melt the butter in a saucepan over low heat, then turn off the heat and add the salt, ½ teaspoon pepper, the parsley, and lemon juice. Mix well. When the broiler is hot, place the piece of mackerel, the scored skin up, in the pan and pour all the butter sauce over it. Broil 5 inches from the heat for 8 minutes on each side.

To serve, cut the piece into four portions and place them on heated plates, spooning some of the pan drippings over each one.

POACHED FISH

TROUT MARGUERY

Made famous by Galatoire's, trout Marguery is Creole cooking at its heartiest and most lavish—fresh poached trout with a rich buttery roux-based sauce full of firm well-seasoned boiled shrimp. It simplifies preparation to have the boiled shrimp prepared ahead; then you need only add them to the sauce and warm them through.

(for 4)

---

2 small to medium-sized speckled trout,*
tenderloined

POACHING LIQUID

2½ c. water
¼ c. dry white wine
1 Tbs. salt butter
1 tsp. salt
3 whole black peppercorns
1 whole bay leaf, broken in half
⅛ tsp. dried thyme
1 slice fresh lemon (¼ inch thick)

MARGUERY SAUCE

½ c. (1 stick) salt butter
¼ c. flour
2½ c. hot liquid (the strained poaching liquid plus enough boiling water to make 2½ c.)
2 large egg yolks, lightly beaten
1 Tbs. fresh lemon juice
¼ tsp. salt
1 lb. fresh shrimp, boiled (page 75)
½ c. fresh mushrooms, sliced (if fresh are unavailable, substitute high-quality canned; drain them very well)

To poach the trout fillets, combine all the ingredients for the poaching liquid in a large heavy skillet or sauté pan. Bring to a boil over high heat, then reduce the heat so that the liquid is just at a simmer. Lower the trout fillets into the liquid with a spatula and cook at a low simmer for 5 to 6 minutes. The fish will flake easily when pricked with a fork if it is done; do not overcook. Remove the fillets from the poaching liquid by lifting them out carefully on a slotted spatula, tipping it to let the excess liquid drain off. Place the fish on a platter and set aside in a preheated 175° oven to keep warm while you prepare the sauce. Strain and reserve the poaching liquid.

In a heavy 2- to 3-quart saucepan, melt 3 tablespoons of the butter over low heat. Add the flour and stir with a wooden spoon until smooth; do not brown. Slowly add the hot liquid, stirring constantly with a wire whisk or a spoon to keep a perfectly smooth texture. Cook over low heat until thickened (about 5 to 7 minutes), stirring constantly, then remove the pan from the heat. Add the egg yolks, lemon juice, and salt and blend well with a whisk. In a separate small saucepan melt the remaining 5 tablespoons butter over low heat. Return the large saucepan to the heat and slowly add the melted butter, keeping the heat very low. Blend well, then add the boiled shrimp and sliced mushrooms. Cook over very low heat, stirring gently, until the

*For suggested substitutes in other areas, see the chart on page 83.

shrimp and mushrooms are heated through (about 4 to 6 minutes). Do not allow the sauce to boil.

To serve, place the fish on heated plates and pour equal quantities of the sauce over each portion.

NEW ORLEANS TROUT SAUCE NORMANDE

Norman style dishes were popular in nineteenth-century New Orleans. This dish combines poached trout with a flamed cream sauce made with Calvados, the French apple brandy.

(for 4)

2 small to medium-sized speckled trout,*
tenderloined and poached as for
Trout Marguery (page 100)

SAUCE NORMANDE

2 Tbs. salt butter
2 Tbs. flour
¼ tsp. salt
¼ tsp. freshly ground white pepper
1½ c. strained poaching liquid
1 c. heavy cream
7 Tbs. Calvados or applejack

After poaching the trout, strain and reserve the poaching liquid. Set the fish in a 175° oven to keep warm while you prepare the sauce. In a heavy 2-quart saucepan, melt the butter over low heat. Gradually add the flour, stirring to keep the mixture smooth, then remove the pan from the heat and add the salt and pepper. In a separate small saucepan, heat 1½ cups of the reserved poaching liquid. Return the larger pan to the heat and add the poaching liquid slowly, stirring constantly, then cook over low heat until the sauce begins to thicken. Add the cream, blend well, and mix in 3 tablespoons of the Calvados. Cook over low heat for 2 to 3 minutes more, then remove the pan from the heat.

When ready to serve, put the fish in a flambé pan or a large heavy skillet and pour the sauce over it. Set the pan on an alcohol burner or on the stove over low heat. In a separate small saucepan heat the remaining 4 tablespoons of Calvados to boiling, then pour over the sauce and fish in the serving pan. Ignite immediately. Tip the pan with a slow, circular motion to distribute the flame and to keep it going. When the flame dies out, serve the fish on heated plates with the sauce poured over it.

*For suggested substitutes in other areas, see the chart on page 83.

TROUT VERONIQUE

This dish of poached trout with a glaze hollandaise made with green grapes was introduced by the Pontchartrain Hotel. It is a spectacular fish creation that is surprisingly simple to prepare, if you take it one step at a time. You will need 4 individual flameproof plates or 1 large one for glazing the sauce just before serving.

(for 4)

- 2 small to medium-sized speckled trout,* tenderloined and poached as for Trout Marguery (page 100)
- 3 c. Blender Hollandaise (page 114) or Handmade Hollandaise (page 115)
- 1½ c. green seedless grapes, cut in half lengthwise (dark seedless grapes may be substituted if the green are not available)

After poaching the trout, set in a 175° oven to keep warm while preparing the sauce.

Add the grapes to the sauce and mix very gently to distribute them evenly. Place each fillet on an individual flameproof plate or use one large flameproof plate for all. (If you use a single large plate, have 4 heated dinner plates ready for serving the portions.) Cover each fillet with a fourth of the Veronique sauce. To glaze, place the plates (or plate) under a preheated broiler 3 to 4 inches from the heat for about 30 seconds, or just until the top of the sauce begins to brown. Remove immediately from the heat and serve. (If you use a single plate, remove the portions by sliding a long spatula under each one and lifting it, along with its glazed sauce covering, onto a dinner plate.)

COLD POACHED REDFISH

Chilled poached fish is particularly delicious with a piquant sauce, such as cream horseradish sauce. To vary the sauce a bit and give it an unusual texture, add 3 tablespoons very finely chopped pecans to it. We like this dish as a main course or as an appetizer. *(for 4 as a main dish; for 8 as an appetizer)*

- 2 small to medium-sized redfish,* tenderloined and poached as for Trout Marguery (page 100)
- 1⅓ c. Cream Horseradish Sauce (page 120)

After poaching the redfish, drain thoroughly and refrigerate on a large platter covered with several layers of plastic wrap for at least 2 hours. To serve as a main dish, place the fish on dinner plates and pour a bit more than ¼ cup cream horseradish sauce over each portion. For appetizer portions, divide the quantities of fish and sauce in half.

*For suggested substitutes in other areas, see the chart on page 83.

POMPANO EN PAPILLOTE

When the French balloonist Alberto Santos-Dumont visited New Orleans in 1901, Antoine's honored him with a dish made to look like a turn-of-the-century flying balloon—a dish that became one of Antoine's most famous creations. The fish is poached in a very rich sauce inside a closed envelope made of baking parchment. A marvelous aroma fills the room when the papillote (paper bag) is cut open at the table. This dramatic dish tastes just as good with a less expensive fish such as redfish, trout, or red snapper. Prepare the boiled shrimp ahead of time. *(for 4)*

---

4 12-inch squares of baking parchment
6 Tbs. (¾ stick) salt butter
¼ c. flour
⅔ c. finely minced shallots (scallions)
1 Tbs. finely minced fresh parsley
1 Tbs. dry white wine
¼ tsp. salt
½ tsp. freshly ground white pepper
⅛ tsp. cayenne
2 large egg yolks, lightly beaten
6 Tbs. heavy cream
1 c. boiled fresh shrimp (see page 75), broken into thirds
½ c. choice lump crabmeat
½ c. fresh shucked small oysters (about 1½ doz.), drained
2 small or 1 medium-sized pompano, tenderloined (divide fillets of medium-sized pompano into 2 pieces)
Extra butter for greasing inside of papillotes

To form the papillotes, trim each square of baking parchment into the shape of a heart, and crease down the center. Set aside while you prepare the sauce in a large heavy saucepan. Melt the butter over low heat, gradually add the flour, stirring constantly, and cook for 2 minutes. Add the shallots and parsley and cook 5 minutes longer, stirring frequently. Remove the pan from the heat. Add the wine, salt, pepper, cayenne, egg yolks, and cream. Mix thoroughly. Then return the pan to low heat and add the shrimp, crabmeat, and oysters. Cook for about 5 minutes, stirring gently. Remove the pan from the heat.

Butter the inside of each papillote, then fold in half, buttered side in. Fold up the edge of the bottom half to form a lip about ¾ inch deep. Pour half the sauce, in equal quantities, on the bottom half of each papillote. Place a piece of fish on the sauce, then pour the remaining sauce over the fish. Fold down the top half of the papillote. Bring the top and bottom edges together, folding them over tightly, several times. Be sure the pointed tip is tightly closed; fold the point over twice to make sure. Put the sealed papillotes in a large shallow baking dish or heavy baking pan, and bake in a preheated 425° oven for about 18 to 20 minutes, or until the baking parchment begins to brown. (Some baking parchment does not get visibly brown. Do not bake the papillotes any longer than 20 minutes.) Bring to the table, closed, on individual dinner plates and open at the table.

REDFISH EN PAPILLOTE

Prepare according to directions for Pompano en Papillote (see above), substituting 2 small or 1 medium-sized redfish for the pompano. Cut the fish into 2- or 3-inch-square pieces and arrange them in the shape of a single fish fillet when filling each papillote to allow for more even poaching.

TROUT EN PAPILLOTE

Prepare according to directions for Pompano en Papillote (see page 103), substituting 2 small or 1 medium-sized trout for the pompano. Increase the parsley to 2 tablespoons, omit the oysters, and cut larger fish into pieces.

RED SNAPPER EN PAPILLOTE

Prepare according to directions for Pompano en Papillote (see page 103), substituting 2 small or 1 medium-sized red snapper for the pompano. If only very large red snappers are available, get a steak of about 1¾ to 2 pounds, skin removed. Cut the steak into four parts, then slice the pieces about ½ inch thick and place them side by side on the sauced bottom half of the papillote.

POACHED RED SNAPPER WITH NANTUA SAUCE

Red snapper is excellent poached and served with this crawfish sauce. Use either small or medium-sized fish, or if only large red snapper is available, a steak of about 2 pounds, for this dish. You can prepare the sauce several hours ahead of time and refrigerate it. To reheat it, put the sauce in a heavy saucepan over *very* low heat, add about 2 teaspoons water, and cook just until it is warmed through. (If you let it come to a boil, it will separate.) Save the solids you strain out for crawfish stuffing; the solids will keep under refrigeration for several days. *(for 4)*

⅓ c. dry white wine
3 c. water
1 small onion, thinly sliced
4 sprigs parsley, torn into 1-inch pieces
1½ tsp. salt
2 whole cloves
4 whole black peppercorns
1 whole bay leaf, broken in half
⅛ tsp. dried thyme
1 slice fresh lemon (¼ inch thick)
2 small or medium-sized red snappers,* tenderloined, or 2 red snapper* steaks, skin removed, cut into ½-inch slices
2 c. Nantua Sauce (page 118), warmed

Put all the ingredients except the fish and the Nantua sauce in a large heavy skillet or sauté pan and bring to a boil over high heat. Reduce the heat and simmer for 15 minutes, then remove the solids with a fine-mesh skimmer or a slotted spoon. Keeping the liquid at a simmer, lower the fish into the pan with a spatula. Simmer for 8 to 10 minutes, just until the fish flakes easily when pricked with a fork, spooning some of the liquid over the top of the fish from time to time during cooking. Remove the fish from the pan by lifting it out carefully with a large slotted spatula. (If you use an unslotted spatula, tip it slightly as you lift to allow the excess liquid to drain off.)

To serve, place the fish on heated plates and top each portion with ½ cup warm Nantua sauce.

*For suggested substitutes in other areas, see the chart on page 83.

REDFISH COURTBOUILLON

The great New Orleans boiled fish dish. The spicy roux-based courtbouillon is cooked for over half an hour before the redfish slices are added, which gives the fish a lovely, heady flavor. Serve redfish courtbouillon in soup bowls with plenty of liquid, and supply soup spoons. If you have any left over, refrigerate it and, the next time you serve, reheat it *very* briefly, to avoid destroying the texture of the fish. Swordfish, turbot, bluefish, and halibut will all work beautifully. *(for 4)*

ROUX-BASED COURTBOUILLON

- 1/3 c. vegetable oil
- 1/2 c. flour
- 1 3/4 c. chopped onion
- 1 c. thinly sliced green shallot (scallion) tops
- 3/4 c. chopped green pepper
- 1 Tbs. finely minced garlic
- 1/3 c. chopped celery
- 1 one-lb. can peeled whole tomatoes (about 2 1/4 c.), coarsely chopped
- 1 Tbs. finely minced fresh parsley
- 3 whole bay leaves, broken into quarters
- 1/2 tsp. dried thyme
- 1/4 tsp. dried marjoram
- 6 whole allspice
- 2 tsp. salt
- 1/2 tsp. freshly ground black pepper
- 1/8 tsp. cayenne
- 1/2 tsp. dried basil
- 2 1/2 Tbs. fresh lemon juice
- 3/4 c. dry red wine
- 2 1/2 c. water

- 1 medium-sized redfish,* cleaned and cut into 2-inch slices across
- 8 slices fresh lemon, each about 1/8 inch thick

In a heavy 4- to 5-quart pot or kettle, heat the oil. Add the flour, stir, lower the heat, and cook over low heat, stirring constantly, until a roux the color of rich peanut butter is formed (about 25 minutes). Add the onion, shallot tops, green pepper, garlic, and celery and brown for another 8 to 10 minutes, stirring constantly. Add the chopped tomatoes, parsley, bay leaves, thyme, marjoram, allspice, salt, pepper, cayenne, basil, lemon juice, and red wine. Stir to mix thoroughly, then slowly add the water, mixing well. Bring to a boil, then lower the heat, and simmer uncovered for 35 minutes. Stir frequently and scrape the sides and bottom of the pot with a wooden spoon or spatula to prevent scorching and to allow the sauce to thicken evenly.

Rinse the redfish steaks under cold running water and shake them dry. Add them to the courtbouillon along with the lemon slices. Cook at a low simmer for exactly 10 minutes, then remove the pot from the heat. Serve 2 slices of redfish per person with about 1 cup of sauce poured over.

*For suggested substitutes in other areas, see the chart on page 83.

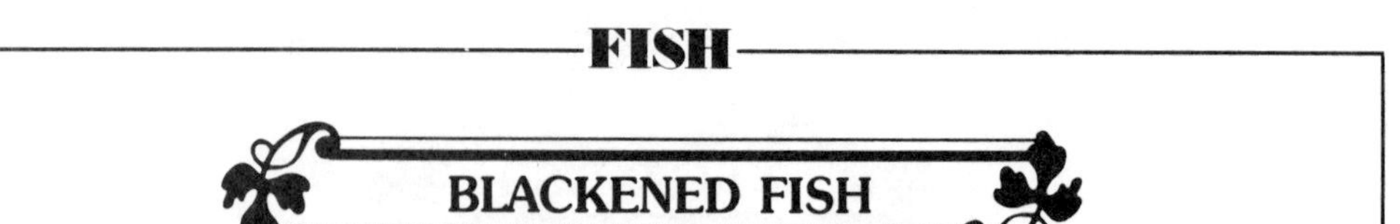

BLACKENED NON-REDFISH

Please do not use redfish or even try to buy redfish for blackening. The popularity of the dish has made redfish an endangered species; besides, virtually everything works better in this dish than New Orleans' local redfish. We suspect that redfish was originally chosen because it was a little known and rarely used local fish. Many of us loved the fish, which is so good that simple broiling or grilling is the best possible preparation. The problems with New Orleans redfish are its size and its new popularity. The best eating redfish are the small (under 2 pounds) young fish. One cannot blacken such a small fish—it will simply disintegrate under the high heat. The solution has been regrettable. Larger and older redfish, not at all prized for eating but necessary as breeding stock, have attracted commercial fishermen seeking to satisfy restaurants' demand for something called redfish. These larger fish, up to 50 pounds, have only their name in common with the favored small redfish and have never been eaten in New Orleans, except occasionally by fishermen as a baked dish with a strong sauce to use up an incidental catch.

The real redfish is too small to be blackened, the large redfish is too large to be an attractive eating fish. Even the originator of blackened redfish has recommended fresh tuna as a preferable fish for blackening. Many restaurants blacken prime ribs instead of fish, an attractive alternative, since the beef benefits from the seasoning and blackening much more satisfyingly than a delicate fish.

In blackening, the process and the spectacle are the most important ingredients, a phenomenon common in New Orleans cooking, where seasoning, drama, and invention have always been used to transform little known or lowly regarded inexpensive local materials. The national insistence on a particular fish owes more to California's new food style, with its emphasis on specific natural ingredients, than to the cooking process. Like most New Orleans food, blackened non-redfish has already become a variation dish. Besides the fish used, and the amount of charring, the most important variations are in the seasoning of the marinade, which varies from simple (fresh black and white pepper) to characteristic (some cayenne) to gross (all of the above plus garlic or garlic powder and whatever else can overwhelm—or impress—the poor initiate). At its best blackened non-redfish is a charred, mildly peppered grilled fish. At its worst it is as attractive and as appealing as highly seasoned burnt toast.

Although this is not really a home dish, you can make a decent version if you are willing to put up with a smoke filled house or have access to a well-vented grill or griddle that can sustain high heat (above 600°). Choose the fish or meat to be blackened, let it stand for about 3 hours in a marinade of melted butter and white, black, and (sparingly) cayenne pepper. Pre-boil or pre-bake the fish or meat for about two-thirds of its normal cooking time. Heat a grill, griddle, or cast iron skillet to smoking, then quickly place the fish on the heat for no more than 10 seconds. Turn over for 5 more seconds, then remove and serve while still hot and sizzling.

BAKED SHEEPSHEAD (GASPERGOU)

At one time sheepshead was widely served in New Orleans restaurants. It is still caught by local fishermen and prepared at home, baked, with seasonings somewhat similar to those used in redfish courtbouillon. Bring it to the table in the baking dish right from the oven—the whole fish surrounded by the tomatoey sauce and garnished with lemon slices is an impressive sight. The trick here is to slice the fish and reassemble it before you bake it so that the sauce permeates the fish with its marvelous combination of flavors. Serving the fish is simple: just lift the slices out.

(for 4 or more)

SAUCE

¼ c. (½ stick) salt butter
¼ c. olive oil
½ c. flour
3 small onions, peeled and sliced about ⅛ inch thick
¾ c. sliced green shallot (scallion) tops
1 Tbs. finely minced garlic
3 Tbs. finely minced fresh parsley
½ c. chopped green pepper
1 one-lb. can peeled whole tomatoes (about 2¼ c.), coarsely chopped
4 whole bay leaves, broken into quarters
¾ tsp. dried thyme
1 tsp. dried basil
3 Tbs. fresh lemon juice
2 tsp. salt
¾ tsp. freshly ground black pepper
¼ tsp. cayenne

---

1 whole sheepshead (3 lb.),* split and cleaned, head and tail left on, eyes removed
¼ to ½ c. water, approximately
10 slices fresh lemon, each about ⅛ inch thick

Preheat the oven to 375°. Meanwhile, in a heavy sauté pan melt the butter over low heat, then mix in the olive oil. Gradually add the flour and cook over low heat, stirring constantly, until a golden brown roux begins to form (about 20 minutes). Quickly add the onions, shallot tops, garlic, parsley, and green pepper and continue cooking over low heat, just until the vegetables begin to turn soft. Remove the pan from the heat and stir in the chopped tomatoes, bay leaves, thyme, basil, lemon juice, salt, black pepper, and cayenne. Mix thoroughly, then add about ¼ cup water. Pour the contents of the pan into a large rectangular or oval baking dish about 3 inches deep and long enough to hold the whole sheepshead comfortably.

Using a sharp knife and beginning just below the head, carefully slice the sheepshead, all the way through crosswise, into steaks about 2 inches thick. Then place the fish with the slices carefully reassembled in the baking dish, partially immersed in the sauce. (At this point the fish should appear to be whole.) Arrange the lemon slices on top of the fish in a decorative pattern, then place the baking dish in the preheated oven and bake for about 25 to 30 minutes. (If the sauce begins to appear too thick, add a few tablespoons of water.) Test to see if the fish is done by pricking with a fork or toothpick; if it flakes easily, it is sufficiently cooked. Remove the baking dish from the oven and bring to the table. Serve individual slices with sauce and a piece of lemon on top.

*For suggested substitutes in other areas, see the chart on page 83.

BAKED RED SNAPPER

Red snapper is delicious done the way we prepare sheepshead. Since red snapper tends to be a bit less firm than sheepshead, we have found that a red snapper of 3½ to 4 pounds works better than a smaller one. *(for 6 or more)*

Prepare according to the directions for Baked Sheepshead (see page 107), substituting a 3½- to 4-pound red snapper for the sheepshead. It is not necessary to increase the quantities for the seasonings, although you may have to add about ¼ to ⅓ cup more water toward the end of baking time.

BAKED BLACK FRESHWATER BASS

An unusual baked fish dish from the Cajun country, black bass larded with salt pork and baked whole. The stuffing, which is made of bacon, onions, bread crumbs, and seasonings, flavors the fish from the inside during cooking. Many people discard it, but you can serve it along with the fish, moistened with some of the pan drippings. *(for 6 to 8)*

---

1 black bass (3 to 4½ lb.), cleaned and left whole
Salt and freshly ground black pepper

STUFFING

1 small onion, finely chopped
1 Tbs. melted salt butter
1 c. crumbled white bread
2 thin slices bacon, chopped
1 Tbs. finely minced fresh parsley
¼ tsp. dried thyme
1 tsp. Worcestershire sauce
3 Tbs. beef stock

¼ lb. salt pork, cut into 10 strips
3 Tbs. melted salt butter

Rinse the fish and dry it thoroughly inside and out with paper towels, then sprinkle it generously with salt and freshly ground black pepper. Combine the ingredients for the stuffing in a bowl and mix well. Stuff the cavity of the fish with the mixture and sew up the opening. Make 5 diagonal slashes ⅓ inch deep on each side of the backbone and wedge the strips of salt pork into the openings.

Brush a baking pan with some of the melted butter. Place the fish on its side in the baking pan. Pour the remaining melted butter over it and bake in a preheated 400° oven for 30 minutes. Baste frequently with the pan drippings and turn the fish over after 15 minutes.

To serve, remove the fish from the center bone in large pieces with a serrated knife and place on heated plates. Stir the pan drippings to mix and pour a tablespoon or so over each portion.

Note: You can also serve the fish in thick slices, with the bone. Try to find places along the backbone that yield easily to the slicing knife before you cut the fish.

SAUTÉED TROUT ROE

From May to September fresh trout roe is available in New Orleans. The roe of speckled trout is quite small, no longer than your little finger and about 3/8 inch wide; you need about 8 pieces for a single portion. *(for 4)*

---

2 doz. pieces speckled trout roe
Salt and freshly ground black pepper
Flour for dusting
3/4 c. (1 1/2 sticks) salt butter

Sprinkle the roe liberally with salt and pepper, then dust lightly on all sides with flour. Melt the butter over medium heat in a large heavy skillet and heat until it begins to sizzle. Add the roe to the pan, sauté for 3 minutes on each side, then remove and put it on heated plates. Cook the butter remaining in the pan until it turns brown, then remove the pan from the heat. Mix the browned butter well and pour an equal amount over each portion of roe.

SAUTÉED SHAD ROE

When we occasionally get shad roe in New Orleans, we like to prepare it the same way as Sautéed Trout Roe (see above), but without the flour coating. One or two pieces of shad roe make a good single portion. Just sprinkle the roe with salt and freshly ground black pepper, heat plenty of salt butter in a skillet, then sauté the roe just 3 to 3 1/2 minutes on each side. Brown the butter remaining in the skillet for a minute, then pour it over the roe.

FRIED TROUT ROE

Another good way to prepare trout roe is deep fried. To get a crisp crust, dip the roe in egg and water before rolling it in seasoned flour. *(for 4)*

---

2 eggs
2 Tbs. cold water
2 doz. pieces trout roe
1 1/2 c. flour
1 tsp. salt
1/2 tsp. freshly ground black pepper
Vegetable oil for deep frying
Meunière Sauce (optional, page 113)

Put the eggs and water in a pie dish and beat lightly with a fork; combine the flour and seasonings in a bowl and mix with a whisk. Dry the trout roe well with paper towels. Dip first in egg and water, then in seasoned flour to coat evenly, and put on a platter to dry for a few minutes.

Meanwhile, preheat oil in a deep fryer or deep skillet to 375°. Fry according to the directions on page 85 until golden brown (about 2 to 3 minutes), then drain on paper towels. Serve plain or with a bit of meunière sauce.

Note: This may also be prepared with mullet roe.

FROG'S LEGS MEUNIÈRE

This is the way we prepare the best frog's legs, the small tender ones. Soaking them in cold milk for about 1½ hours before frying seems to make them even more tender. *(for 4)*

12 pairs small frog's legs
Cold milk for soaking

---

1 c. flour
1 tsp. salt
¼ tsp. freshly ground black pepper
Scant ⅛ tsp. cayenne
Vegetable oil for deep frying

MEUNIÈRE SAUCE

1 c. (2 sticks) salt butter
5 tsp. fresh lemon juice
2 tsp. finely minced fresh parsley

With a sharp knife, cut off the bottom joint of the frog's legs, discarding the part with the feet, and separate the pairs. Rinse thoroughly under cold running water and pat dry with paper towels. Place in a wide-bottomed dish or bowl, add cold milk to cover, and soak for 1½ to 2 hours.

Combine the flour, salt, pepper, and cayenne in a bowl, and preheat oil in a deep fryer to 375°. Remove the frog's legs from the milk about 4 at a time and roll them in seasoned flour to coat thoroughly. Fry about 4 at a time in the hot oil until golden brown (about 5 to 8 minutes per batch, depending on the size of the frog's legs), turning often during frying with tongs to ensure even browning. Drain, then place on a platter lined with paper towels and put in a 200° oven to keep warm, along with 4 individual gratin dishes or dinner plates with raised edges.

Melt the butter slowly over low heat and cook until it begins to turn a light brown (the color of hazelnuts). Remove the pan from the heat and add the lemon juice and parsley, then return to the heat and cook for 1 minute longer. Stir to mix thoroughly and remove from the heat.

To serve, put 3 pairs of frog's legs in each individual dish or bowl and pour ¼ cup of the sauce over them.

FROG'S LEGS SAUCE PIQUANTE

A good way to prepare frog's legs when you get the tougher, larger ones. The frog's legs are salted and browned in oil before they are added to the sauce piquante pot. *(for 4)*

2 Tbs. vegetable oil
8 pairs medium to large frog's legs
Sauce Piquante (page 77)

Heat the oil in a large skillet and brown the frog's legs on all sides, then set to drain on paper towels while you prepare the sauce. Simmer for 30 to 40 minutes after you add the frog's legs, just until they are tender. Test with a fork.

8

SAUCES

"First you make a roux," the often quoted maxim of Creole cooking, is indeed true for many of our most characteristic dishes–gumbos, stews, étouffées, bisques. Brown rouxs are made with butter or oil and flour, then cooked and stirred for almost half an hour until we get the right rich brown color. Then we quickly add mountains of freshly chopped vegetables to arrest the browning. It's surprising to realize that gumbo, for example, is a dish that has a sauce–the roux. Properly prepared, the roux is completely absorbed, but its taste and texture are an essential part of the gumbo. Another "hidden" sauce is courtbouillon, the highly seasoned liquid in which we boil shellfish, often used again in more complex sauces such as those for trout Marguery or pompano en papillote. Two classic French sauces, hollandaise and béarnaise (pages 114–15), appear in many of our fancy dishes, prepared with more lemon and pepper than their French counterparts. And we are fearless about the way we use our sauces: béarnaise is put on meat and crabmeat, beef stock sauces on fried fish and fried oysters, butter sauces on just about everything. New Orleans butter sauces are quite simple to prepare once you learn the secret of their distinctive taste: they are made with unclarified salt butter, the salt butter found in all American markets. These sauces aren't

difficult to make, and many of them are prepared as readily at home as in good restaurant kitchens because they are so much a part of Creole and Cajun cooking. Once you master them, you can go on to use them in your own way. After all, innovation is the very spirit of Creole cooking.

MEUNIÈRE SAUCE

The basic New Orleans butter sauce, used with fish, shellfish, meat, and poultry. The browned solids are part of the sauce; stir well and be sure to pour some of the solids over the dish, along with the browned butter. *(about 1½ cups)*

1½ c. (3 sticks) salt butter
1 tsp. freshly ground black pepper
¼ c. fresh lemon juice
4 Tbs. finely minced fresh parsley

In a small heavy saucepan melt the butter slowly over low heat, then cook over low heat until the butter begins to turn a light brown (the color of hazelnuts). Remove the pan from the heat and add the pepper, lemon juice, and parsley. Stir; the sauce will foam up. When the foaming subsides, return the pan to low heat for about a minute. Stir to mix thoroughly, then remove the pan from the burner.

BROWN MEUNIÈRE SAUCE

A roux-based beef stock sauce used on fried fish and shellfish. This sauce takes about an hour to prepare and comes out best when cooked in a large quantity. It keeps well under refrigeration for several days, so prepare it a day or half day in advance and keep what's left over in a closed freezer container for another meal. Stir well before you pour out what you plan to serve and add a few teaspoons of water when reheating. The sauce should be quite smooth and have the consistency of heavy cream. *(about 3½ cups)*

STOCK BASE

3 c. beef stock (or use beef concentrate with water)
¼ c. finely chopped celery
⅓ c. finely chopped carrots
1 tsp. finely minced fresh parsley
½ tsp. salt
4 whole black peppercorns
⅛ tsp. dried thyme
1 small onion, cut in quarters
1 to 1½ c. boiling water, approximately

ROUX

½ c. (1 stick) salt butter
½ c. flour
½ tsp. salt
¼ tsp. freshly ground black pepper

Combine the ingredients for the stock base in a medium-sized saucepan. Bring to a boil over high heat, then reduce the heat and simmer for 20 minutes; the liquid will be reduced by about ½ to ¾ cup, or more. Remove the pan from the heat and strain the stock into a bowl. Measure and add sufficient boiling water to the stock to make 3¼ cups, then pour back into the original pan and set aside.

In a heavy 3- to 4-quart saucepan melt the butter over low heat. Stir in the flour, salt, and pepper. Cook over low heat, stirring constantly, until a rich brown roux is formed (about 20 to 25 minutes), then remove the pan from the heat.

Warm the stock base for a minute or so without allowing it to boil, then gradually add it to the pan containing the roux, stirring constantly to keep the mixture smooth. Return the pan to low heat and cook, stirring, until the sauce is thoroughly blended and heated through (about 12 to 15 minutes). Let the sauce cool at room temperature for 10 minutes, then refrigerate in a tightly covered freezer container or jar.

AMANDINE SAUCE

This is a meunière sauce with almonds. Blanched slivered almonds work best here, and the simplest way to brown them is to add them just a few minutes before the sauce is completed. For dishes where you wish to arrange the almonds on the dish to be sauced, add them right after the butter is completely melted and watch their color; when the almonds turn light brown, remove them with a slotted spoon and reserve them in a bowl or cup while you finish browning the butter. Then place them where you wish and pour the browned butter over the entire dish. *(about 1½ cups)*

- 1½ c. (3 sticks) salt butter
- 1 tsp. freshly ground black pepper
- 3 Tbs. fresh lemon juice
- 2 Tbs. finely minced fresh parsley
- 1 c. blanched slivered almonds

In a medium-sized heavy saucepan, melt the butter over low heat, then cook over low heat until the butter begins to brown. Remove the pan from the heat and add the pepper, lemon juice, and parsley. Stir; the sauce will foam up. When the foaming subsides, add the almonds and return the pan to low heat. Cook until the almonds and butter are browned, then remove the pan from the heat and stir to mix.

BLENDER HOLLANDAISE

We prefer making hollandaise this way, in an electric blender. The sauce has a headier flavor since no water is necessary to stabilize it, and a fluffier texture because of the air it absorbs. Be sure the butter is quite hot when you add it to the egg yolks, and turn the blender on and off with a regular rhythm during the thickening process.

Hollandaise cannot be reheated, so prepare it just before you plan to use it. The sauce can be kept warm for up to 15 minutes by setting the blender container in warm water. *(about ⅔ cup)*

- ½ c. (1 stick) salt butter
- 3 large egg yolks
- 1 Tbs. fresh lemon juice
- Scant ⅛ tsp. cayenne

In a small heavy saucepan, melt the butter over low heat, then remove from the heat. Combine the egg yolks, lemon juice, and cayenne in a blender container. Cover the container and switch the blender on and off quickly several times, just to break the yolks and mix the ingredients lightly. Remove the blender cover (or the detachable center section of the cover, if it has one), turn on high speed, and gradually pour in the hot melted butter in a steady stream. Cover again and switch the blender on for 60 seconds and then off for 30 seconds. Repeat (as many as 10 to 12 on-off cycles may be necessary) until the sauce thickens to a consistency where it does not drip readily from a spoon.

HANDMADE HOLLANDAISE

Hollandaise made with a wire whisk is no more difficult than blender hollandaise; you simply have to watch for different things. The saucepan must be kept warm while you beat the butter into the egg yolks. A lined copper saucepan is excellent, since it will retain the heat long enough after you remove it from the burner to allow you to finish the sauce. With other pans, keep the heat on low and move the pan off the heat for 60 seconds, then back on for 30 seconds several times as you beat in the butter. The melted butter should be warm but not hot, or it will cook the egg yolks.

(about ⅔ cup)

3 large egg yolks
2 Tbs. cold water
½ c. (1 stick) salt butter
2 tsp. fresh lemon juice
Scant ⅛ tsp. cayenne

Put the egg yolks and water in a heavy 2- to 3-quart saucepan. In a separate small saucepan melt the butter over low heat. When all of it is melted, remove from the heat. Put the pan containing the egg yolks and water on another burner over very low heat and begin beating with a wire whisk. Beat steadily for 2 to 3 minutes, until the yolks get thick and pale. Pour in about 2 tablespoons of the warm butter, beating constantly. Remove the pan from the heat and continue beating, adding the butter in small amounts as you beat. When you add the last bit of butter, put the pan back on very low heat. Add the lemon juice and cayenne and beat a bit more, slowly, until the sauce is well blended. (It should look glossy and stand in little peaks when you pull out the whisk.) If necessary, set the pan in a basin or bowl of warm water until served. When you are ready to use the sauce, beat it evenly with a wire whisk for 30 seconds before spooning it out.

BÉARNAISE SAUCE

(about ⅔ cup)

GLAZE

1½ Tbs. finely minced green shallot (scallion) tops
¼ tsp. finely minced garlic
2 tsp. fresh lemon juice
¼ c. dry white wine
½ Tbs. dried tarragon
½ Tbs. dried chervil
⅛ tsp. salt
¼ tsp. freshly ground white pepper

½ c. (1 stick) salt butter
3 large egg yolks
Scant ⅛ tsp. cayenne

In a small heavy saucepan combine the ingredients for the glaze and cook over medium heat until the mixture is reduced to about 2 tablespoons; it will have almost no liquid. In a separate saucepan, melt the butter over medium heat, then remove from the heat. Put the egg yolks and cayenne in the blender container. Cover and blend on high speed for a few seconds, just to break the yolks. Add the glaze, cover again, and turn the blender on high for a few seconds more. Remove the blender cover, turn on high speed, and gradually pour in the hot melted butter in a steady stream. Cover the blender and switch on for 60 seconds and then off for 30 seconds. Repeat the on-off procedure until the sauce is quite thick.

MARCHAND DE VIN SAUCE

A rich heady "wine merchant's" sauce made famous by Antoine's, where it is served on tournedos. Make the beef stock with 3 or 4 soup bones, then scoop out the bone marrow and add it to the stock for extra richness. The sauce should be a bit thicker than heavy cream, with a slightly rough texture because of the tiny bits of ham in it. *(2 cups)*

- ½ c. (1 stick) salt butter
- 3 Tbs. flour
- ¼ c. very finely minced lean baked ham
- ½ c. finely minced green shallot (scallion) tops
- 3 Tbs. finely minced onion
- ¼ c. finely minced garlic
- 1 tsp. salt
- ¼ tsp. freshly ground black pepper
- ⅛ tsp. cayenne
- 1 c. rich beef stock, made from soup bones
- Marrow from the soup bones
- ½ c. dry red wine

In a large heavy saucepan melt the butter over low heat. Gradually add the flour, stirring constantly, and cook over low heat until a light brown roux begins to form. Quickly add the ham, shallot tops, onion, and garlic and cook, still stirring, for about 5 minutes more. Add the salt, pepper, and cayenne and blend thoroughly. Keep the mixture simmering and very gradually add the beef stock, bone marrow, and red wine, stirring constantly to keep the sauce as smooth as possible. (It should have a slightly rough texture because of the minced ham.) When the sauce is thoroughly blended, cook over very low heat for about 30 minutes, stirring from time to time to prevent scorching.

SAUCE PARADIS

The richest sauce in Creole cuisine, made with Madeira wine, currant jelly, green grapes, beef stock, and truffles. When green seedless grapes are in season, we buy them in quantity and freeze them, for this sauce and also for Trout Veronique (see page 102). The truffles are a grand touch but do not change the flavor of the sauce, so if you have none on hand don't be deterred. We like sauce paradis on squab, quail, duck, and chicken. *(about 3 cups)*

- ¼ c. (½ stick) salt butter
- ¼ c. flour
- 2 c. rich beef stock
- ½ c. Madeira wine
- 3 Tbs. red currant jelly
- ⅛ tsp. freshly ground white pepper
- 1 c. green seedless grapes (drained, if they have been frozen)
- 3 large truffles, sliced thin (optional)

In a heavy 2- to 3-quart saucepan melt the butter over low heat, then add the flour, stirring to keep the mixture smooth. Cook over low heat, stirring constantly, for 10 minutes, then slowly add the beef stock, stirring as you pour. Cook over low heat until the sauce thickens slightly (about 6 minutes), then add the wine, currant jelly, and pepper and mix thoroughly. Cook until the jelly has melted, then add the grapes and truffles. Continue cooking for about 3 minutes more, just long enough to heat the grapes and truffles through. Remove the pan from the heat. Right before serving, stir gently to mix.

BORDELAISE SAUCE

New Orleans bordelaise sauce is made with butter, olive oil, and garlic. We like it best on pasta; it can also be used for meat and shellfish. Don't cook the garlic too long; once it browns, the flavor gets milder the longer you cook it. The parsley should be added at the very end. *(about ⅓ cup)*

¼ c. (½ stick) salt butter
2 Tbs. olive oil
3 large or 5 small cloves garlic, coarsely chopped
½ tsp. salt
¼ tsp. freshly ground white pepper
1 Tbs. finely minced fresh parsley

In a small heavy saucepan melt the butter over low heat. Add the olive oil and warm for about 2 to 3 minutes, then add the garlic, salt, and pepper. Cook over low heat for 4 to 5 minutes, or just until the garlic begins to brown. Turn off the heat and quickly remove the garlic with a slotted spoon or fine mesh skimmer. Add the parsley and mix.

NEW ORLEANS BÉCHAMEL SAUCE

This butter and flour sauce is the basis of Creole sauces made with a white roux, such as marinière, Marguery, and ravigotte. It can also be used in the preparation of cream vegetable soups. Measure the Tabasco very carefully; one drop too much can easily throw the sauce out of balance. *(1 cup)*

---

2 Tbs. salt butter
1½ Tbs. flour
¾ c. milk
4 drops Tabasco
½ tsp. salt
⅛ tsp. freshly grated nutmeg

In a heavy 2-quart saucepan melt the butter over low heat; do not brown. Add the flour gradually, stirring constantly to keep the mixture smooth; do not allow the flour to cook. Once all the flour is blended in, gradually pour in the milk, stirring constantly with a wire whisk or wooden spoon to keep the sauce perfectly smooth. Move the whisk around in the pan as you stir to blend the sauce at the bottom and sides. Once all the milk has been added, cook over low heat until the sauce thickens, then remove from the heat and stir in the Tabasco, salt, and nutmeg. Blend thoroughly.

BEURRE BLANC

A rich creamy butter sauce with a slightly tart flavor, perfect with broiled or poached fish. Take the butter out of the refrigerator 20 to 30 minutes in advance; it should be soft but not melted. Cut it into small pieces when you are ready to start.

The secrets of a smooth beurre blanc are simple: add the butter very gradually and keep the saucepan warm but not hot as you beat. A lined copper pan will stay warm for quite a while after you take it off the heat. If you use another kind of pan, keep the burner at a low setting and move the pan onto the heat for about 30 seconds, then off for 30 seconds; repeat until you have beaten in all the butter. Beurre blanc is served warm. It cannot be reheated or set to keep warm in warm water. Put the pan on the stove near, but not directly over, the pilot. *(about ⅔ cup)*

GLAZE

¼ c. dry white wine
1½ Tbs. very finely minced shallots (scallions)
½ tsp. very finely minced garlic

¼ tsp. freshly ground white pepper
½ c. (1 stick) salt butter, softened

Combine the ingredients for the glaze in a small heavy saucepan. Cook over medium heat until most of the liquid has evaporated and about 2 tablespoons or a bit less of the glaze is left (about 10 to 15 minutes). Remove the pan from the heat, add the pepper, and stir once.

Cut the softened butter into small pieces. Gradually incorporate the butter into the glaze by adding a piece at a time while beating with a wire whisk. (The saucepan should remain warm while you beat. If necessary, return it to low heat at regular intervals for half a minute, then remove.) The finished sauce should be thick (like hollandaise) and rather pale, with a slightly iridescent cast.

NANTUA SAUCE

A smooth rich crawfish sauce made with butter, heavy cream, and a touch of brandy. To get the richest possible flavor, chop the crawfish tails very fine before you mash and cook them. Save the crawfish solids you strain out after cooking and use them to prepare crawfish "stuffing" (topping) for fish (see page 96).

(about 2 cups)

---

1 lb. crawfish tails, parboiled for 3 minutes, then chopped very fine
6 Tbs. (¾ stick) salt butter
¾ c. heavy cream
1 Tbs. brandy
1 tsp. salt
¼ tsp. freshly ground white pepper
⅛ tsp. cayenne
5 Tbs. fish stock, strained fish poaching liquid, or water
¼ c. flour

Mash the chopped crawfish in a bowl with the back of a wooden spoon and set aside. Melt the butter in a large heavy sauté pan or saucepan over low heat. Add the mashed crawfish and any liquid in the bottom of the bowl to the butter and mix, then add the cream, brandy, salt, pepper, and cayenne. Raise the heat and bring the mixture to a simmer, then cover the pan, reduce the heat to very low, and cook for 35 minutes, uncovering to stir every 5 minutes or so.

At the end of 35 minutes, uncover the pan, add the fish stock, and mix thoroughly. Cook for 3 minutes more, then remove from the heat and strain the contents of the pan into a small to medium-sized heavy saucepan. (Reserve the solids in the strainer for crawfish "stuffing," if desired.) Put the pan on low heat, gradually stir in the flour, and cook over low heat, stirring constantly, for about 4 minutes. Serve over poached fish.

MAYONNAISE

Rich homemade mayonnaise, prepared with a light olive oil. (The French Plagniol is excellent.) If you prefer a lighter effect, use equal parts of olive oil and vegetable oil.

Mayonnaise is not difficult to prepare if you follow a few simple procedures. First, be sure all the ingredients are at room temperature; this means taking the eggs out of the refrigerator at least half an hour in advance. Second, all utensils should be warm, as indicated in the recipe directions. Third, use a small deep bowl (about 6 inches in diameter for the quantity given here) and a large whisk in relation to the bowl (about 10 inches long) or an electric beater; this will enable you to beat easily and effectively and will keep the entire mass of the sauce moving during beating. Fourth, add the oil in very small amounts, about 1 teaspoon at a time at the beginning. As the sauce thickens, you can increase it to a tablespoon at a time. It is not essential to pour steadily and beat without resting; the main thing is to incorporate each bit of oil thoroughly before you add the next amount. Refrigerate the mayonnaise in the bowl, tightly covered with plastic wrap. Beat it quickly for just a few seconds before serving.

(about 2 cups)

2 large egg yolks
1 tsp. salt
1 tsp. dry mustard
¼ tsp. freshly ground white pepper
Scant ⅛ tsp. cayenne
1 Tbs. fresh lemon juice
1½ c. olive oil
1½ Tbs. white wine vinegar

Have all ingredients at room temperature. Warm a 6-inch stainless steel or porcelain bowl, a 10-inch wire whisk, and a 2-cup measuring cup in a 200° oven for about 4 minutes, then remove them from the oven and let them cool for about 1 minute.

Put the egg yolks in the bowl and beat with a whisk or electric beater until they are thick and lemon colored. Add the salt, mustard, pepper, cayenne, and lemon juice and beat for about 1 minute. Begin adding the oil from the warmed measuring cup, a bare teaspoon at a time, beating evenly and quickly after you add each bit of oil. After about ¼ cup of oil has been added, the sauce should begin to get quite thick. At that point, increase the oil added to about 2 teaspoons, always beating after each addition. When you have added over 1 cup of the oil, begin adding the wine vinegar, about 1 teaspoon at a time, between the oil additions. When you have added all the oil, the mayonnaise should be creamy, moderately thick (like light hollandaise), and quite glossy. Beat lightly for about 45 seconds longer, then cover the bowl with plastic wrap and refrigerate.

CREAM HORSERADISH SAUCE

Prepared horseradish, Creole mustard, and heavy cream combined in a sauce that is excellent with boiled brisket of beef. We also like it with chilled poached fish. Use white prepared horseradish and check the label—extra hot will not work in this sauce. If you cannot get Creole mustard, use regular prepared mustard and add ¼ teaspoon white wine vinegar and a bit less than ⅛ teaspoon dry mustard to it. Let the other ingredients steep together for a little while before you add the cream.

This sauce should be prepared in advance because it tastes better after it has been refrigerated a few hours. It keeps very well under refrigeration for 3 to 4 days if you put it in a tightly closed china or stainless steel container. When you plan to use it, stir well and pour off only what you need. Do not try to put any leftover sauce back again.

(about 1 cup)

- 6 Tbs. prepared white horseradish, preferably Zatarain's
- 1 Tbs. Creole mustard
- 3 Tbs. white wine vinegar
- ¼ tsp. freshly ground white pepper
- ⅛ tsp. cayenne
- ⅛ tsp. sugar
- ½ c. heavy cream

Combine all the ingredients except the cream in a gravy boat or deep sauce dish. Mix thoroughly and let stand at room temperature for 15 minutes, then add the heavy cream slowly, stirring constantly. Cover the dish with plastic wrap and refrigerate for at least 1 hour before serving.

9

MEATS AND SAUSAGES

Because of a lack of prime beef, New Orleans cooks have developed economical and imaginative ways of making what they have go a long way. Meat dishes prepared at home and in modest restaurants have traditionally used the less expensive cuts: soup meat served with a good strong horseradish sauce or in the soup surrounded by an array of vegetables; ground meat highly seasoned, cooked with plenty of onions, and eaten with rice or beans or on French bread as the New Orleans style hamburger; and the great roast beef poor boy, a tough cut of beef cooked slowly, sliced thin, and eaten on warm French bread with the rich natural gravy, shredded lettuce, tomatoes, and mayonnaise—a gargantuan, leaky, absolutely delicious whole-meal sandwich.

We pound out our veal and fry it as crisp panéed veal or simmer it slowly as grillades, served with grits to soak up the gravy. Seasoning meat—fatty chunks of ham or fresh pork—is sold packaged in local food stores because everyone uses it to make bean dishes and pot dinners. And New Orleanians love sausage, consuming it in enormous quantities, in bean dishes, in gumbos, as an accompaniment to pot dinners, or else smothered with lots of fresh vegetables.

Meat dishes in elegant restaurants are traditionally richly sauced—tournedos marchand de vin, fillet with béarnaise—and the best steak houses vie with one another in the complexity of their steak sauces. We have no tradition of *pâtés* or *terrines*, probably because of the warm climate. Our classic cold meat dish is daube glacé, a very highly seasoned form of beef in aspic made from daube, a larded, seasoned, slow-cooked pot roast. Another cold favorite is Creole hogshead cheese, one of the spiciest versions of this dish to be found anywhere.

In this chapter you will find recipes for the traditional New Orleans meat dishes, as well as instructions for preparing the classic local sausages. All these dishes can be prepared with ingredients found in markets throughout the country.

COCHON DE LAIT (ROAST SUCKLING PIG)

Cochon de lait is a Cajun specialty associated primarily with one Cajun town, Mansura. There the art of preparing this dish is practiced seriously: just about everyone in town turns out to watch the preparations and to enjoy the feast. There are two secrets to the beautifully crisp, unbelievably delicious-smelling suckling pig for which Mansura is famous: huge amounts of seasoning on the inside, the outside, and under the skin; and very slow roasting, about 5 to 6 hours for a 20-pound pig.

When the weather is good, Mansurans often roast cochon de lait on a spit over an open wood fire; when it's not, they get the same results in a slow oven.

Ask your butcher for a plump pig no more than 22 pounds in size; anywhere from 15 to 20 pounds is ideal. Have the butcher clean the pig for you. You will need a large roasting pan and a rack to hold the pig out of the grease which collects in the pan. You can garnish the finished pig with all manner of things—apple balls, fruit cups made with hollowed-out oranges, bouquets of parsley and shallots, even decorative figures made with baked sweet potatoes. Or you can simply do as we do—put the glorious roasted pig on a large serving platter and bring it to the table whole and unadorned to be admired, then take it back into the kitchen to carve it for serving. It's probably risky for even the most practiced carver to tackle a cochon de lait at the dinner table.

(for 10 or more)

- ½ c. large pieces of garlic (peeled and sliced ⅛ inch thick)
- 1 suckling pig (about 15 to 20 lb.) cleaned for cooking
- ½ c. salt, approximately
- ½ c. freshly ground black pepper, approximately
- 4 Tbs. (2 oz.) cayenne, approximately
- 1¼ c. olive oil
- 4 small poultry skewers
- String for trussing and tying up the pig

Preheat the oven to 325°. Stuff the pieces of garlic under the skin of the pig's legs and body by sliding them in carefully with your fingers; be careful not to break the skin. Sprinkle about half of the salt, pepper, and cayenne on the inside of the pig, then sprinkle the remaining seasonings as evenly as possible over the outer skin. Pin the ears back with small poultry skewers and truss the body and neck cavities with skewers and string. Tuck the front feet under and the back feet forward, then tie together from the underside with string. Set the pig on its side on a raised roasting rack and set the rack in a large roasting pan. Pour half the olive oil over the upper side and place in the oven. Baste after 15 minutes, then at 30 minutes, remove the pig from the oven and turn it over; baste with the remaining olive oil and put it back in the oven. Baste every 15 to 20 minutes for the first 2 hours. Allow 15 minutes per pound for total cooking time. When the pig is cooked, remove from the oven, take out the skewers and string, and set it on a large preheated platter.

BOILED BRISKET OF BEEF

New Orleans' most popular old time meat dish. The brisket is cooked slowly with lots of fresh vegetables and seasonings. We generally serve the meat drained and sliced about ⅓ inch thick, with some of the broth spooned over it and accompanied with a creamy horseradish sauce. Save some of the broth for reheating left-over brisket; use the rest as a soup course for another meal. Most of the vegetables cook into the stock and disappear; use any bits that remain in the soup.

(for 4 or more)

- 1 brisket of beef (5 to 6 lb.)
- 2 Creole (beefsteak, Jersey) tomatoes, cut in quarters
- 2 medium onions, cut in quarters
- 6 carrots, cut in half across, then in quarters
- 6 shallots (scallions), cut into 3- to 4-inch lengths
- 4 stalks celery, cut in half across, then quartered
- 8 to 10 sprigs parsley, stems included, torn into 2- to 3-inch lengths
- 2 Tbs. salt
- 1½ tsp. freshly ground black pepper
- 4 whole bay leaves, crushed
- 1 tsp. dried thyme
- 6 whole cloves
- 6 whole allspice
- ¼ tsp. cayenne
- ¼ tsp. mace
- 2 qt. water, approximately

Place the brisket in a deep heavy kettle or stock pot of about 5- to 6-quart capacity. Place the vegetables and parsley on top of and around the brisket (the brisket and vegetables should be crowded in the bottom of the pot), then add the seasonings and enough water just to cover the meat. Bring to a boil, lower the heat, and simmer 2½ to 3 hours, or until the meat is fork tender. Serve sliced with Cream Horseradish Sauce (see page 120) on the side. Save the broth and vegetables and serve as a soup course.

DAUBE

A flavorful, less tender cut of beef larded with salt pork fat and braised, then slowly cooked with vegetables and seasonings. Save the stock and pieces of fat and vegetables for making daube glacé. Daube is generally served thinly sliced, with spaghetti and Italian tomato sauce. It would also be excellent with rice and gravy.

(for 8 or more)

- ¼ lb. salt pork fat
- 1 shoulder roast of beef (5 to 6 lb.)
- 3 c. finely chopped onion
- 2 Tbs. finely minced garlic
- ½ tsp. ground bay leaves
- ½ tsp. cloves
- ½ tsp. ground thyme
- 4 tsp. salt
- ¾ tsp. freshly ground black pepper
- 2 Tbs. lard
- 5 carrots, pared and cut into ½-inch cubes
- 1 Tbs. finely minced fresh parsley
- ⅛ tsp. cayenne
- ¾ c. dry red wine
- 1½ qt. boiling water, approximately

Cut the salt pork into ¼-inch strips about 3 inches long. To lard the beef, make incisions about 3 inches long and 1½ inches deep every 1½ inches, and insert the strips of salt pork. Combine 1 cup of the chopped onion, 1 tablespoon of the minced garlic, ¼ teaspoon each of the ground bay leaf, cloves, and thyme, ½ teaspoon of the salt, and ¼ teaspoon of the pepper. Mix thoroughly. Insert some of this mixture into each larding incision, pressing it into the strips of fat.

In a heavy 7- to 8-quart pot or kettle melt the lard over medium heat. Brown the beef roast in the hot lard, turning several times to allow browning on all sides. Add the carrots, parsley, and remaining seasonings and cook until the carrots and all the seasonings are browned. Add the red wine and just enough boiling water to barely cover the beef. Cover the pot and simmer over low heat for 3 to 3½ hours or until the beef is very tender but not quite falling apart.

When the meat is done, lift it out of the pot with a long fork, holding it over the pot for a minute to let the excess liquid drain off. Slice ¼ to ⅓ inch thick and serve with spaghetti and tomato sauce.

DAUBE GLACÉ

The classic Creole cold meat dish, prepared with cooked daube and plenty of additional spices. Some small local markets sell homemade daube in two degrees of hotness, regular (hot) and hot (very hot). This is our version of the regular, which we prefer. Once you cook the daube, making daube glacé is quite simple. Try to reserve about half the meat from the daube along with the stock, fat, and vegetables for a really meaty daube glacé, although you can manage with a bit less meat if you have to. We find that 2 three-quart molds work better than a single large one. The traditional daube glacé mold is rectangular, but round or square molds are fine. Because it must chill for at least 12 hours before you unmold it, plan to start your daube well ahead; it will keep for about 5 days under refrigeration if you cover the platter with plastic wrap, using several layers wrapped tightly (or everything in the refrigerator will take on the pungent aroma). *(for 8)*

- 3 lb. tender cooked Daube (page 124), approximately
- 1½ qt. stock from the daube, including vegetables and fat
- 3 envelopes (3 Tbs.) unflavored gelatin, dissolved in 1 c. cold water
- ¼ tsp. cayenne
- 2½ tsp. salt
- ½ tsp. freshly ground black pepper
- 1 tsp. crushed red pepper pods
- 1 Tbs. Worcestershire sauce
- 2 Tbs. finely minced fresh parsley
- 1 tsp. finely minced garlic

Shred the meat and cut it into lengths of approximately 3 inches. Combine with the rest of the ingredients and mix thoroughly, then pour into 2 deep rectangular 3-quart molds. Cover with plastic wrap and chill in the refrigerator for at least 12 hours.

Before serving, remove the thin layer of congealed fat that will have settled at the top. Loosen the daube glacé from the mold by sliding a thin knife all around the sides. Place a serving platter over the mold and turn it upside down, then tap to unmold the daube glacé onto the platter. Serve in ¾ to 1-inch slices, with plenty of French bread and butter.

TOURNEDOS MARCHAND DE VIN

The best American beef with a glorious rich wine merchant's sauce—an unusual combination made famous by Antoine's. Prepare the sauce first, then reheat it for about 45 seconds over high heat and pour it over the steak right before serving.

(for 4)

Marchand de Vin Sauce (page 116)
4 tournedos (the tenderloin portion of T-bone steak), cut 1½ to 1¾ inches thick
Salt and freshly ground black pepper
6 Tbs. (¾ stick) melted salt butter

Preheat the broiler, broiling pan, and rack. Meanwhile, sprinkle both sides of each tournedos liberally with salt and freshly ground black pepper. When the broiler is hot, remove the broiling pan and rack from the broiler, brush the rack with some of the melted butter, and place the steaks on it. Pour the remaining butter evenly over the steaks and broil, about 4 inches from the flame, about 5 to 6 minutes on each side for rare, 7 to 8 for medium. (We do not recommend cooking this cut until it is well done.) When cooked to the desired degree of doneness, remove immediately from the broiler.

To serve, put the tournedos on prewarmed plates and pour the juice and butter from the broiling pan over them. Then top each steak with ½ cup of the marchand de vin sauce.

STEAK WITH BÉARNAISE

This combination of steak with a heady béarnaise sauce is simple to prepare and very festive to serve. Make the béarnaise just before you grill the meat; keep the sauce warm by setting the blender container in a basin or bowl of warm water.

(for 4)

2 c. Béarnaise Sauce (page 115)

2 fillets or sirloin strips, cut 1½ to 1¾ inches thick
Salt and freshly ground black pepper
6 Tbs. (¾ stick) melted salt butter

Preheat the broiler, broiling pan, and rack. Meanwhile, sprinkle the steaks liberally on both sides with salt and pepper. Prepare the béarnaise sauce and set the blender container in warm water while you broil the steaks. Using the melted butter, broil according to the directions for the recipe above.

To serve, put the cooked steaks on heated plates and pour ½ cup béarnaise sauce over each one.

STEAK WITH NEW ORLEANS STYLE BUTTER SAUCE

Our version of the favorite local grilled steak, covered with New Orleans meunière sauce heightened with lemon, parsley, and "Lea and Perrins," the local name for Worcestershire of any brand. If you use a timer for broiling the steak (see page 126 for suggested times), you can prepare the sauce while the steak is in the broiler.

(per portion)

STEAK SAUCE

3 Tbs. salt butter
1 tsp. fresh lemon juice
1 tsp. finely minced fresh parsley
1½ Tbs. Worcestershire sauce

---

1 fillet, sirloin strip, T-bone, etc.

Put the butter in a small saucepan and turn the heat on to medium under the pan as soon as you put the steak in the broiler. When almost all the butter is melted, add the remaining ingredients and continue cooking until the sauce turns a light brown, then remove the saucepan from the heat and mix well.

To serve, put the cooked steak on a heated plate. Pour the sauce over it and serve immediately.

STEAK TARTARE

The freshest ground beef you can get, mixed with pungent seasonings and a light olive oil such as the French Plagniol. This dish is called *steack américain* in France and a "cannibal special" in New Orleans. Top round steak is a good choice for steak tartare; so is sirloin, if you trim away the fat. Have the butcher grind the meat before your eyes if you don't own a home meat grinder; it should be ground and mixed with the seasonings within a period of about 15 minutes. *(for 4)*

---

1 lb. freshly ground top round or sirloin
2 large egg yolks
1½ Tbs. hot mustard
½ large onion, finely chopped (about ⅔ c.)
2 tsp. fresh lemon juice
3½ Tbs. olive oil
1 tsp. salt
½ tsp. freshly ground black pepper
½ tsp. fines herbes
2 tsp. very finely minced garlic
2½ tsp. finely minced fresh parsley

GARNISH

Fresh cucumber slices or kosher style pickle slivers

Put the freshly ground beef into a large stainless steel or porcelain bowl. Add the egg yolks and toss gently with a fork. Add all the other ingredients except the garnish and mix gently with a wooden spoon until evenly blended, taking care not to overbeat the mixture; it should remain light and airy. Cover the mixing bowl with plastic wrap and chill on the top shelf of the refrigerator for 8 to 10 minutes.

To serve, divide into 4 portions and shape gently into patties about 1½ inches high. Serve garnished with 3 or 4 slices of fresh cucumber or slivers of kosher style pickles.

PANÉED VEAL

Veal rounds pounded out thin, well seasoned, rolled in bread crumbs, and fried crisp and brown—the traditional New Orleans breaded veal dish. This dish works as well with average, not-so-young American veal as it does with white baby veal, which is increasingly difficult to find. If you don't own a mallet for pounding out meat, use the flat side of a cleaver or the bottom of a heavy rounded mixing bowl. Let the coated pieces of veal dry for about 10 minutes before frying. *(for 4)*

1½ to 2 lb. veal round, cut about ⅜ inch thick
Salt and freshly ground black pepper
1 large egg, beaten with 3 Tbs. cold water
Italian bread crumbs
Vegetable oil for deep frying

GARNISH
Lemon wedges

Trim all fat from the veal round and cut into pieces about 2 by 4 inches. Pound out to half their thickness with a mallet, using the fine scoring side. Sprinkle both sides with salt and pepper, then dip the pieces of veal first in the egg and water mixture, then in the seasoned bread crumbs. Take care to coat each piece thoroughly with crumbs; then shake off the excess. Place the coated pieces of veal in a single layer on a large platter to dry for 10 minutes.

Meanwhile, heat oil in a deep fryer to 360° to 375°. Fry the veal one to two pieces at a time until golden brown (about 4 minutes). Place on a platter lined with several layers of paper towels, and put it in a preheated 200° oven to keep warm while frying the rest of the veal. Serve very hot, with lemon wedges.

MIGNONNETTES OF VEAL NORMANDES

This French veal dish was popular in New Orleans in the nineteenth century. The veal is shaped into ovals, sautéed in butter, then topped with a glorious sauce combining Calvados (apple brandy), heavy cream, and mushrooms. One of our favorite festive dinners. *(for 4)*

---

1 round of veal (about 1½ lb.), sliced ⅜ inch thick
Salt and freshly ground white pepper
Flour for dusting
6 Tbs. (¾ stick) salt butter
¼ c. Calvados
¼ tsp. salt
½ lb. fresh mushrooms, sliced (about 2½ c.; if fresh are not available use good quality canned, well drained)
⅛ tsp. freshly ground white pepper
1 c. heavy cream

Trim all fat and gristle off the veal round and discard. (If there is a marrow bone, save it for making veal stock.) Cut the meat into 4 rectangles and shape the rectangles into ovals (mignonnettes) with your fingers; if the veal is not very tender, you may have to cut off the corners with a knife to get the desired shape. (Save the cuttings for use in dishes requiring seasoning meat.) Sprinkle each mignonnette lightly with salt and pepper on each side, then dust each side lightly with flour.

In a large heavy skillet or sauté pan melt the butter over low heat. Raise the heat for a minute or so to let the melted butter heat, then add the pieces of veal and surround with the sliced mushrooms. Cook over low heat for about 8 minutes, turning the meat over several times to get an even light brown color on both sides. Turn the mushrooms over as well. When the veal is nicely browned, lift it out with a fork, letting the butter drain back into the skillet. Place on dinner plates and set the plates in a 200° oven to keep warm while you prepare the sauce.

Add the Calvados to the butter and mushrooms in the skillet and mix thoroughly, then add ¼ teaspoon salt and ⅛ teaspoon pepper. Keeping the heat at low, slowly pour in the cream, stirring constantly. Raise the heat to medium. When the sauce begins to simmer, reduce the heat just enough to keep the simmer going and cook for about 6 minutes or until the sauce thickens slightly and is reduced by about one-third. Stir frequently.

Just before serving remove the veal from the oven and spoon the sauce evenly over the portions.

GRILLADES AND GRITS

The old time New Orleans version of smothered steak—veal or beef round pounded out thin, browned in hot fat, then slowly cooked with onions and fresh tomatoes. Grillades are always served with grits to soak up the rich natural gravy. They make a hearty inexpensive supper or a grand old fashioned Sunday breakfast.

(for 4)

- 1¼ to 1¾ lb. round of veal or beef
- 2 tsp. salt
- 1 tsp. freshly ground black pepper
- ⅛ tsp. cayenne
- 1 Tbs. finely minced garlic
- 2 Tbs. flour
- 1½ Tbs. lard
- 1 c. chopped onion
- 1 large ripe Creole (beefsteak, Jersey) tomato, coarsely chopped
- 1 c. water, more if necessary
- 2½ to 3 c. cooked grits

Trim all the fat off the meat and remove any bones. Cut into pieces about 2 inches square and pound out with a mallet to about 4 inches square. Rub the salt, black pepper, cayenne, and garlic into the pieces of meat on both sides, then rub in the flour.

In a large heavy skillet or sauté pan, melt the lard over medium heat and brown the grillades well on both sides. Lower the heat and add the onion, tomato, and water. Bring to a simmer, cover loosely, and cook over low heat for about 30 minutes, uncovering to turn the meat over every 10 minutes. A rich brown gravy will form during cooking; if it appears too thick, add water a little bit at a time.

When the meat is cooked, remove it to a heated platter and place in a preheated 200° oven to keep warm. Prepare the grits according to package directions. Just before serving reheat the gravy in the skillet, then pour it over both the meat and the grits.

HOGSHEAD CHEESE

Creole hogshead cheese is one of the hottest versions of this country style delicacy to be found anywhere. Have your butcher clean and quarter the hog's head for you. Allow about 4 hours for cooking, and at least 6 hours in the refrigerator to let it set properly. Hogshead cheese will keep for about 4 days under refrigeration.

We like hogshead cheese as a serve-yourself appetizer before dinner. Just put it out on a platter with a long serrated knife for slicing and provide forks and small plates. You may want to reduce the cayenne a bit the first time you prepare it.

(for 8 or more)

1 hog's head, cleaned (brains, ears, eyes, and tissue removed) and quartered
4 hog's feet

COURTBOUILLON

Cold water
3 tsp. salt
1 tsp. freshly ground black pepper
½ tsp. cayenne
½ tsp. chili powder
¼ tsp. allspice
½ tsp. mace
3 whole bay leaves, crushed
1 tsp. dried thyme
½ lemon
1 Tbs. lard
1 c. chopped onion
3 Tbs. finely minced garlic
¼ c. finely minced fresh parsley
¾ c. thinly sliced green shallot (scallion) tops
2 Tbs. fresh lemon juice
1 lb. lean ham, cut into ¾-inch cubes

Wash the hog's head and feet thoroughly in cold water. Put into a heavy 6- to 8-quart saucepan or stock pot and add cold water just to cover, then add the salt, pepper, cayenne, chili powder, allspice, mace, bay leaves, thyme, and the lemon half. Bring to a boil and cook for about 3 hours, or until the meat begins to fall off the bones. Remove the meat from the liquid with a slotted spoon and set to cool on a platter, then cut into chunks about ¾ inch across. Boil the cooking liquid until it is reduced to about one-fourth its original quantity and set aside.

In a large skillet, melt the lard and add the onion, garlic, parsley, shallots, lemon juice, and ham. Cook over low heat until the vegetables are quite soft, but not brown. Put the cooked vegetables and ham into a large saucepan along with the cut-up meat and the reduced cooking liquid. Simmer for 30 minutes more, then mix thoroughly and pour into 2 large or several small molds and allow to cool at room temperature for about half an hour. Then cover the molds with plastic wrap and refrigerate for at least 6 hours.

When ready to unmold for serving, loosen the head cheese by sliding a knife around the edges of each mold, then cover the mold with a plate larger than the mold and invert. If head cheese does not slip out readily, tap the mold sharply to loosen. Serve well chilled.

TRIPE À LA CREOLE

This tripe stew was widely served in New Orleans in the nineteenth century; it is still prepared at home today. The tripe is simmered in a courtbouillon enriched with beef stock until tender, then added to the sauce and cooked a bit longer. Cleaned, partially precooked tripe is available in many of the better markets across the country, and shortens preparation time considerably. Don't overcook the tripe; it should have a pleasant chewy texture. Serve with boiled rice to soak up the heady sauce. *(for 4)*

COURTBOUILLON

- 3 qt. water, approximately
- 1⅔ Tbs. salt
- 1 Tbs. white wine vinegar
- ½ onion, cut into quarters
- ½ tsp. freshly ground black pepper
- ⅛ tsp. cayenne
- ¼ tsp. finely minced garlic
- 2 Tbs. rich beef stock (if you have none on hand use beef concentrate)
- 2½ to 3 lb. honeycomb tripe

SAUCE

- 2 Tbs. salt butter
- 2 medium-sized onions, sliced (about 3 c.)
- ½ c. chopped green pepper
- ¾ tsp. finely minced garlic
- ½ c. finely chopped seasoning ham (about ¼ lb.)
- 2 whole bay leaves, crushed
- 2 Tbs. minced fresh parsley
- 1 tsp. dried thyme
- 1¾ tsp. salt
- ¾ tsp. freshly ground black pepper
- ⅛ tsp. cayenne
- ¼ tsp. dried basil
- 2 one-lb. cans peeled whole tomatoes, undrained

Boiled Rice (page 17)

In a heavy 5- to 6-quart saucepan, combine the ingredients for the courtbouillon. Bring to a boil over high heat, then add the tripe. Reduce the heat to low and cook for 2 to 3 hours, or until the tripe is tender.

Meanwhile, in another heavy saucepan about 4 to 5 quarts in capacity melt the butter over low heat. Add the sliced onions and sauté until soft, then add all the other ingredients except the tripe. Continue sautéing for 20 minutes more, stirring frequently.

Remove the tripe from the courtbouillon and drain. Allow to cool slightly before handling, then cut into pieces about 2 inches long and ½ inch wide. Add to the pan with the sauce, cover, and cook the tripe in the sauce for 25 minutes. Serve with boiled rice.

BRAISED SWEETBREADS MEUNIÈRE

Sweetbreads are a delicacy few people get to enjoy—the tough tasteless ones served in many restaurants are enough to discourage you for life. Try preparing them at home this simple way and you'll quickly understand why lovers of sweetbreads consider them an extra special dish. Sweetbreads are generally sold frozen; thaw them thoroughly before cooking or they'll taste rubbery. If you parboil the sweetbreads for a few minutes, then rinse them under cold running water, cleaning them will be easy.

(for 4)

- 2 lb. sweetbreads
- Salt and freshly ground white pepper
- Flour for dusting
- ¼ c. (½ stick) salt butter
- ¼ c. dry white wine
- ½ c. light beef stock
- 2 Tbs. finely minced fresh parsley
- ¼ tsp. salt
- ⅛ tsp. freshly ground white pepper
- ⅛ tsp. mace
- 1⅓ c. Meunière Sauce (page 113)

Parboil the sweetbreads in boiling salted water for 3 minutes, then drain in a colander and rinse quickly under cold running water. Clean by peeling off all the membrane and cutting away the connective tissue. Pat dry between paper towels. Sprinkle generously on both sides with salt and white pepper, then dust evenly with flour.

In a large heavy sauté pan or skillet melt the butter over medium heat until sizzling, then cook the sweetbreads in hot butter on both sides until lightly browned. Turn the heat to low and add the wine, beef stock, parsley, salt, pepper, and mace. Cook over low heat for 30 minutes, turning the sweetbreads over carefully with a large spoon several times. Remove to individual serving ramekins with a slotted spoon, allowing the liquid to drain back into the pan, and place in a preheated 200° oven to keep warm while you prepare the meunière sauce.

To serve, spoon ⅓ cup sauce over each portion.

CREOLE SWEETBREADS

A nineteenth-century New Orleans dish—sweetbreads braised in oil and butter, then cooked with diced vegetables, beef stock, brandy, and red wine. *(for 4)*

- Cold water
- Juice of ½ lemon
- ½ tsp. salt
- 2½ to 3 lb. calf's sweetbreads
- ¼ c. (½ stick) salt butter
- ¼ c. vegetable oil
- Flour for dusting
- ⅔ c. finely chopped onion
- ½ c. thinly sliced green shallot (scallion) tops
- ½ c. finely diced carrots
- 1 tsp. finely minced garlic
- 3 Tbs. finely minced fresh parsley
- 1 tsp. salt
- ¼ tsp. freshly ground white pepper
- ¼ tsp. freshly ground black pepper
- ⅛ tsp. cayenne
- ⅛ tsp. cloves
- ½ tsp. dried marjoram
- 1 tsp. dried thyme
- 2 c. rich beef stock
- 1 c. dry red wine
- 6 Tbs. brandy
- 4 tsp. fresh lemon juice

Bring cold water containing the juice of half a lemon and ½ teaspoon salt to a boil, add the sweetbreads, and parboil for 10 minutes. Remove them from the boiling water and plunge into a bowl of ice water. Drain and clean them by peeling off the membrane and trimming away all connective tissue.

In a large sauté pan or skillet melt the butter over medium heat. Mix in the oil. Dust the sweetbreads with flour and braise them in the hot butter and oil until golden brown on both sides. Remove them to a platter with tongs and set aside. Add the vegetables and dry seasonings to the pan and cook over medium heat, stirring constantly, for 10 minutes. Stir in the remaining ingredients and cook for 5 minutes more. Add the sweetbreads, reduce the heat to low, and cook for 35 minutes, stirring frequently and turning the sweetbreads over several times.

To serve, spoon about 3 tablespoons of sauce and vegetables over each portion of sweetbreads.

CREOLE QUENELLES

These poached meat dumplings made with calf's liver and pork were popular locally before the turn of the century. We like them as a main dish or as an accompaniment to fish or poultry. You can prepare the quenelles an hour in advance and keep them warm in the oven.

(for 4)

- 1 lb. calf's liver
- ½ lb. salt pork
- 1 c. finely chopped onion
- ½ tsp. dried thyme
- 3 Tbs. finely minced fresh parsley
- ⅛ tsp. ground bay leaf
- ¾ tsp. freshly grated nutmeg
- 1 tsp. freshly ground black pepper
- 3 large eggs plus 2 large egg yolks
- ¼ c. heavy cream
- 2 Tbs. salt butter
- Flour for dusting

Cut the calf's liver and salt pork into small chunks and pass twice through the fine blade of a meat grinder. Add the onion, thyme, parsley, bay leaf, nutmeg, and black pepper and toss well to mix thoroughly. Add the eggs, egg yolks, and heavy cream and mix again. In a large heavy skillet or sauté pan melt the butter over low heat. Add the seasoned ground meat mixture and cook over low heat for 15 minutes, stirring frequently, until the meat is light brown in color and the onions are tender. Remove the pan from the heat and allow to cool.

Roll the ground meat mixture into dumplings of cylindrical shape, about 3 inches long, 2 inches wide, and ½ inch thick. Dust each dumpling lightly on all sides with flour. Put about 2 inches of lightly salted water into a large sauté pan and bring to a boil. Reduce the heat slightly and carefully place the dumplings flat in the lightly boiling water. Poach for 5 minutes, turning the dumplings over gently after 3½ minutes. When done, remove from the poaching liquid with a slotted spoon or spatula and place on a heated platter. Keep warm in a preheated 175° oven until serving time. (To prevent the dumplings from drying out, cover the platter loosely with a large piece of aluminum foil.)

GRILLED LAMB CHOPS BÉARNAISE

New Orleans' only popular lamb dish. *(for 4)*

3 c. Béarnaise Sauce (page 115)
8 double rib lamb chops
Salt and freshly ground black pepper

Prepare the béarnaise sauce and set the blender container in a basin of warm water to keep warm. Preheat the broiler, broiling pan, and rack. Meanwhile, trim the excess fat from the lamb chops and sprinkle the chops generously on both sides with salt and pepper. Broil the chops, about 3½ inches from the heat, 5 minutes on one side and 4 on the other for rare, 6 and 5 minutes for medium.

To serve, put the chops on heated plates and spoon about ¾ cup béarnaise sauce over each portion.

NEW ORLEANS HAMBURGER

The traditional New Orleans hamburger is well seasoned, has lots of chopped onions cooked in with the meat, or sautéed separately and heaped on it, and is eaten on warm French bread. Most New Orleanians like it "dressed"—that is, garnished with shredded lettuce, sliced tomatoes, pickle slices, and gobs of mayonnaise. A deliciously juicy version of an American staple. *(for 4)*

1 c. chopped onion
1 Tbs. vegetable oil (optional), approximately
1 lb. ground beef, preferably chuck
1½ tsp. salt
½ tsp. freshly ground black pepper
Scant ⅛ tsp. cayenne
¼ tsp. paprika
⅛ tsp. chili powder

In a large heavy skillet or on a griddle fry the chopped onion in the vegetable oil until glazed and lightly browned. Put the ground beef in a large mixing bowl and add the browned onions and the remaining ingredients. Mix well by tossing with a long fork or a wooden spoon, then divide into 4 portions and shape into wide patties about ½ inch high. Heat a large skillet or griddle until a drop of water dances on it. Grill the hamburgers on both sides until well browned, flattening them with a spatula while they cook. The hamburgers should be about ⅜ inches thick after cooking and rather crisp at the edges. Serve on French bread.

Variation: Do not fry the onions, but mix them in raw with the meat and seasonings. Grill the hamburgers on slightly lower heat for a few minutes longer than you normally would, to let the onions cook through.

ROAST BEEF POOR BOY

Roast beef poor boys are a New Orleans institution. Everyone loves these huge sandwiches made with slow-cooked beef and lots of meat gravy on hot French bread—loves them so much that many bad ones are eaten along with the good. We include this recipe for those who live elsewhere and would like to know how good poor boys are made. We also include it for fellow New Orleanians who seldom make their own, in the hope that they will insist on the real thing and complain loudly when offered a terrible, dry poor boy on cold bread. If all else fails, we'll just have to practice the fine art of the roast beef poor boy at home.

The loaf of French bread should be as fresh as possible, preferably no more than a few hours out of the oven or just thawed if you bake your own and freeze it (see page 202). As for the meat, it should be sliced from a good tough cut of beef with the right meaty flavor (a shoulder roast, for example), cooked for 4 to 5 hours, so that it makes a good strong gravy. We like to add soup bones to the stock during cooking to make the gravy even thicker and richer. (The meat is probably less crucial than the gravy it produces.) *(1 dressed poor boy about 12 inches long)*

Warm the bread in a moderately hot oven for a few minutes. Split it in half lengthwise and spread a generous layer of mayonnaise on the bottom piece. Spread about ¾ cup shredded lettuce over the mayonnaise, then put 4 to 6 very thin slices of meat on the shredded lettuce. Cover with ½ to ⅔ cup of the thick natural gravy and top with 3 thin slices of tomato. Cover with the top half of the warm French bread—and when you serve, provide plenty of napkins to catch the drippings.

MUFFULETTA

The muffuletta is an Italian sandwich created in New Orleans early in the twentieth century. It consists of a round loaf of bread about 10 inches across filled with Italian salami, olive salad, cheese, Italian ham, and freshly minced garlic.

The key ingredient is the olive salad, which gives the sandwich its special flavor and makes it appealing to the eye. Olive salad is a mixture of broken or chopped green olives and the pimientos that once stuffed them, chopped Greek olives, prepared pickled Italian vegetables, olive oil, oregano, chopped garlic, and parsley. These ingredients form a spicy aromatic mixture that is very colorful and also very liquid. The juice of the olive salad is a kind of Italian vinaigrette dressing, 90 percent olive oil and 10 percent vinegary olive juice.

A filled muffuletta sandwich—another lovely, leaky New Orleans whole-meal sandwich—is almost 3 inches high at the center. *(1 muffuletta; feeds 1 or 2)*

The muffuletta loaf is prepared by several local bakeries. To make the sandwich, you slice the muffuletta across, then dampen the inside of the bread with juice from the olive salad and with minced garlic. Then you put a layer of thinly sliced Italian salami on the bottom half. Cover the salami with lots of olive salad. Put several thin slices of provolone cheese over the salami, and cover the cheese with several slices of Italian ham. If you wish, sprinkle some minced garlic on the salami and ham layers. Cover with the top half of the muffuletta loaf.

SAUSAGES

This section is primarily for those who live outside the Louisiana marketing area and can't purchase chaurice, andouille, or Creole smoked sausage—some of the Creole and Cajun sausages we use in gumbos, jambalayas, or bean dishes, or serve grilled as main-dish meats. For Louisianians, making sausage is purely a labor of love, since all our local sausages are readily available in New Orleans and Cajun markets prepared fresh by small companies, farmers, and local families.

These recipes will enable you to prepare our local sausages at home. All of them freeze well; we find it most practical to wrap them for freezing in half-pound and one-pound packages.

CHAURICE

This Creole pork sausage is a local favorite dating well back into the nineteenth century. Its firm texture and hearty, spicy flavor make it an excellent accompaniment to red or white beans and rice; at our house we also like it grilled as a breakfast sausage. The most practical way to prepare sausage at home is in quantities of about 6 pounds at a time, with an electric or manual meat grinder and a sausage stuffer (or "horn") that fits onto the grinder. There are many inexpensive meat grinders available these days in housewares departments and hardware stores. You will find it delightful to be able to grind your chopped meat fresh right before cooking and to improvise combinations of various raw or leftover cooked meats for sausages or simple sausage patties.

For making sausage, you will also need a wooden pestle with a flat end to push the meat into the machine (these generally come with the grinder), some sausage casing, and string for tying off the sausages. Casing can be purchased from butchers and butchers' supply houses. Check in your own area to find out who carries casings. The two sizes most frequently used in Creole and Cajun cooking are the small hog or sheep casings, about 1 inch wide stuffed, and the large hog casings, about 2 to 3 inches wide; specify which size you want when you buy them.

For home sausage making we find it most practical to fill and tie off one sausage at a time. Remember to soak the casing about an hour in cold water to soften it and to loosen the salt in which it packed. Cut into 3-yard lengths, then place the narrow end of the sausage stuffer in one end of the casing. Place the wide end of the stuffer up against the sink faucet and run cold water through the inside of the casing to remove any salt. (Roll up the casing you do not intend to use; put about 2 inches of coarse salt in a large jar, place the rolled-up casing on it, then fill the rest of the jar with salt. Close tightly and refrigerate for later use.)

Freshly prepared sausage should be refrigerated quickly to keep it from spoiling and should be used within 4 to 5 days. If you plan to keep it any longer, freeze it—it will stay fresh for three months. We find it most practical to wrap sausage for freezing in ½-pound packages, ready to be used in bean dishes, in gumbos, or grilled. Pan grilled or charcoal broiled sausage can be cooked frozen: it will defrost during the first minute or two of cooking.

(about 6 pounds of 10- to 12-inch sausages)

3 yards small sausage casing
4 lb. lean fresh pork
2 lb. fresh pork fat
2 c. very finely chopped onion
4 tsp. very finely minced garlic
1 tsp. cayenne
1 tsp. chili powder
1 tsp. crushed red pepper pods
2⅔ Tbs. salt
2 tsp. freshly ground black pepper
2 tsp. dried thyme
5 Tbs. finely minced fresh parsley
3 whole bay leaves, crushed very fine
½ tsp. allspice

Prepare the casings by soaking them in cold water for an hour, then running cold water through them. Cut off a 3-yard length. (Repack the rest as directed above and refrigerate for later use.)

To prepare the stuffing, cut the pork and fat into small pieces with a sharp knife. Mix together and run once through the coarse blade of the meat grinder, placing a large bowl in front of the grinder to catch the meat. Add the seasonings and mix vigorously with a wooden spoon or a large stiff wire whisk until the stuffing is fluffy and very smooth.

To stuff the sausages, cut the softened casing into 16-inch lengths. Tie a knot in each piece about 2 inches from one end. Fit the open end over the tip of the sausage stuffer and slide it to about 1 inch from the wide end. Push the rest of the casing onto the stuffer until the top touches the knot. (The casing will look like accordian folds on the stuffer.) Fit the stuffer onto the meat grinder as directed on the instructions that come with the machine, or hold the wide end of the stuffer against or over the opening by hand. Fill the hopper with stuffing. Turn the machine on if it is electric and feed the stuffing gradually into the hopper; for a manual machine, push the stuffing through with a wooden pestle. The sausage casing will fill and inflate gradually. Stop filling about 1¼ inches from the funnel end and slip the casing off the funnel, smoothing out any bumps carefully with your fingers and being careful not to push the stuffing out of the casing. Tie off the open end of the sausage tightly with a piece of string or make a knot in the casing itself. Repeat until all the stuffing is used up.

To cook the chaurice, place the sausage in a large heavy skillet or sauté pan with about ¼ inch cold water. Bring to a boil over high heat, cover the pan, then reduce the heat to low and cook for about 15 minutes. Uncover the pan, raise the heat to medium, and cook until the sausage is well browned on all sides (about 10 minutes longer), turning frequently with tongs. Drain on paper towels for a few minutes.

Note: One chaurice per person is an average serving.

CREOLE SMOKED SAUSAGE

New Orleans' most popular sausage, a type of country sausage made with pork, or pork and beef. It's not really smoked, but has a fine smoky flavor that makes it an ideal seasoning meat for our favorite bean dishes, gumbos, and jambalayas. We also like it pan grilled as a breakfast or dinner sausage. Allow about 20 to 25 minutes for grilling. When used as a seasoning meat in other dishes, it requires no precooking.

(about 6 pounds of 6- to 8-inch sausage)

---

3 yards small sausage casing
4 lb. lean pork (or 2 lb. lean pork and 2 lb. lean beef)
2 lb. pork fat
2 tsp. finely minced garlic
2 tsp. freshly ground black pepper
3 Tbs. salt
2 tsp. cayenne
½ tsp. ground bay leaf
¼ tsp. cumin
½ tsp. chili powder
4 tsp. paprika
½ tsp. sugar
5 tsp. Colgin's liquid hickory smoke

Prepare the sausage casings and stuffing according to the directions on page 137. Mix the stuffing ingredients lightly; the stuffing should be slightly coarse in texture. Cut the casing into 12-inch lengths and stuff as directed on page 137. Allow two smoked sausages per serving.

CREOLE HOT SAUSAGE

Similar to Creole smoked sausage, but with a great deal more pepper. We generally cut it into ⅓-inch slices and grill it for about 15 minutes as an accompaniment to bean dishes or smothered vegetables or as a breakfast sausage with grits and eggs. Use it sparingly until you become accustomed to this much pepper. We don't recommend hot sausage as a seasoning meat in the traditional bean dishes or other local pot dinners; it is likely to overwhelm the flavor of the other ingredients.

(about 6 pounds of 6- to 8-inch sausage)

Prepare according to the directions above for Creole Smoked Sausage, adding 1 teaspoon cayenne and 1 teaspoon black pepper; omit the liquid hickory smoke.

ANDOUILLE

Andouille was a great favorite in nineteenth-century New Orleans. This thick Cajun sausage is made with lean pork and pork fat and lots of garlic. Sliced about ½ inch thick and grilled, it makes a delightful appetizer. It is also used in a superb oyster and andouille gumbo popular in Laplace, a Cajun town about 30 miles from New Orleans that calls itself the Andouille Capital of the World.

(about 6 pounds of 20-inch sausage, 3 to 3½ inches thick)

1½ yards large sausage casing, approximately
4 lb. lean fresh pork
2 lb. pork fat
3⅓ Tbs. finely minced garlic
2 Tbs. salt
½ tsp. freshly ground black pepper
⅛ tsp. cayenne
⅛ tsp. chili powder
⅛ tsp. mace
⅛ tsp. allspice
½ tsp. dried thyme
1 Tbs. paprika
¼ tsp. ground bay leaf
¼ tsp. sage
5 tsp. Colgin's liquid hickory smoke

Prepare the sausage casing as directed on page 137. Cut the meat and fat into chunks about ½ inch across and pass once through the coarse blade of the meat grinder. Combine the pork with the remaining ingredients in a large bowl and mix well with a wooden spoon. Cut the casings into 26-inch lengths and stuff as directed on page 137.

To cook, slice the andouille ½ inch thick and grill in a hot skillet with no water for about 12 minutes on each side, until brown and crisp at the edges.

BOUDIN BLANC

A delicious Cajun white sausage made with rice, ground pork, chicken, and vegetables. When you cook it, the casing breaks open and the creamy stuffing becomes a smoky, spicy rice stew. Remove and discard the pieces of casing before serving, if you wish. We like to use heavy cream in preparing boudin blanc; for a slightly stronger flavor you can substitute chicken or veal stock. Use leftover chicken and prepare the rice ahead of time. *(about 4 pounds of 16-inch sausage)*

- 1½ yards small sausage casing
- 1 lb. lean fresh pork
- 1 lb. fresh pork fat
- 1 c. heavy cream
- 1 c. chopped onion
- 5 Tbs. finely minced fresh parsley
- 1 Tbs. finely minced garlic
- ⅓ c. thinly sliced green shallot (scallion) tops
- ⅓ c. water, approximately
- 1 lb. leftover white poultry meat
- 3 c. cooked long grain white rice (page 17)
- ½ tsp. sage
- 4 tsp. salt
- ½ tsp. freshly ground black pepper
- 1 tsp. cayenne
- ¼ tsp. ground bay leaf
- ¼ tsp. dried thyme
- 1/16 tsp. allspice
- ⅛ tsp. mace
- ¼ c. water, more if necessary

Prepare the sausage casings as directed on pages 136–7. Cut the pork and fat into small pieces and put into a heavy 5- to 6-quart saucepan along with the cream, onion, parsley, garlic, shallots, and seasonings. Add about ⅓ cup water. Cook over high heat until the mixture begins to boil. Quickly reduce the heat to low and cook for about 10 minutes, stirring frequently; then remove the pan from the heat. Cut up the poultry meat and add it to the contents of the saucepan, along with the cooked rice. Mix thoroughly, drain in a colander, and let cool for about 10 minutes. Meanwhile, cut the casings into 20-inch lengths, then stuff as directed on pages 136–7, using the coarse blade.

To cook, place the boudin in a medium-sized heavy skillet or sauté pan. Curl it around to fit. Turn the heat on low, add about ¼ cup water, and cook very slowly over low heat for about 20 minutes, until piping hot. Turn the boudin over several times and stir frequently with a wooden spoon, scraping the bottom of the skillet to prevent scorching. Add a few tablespoons of water, if necessary. As the casing breaks open, move the torn pieces to the sides of the pan. To serve, spoon the semi-liquid mixture onto heated plates.

Note: Allow about ½ pound sausage per serving.

10

POULTRY AND GAME

Louisiana is one of the great hunting areas of the world. There are few rules for cooking game Louisiana style, and even fewer for identifying what comes to the table. George A. Sala, an English writer and connoisseur of food, commented on our puzzling habits in *America Revisited*, published in 1882:

So it is with the game, the nomenclature of which is, even when acquired, bewildering to the foreigner; and the confusion of the two tongues makes confusion worse confounded. What at a French restaurant is called a "perdreau" looks like a large quail; in fact, the Creole waiter will gravely tell you that the English for "perdreau" is quail; of the bird termed in European French "caille," he does not seem to have any definite knowledge. . . . I have ceased to strive after accuracy, and have allowed the **garçon** ***to bring me what he would in the way of game. That is the wisest plan to adopt. The Creole restaurant waiter knows infinitely more about local matters edible than you do. He is generally a very good fellow; and if you leave the selection to him he will bring you that which is in season and most toothsome. Still, for the sake of convenience, it might be***

desirable for an independent system of nomenclature—say an Indian one—to be applied to game and fish. I would not mind if a duck were called a "catahoula," a pigeon an "oshibi," a pheasant a "caccassar," a partridge a "tangipahoa," a quail a "chefuncte," a snipe a "lanacoco," a woodcock a "tickfaw," or a snipe an "atchafalaya."

Duck both wild and domestic is a great local favorite, prepared highly seasoned and slowly roasted, or stewed with cabbage or turnips, or used in gumbos and stews. Quail, partridge, and pheasant are braised, smothered with vegetables, or roasted and topped with rich, elaborate sauces. Armadillo, rabbit, and turtle are caught in the Cajun country and generally cooked with sauce piquante, a very peppery sauce that pleases the local palate. Many of our favorite local styles of preparing wild game can also be used with chicken, Rock Cornish hen, farm-raised quail, and domestic duck.

Chicken and game dishes served in grand restaurants, such as chicken Pontalba and pigeonneaux sauce paradis, are great fun to prepare at home and make exciting special occasion dinners. We have included them here along with traditional home favorites such as highly seasoned fried chicken, Cajun chicken maquechoux with fresh corn, smothered chicken, and the classic Cajun roast duckling.

CHICKEN PONTALBA

One of the grandest chicken dishes we know. A layer of vegetables and ham sautéed in butter, then covered with a layer of crisp lightly fried pieces of deboned chicken, the whole then topped with a sea of rich simmering béarnaise sauce. Simple to prepare if you proceed one step at a time. *(for 4)*

½ c. (1 stick) salt butter
1 c. chopped onion
1½ c. thinly sliced shallots (scallions)
1 Tbs. finely minced garlic
1¼ c. diced potatoes (½-inch dice)
1 c. diced lean ham (¾-inch dice)
1¼ c. thinly sliced fresh mushrooms (if not available, substitute high quality canned)
½ c. dry white wine
1 Tbs. finely minced fresh parsley
1 c. flour
1 tsp. salt
½ tsp. freshly ground black pepper
⅛ tsp. cayenne
2 lb. deboned chicken breast, leg, and thigh (about 2 whole small fryers)
1 c. vegetable oil
2 c. Béarnaise Sauce (page 115)

In a heavy 10-inch sauté pan or skillet melt the butter over low heat. Add the onion, shallots, garlic, and potatoes and cook over low heat until the vegetables are browned (about 15 minutes), stirring frequently. Add the diced ham, mushrooms, wine, and parsley and cook for 8 minutes more, then turn off the heat. Remove the vegetables and ham from the pan with a slotted spoon and place in a large gratin dish attractive enough to bring to the table, allowing the excess butter to drain back into the pan. Put the dish in a preheated 200° oven.

In a shallow bowl or pie dish, combine the flour, salt, black pepper, and cayenne. Cut up the larger pieces of deboned chicken so that none are thicker than about ½ inch or longer than about 1½ inches. Dredge the pieces of chicken in the seasoned flour. Add the vegetable oil to the butter in the pan, then heat the oil and butter mixture until it sizzles lightly. Fry the chicken pieces until they are cooked through and golden brown on all sides (about 8 to 10 minutes), turning frequently with tongs. Remove the chicken, drain for a minute on paper towels, then arrange the pieces evenly over the sautéed vegetables in the gratin dish. Put the dish back in the oven while you prepare the béarnaise sauce, then remove the dish from the oven, spoon the sauce evenly over the entire surface, and serve.

CHICKEN MAQUECHOUX

"Maquechoux" is a Cajun word meaning a smothered dish made with fresh corn. This hearty chicken stew is prepared with fresh corn and fresh ripe tomatoes. When you strip the kernels off the cob, save the cob liquid and squeeze as much of it as you can out of the cobs. When fresh corn is not in season, substitute canned or frozen corn and add about 2½ tablespoons heavy cream in place of the corn cob liquid. Serve chicken maquechoux in wide soup bowls with pieces of chicken, kernels of corn, and plenty of liquid from the pot in each. Provide soup spoons—the liquid is delicious and shouldn't be wasted. *(for 6 or more)*

¼ c. vegetable oil
2 small fryers (2½ to 3 lb. each), cut up
3½ to 4 c. fresh corn scraped off the cob, corn cob liquid reserved (substitute 14 to 16 oz. frozen or canned when fresh is unavailable)
2 Tbs. heavy cream
3 c. chopped onion
⅔ c. green pepper, chopped
2 large Creole (beefsteak, Jersey) tomatoes, coarsely chopped
¼ tsp. dried thyme
¼ tsp. dried basil
1 Tbs. finely minced fresh parsley
3 tsp. salt
1 tsp. freshly ground black pepper
2 to 3 Tbs. milk, if necessary

In a heavy 8- to 10-quart pot or kettle heat the oil over medium heat. Brown the chicken parts in the hot oil, turning frequently with tongs to brown evenly. Reduce the heat to low once the chicken begins to brown (about 15 to 20 minutes), then lower heat still further and add the corn, corn liquid, and cream. Mix thoroughly. Add the onion, green pepper, tomatoes, herbs, salt, and pepper and cook over low heat for 30 to 45 minutes, or until chicken is very tender, stirring frequently. If the mixture seems to be becoming too dry, add 2 to 3 tablespoons of milk toward the end of the cooking period. Serve hot in soup or gumbo bowls.

FRIED CHICKEN

New Orleans' favorite form of fried chicken—crisp and well seasoned, with a thin crust. This is much closer to soul fried chicken than to the batter fried chicken popular elsewhere in the South. The trick is to get the seasonings *into* the chicken, not just on top, so season the cut-up chicken for at least 2 hours before you plan to fry it, 4 to 5 hours if possible. Later dredge the pieces in flour and fry. Simple and delicious. You can keep fried chicken warm *and* crisp in the oven for almost an hour. Just put it uncovered on a large platter lined with several layers of paper towels. *(for 4)*

---

2 small fryers (about 2½ to 3 lb. each), cut up
Salt, freshly ground black pepper, and cayenne
½ tsp. finely minced garlic, approximately
Lard or vegetable oil for deep frying
Flour for dredging

Wash the chicken parts, and shake off excess water. Sprinkle each piece on one side very generously with salt, pepper, cayenne, and a small amount of garlic. Place the pieces flat, seasoned sides down, in a single layer on a large platter. Season the upper sides of the pieces the same way, then cover the platter loosely with plastic wrap and refrigerate for at least 2 hours before frying.

When ready to fry, put lard to a depth of 4 to 5 inches in a deep fryer and heat to 375°. Dredge the pieces of chicken in flour to coat evenly and fry 2 to 4 pieces at a time until golden brown; do not crowd the fryer basket. Large pieces such as breasts should take about 12 to 15 minutes, smaller ones such as backs and wings 9 to 10 minutes. As each batch is completed, drain thoroughly and place on large platter lined with several layers of paper towels. Place in a preheated 200° oven to keep warm until ready to serve.

Variations: Use "pearly meal," a combination of yellow corn flour and yellow corn meal for dredging: 1 cup yellow corn flour to 1 cup yellow corn meal. Optional seasonings for the meal: 1 teaspoon salt, ½ teaspoon freshly ground black pepper, ⅛ teaspoon cayenne.

Use Fish-Fri (yellow corn flour) in place of flour. Add no seasonings to the Fish-Fri.

Use yellow corn meal with a bit of color added for dredging. To 2 cups yellow corn meal, add ¼ cup finely minced fresh parsley, 1 teaspoon salt, ½ teaspoon freshly ground black pepper, and 1 teaspoon paprika.

OLD STYLE BROILED CHICKEN

A simple dish unusually seasoned. Be sure to save the pan drippings, a delicious mixture of butter and all the seasonings from the chicken; pour about 1½ tablespoons over each portion. *(for 4)*

---

1 fryer (3 to 3½ lb.), quartered
1½ tsp. salt
1¼ tsp. freshly ground black pepper
¾ tsp. very finely minced garlic
½ tsp. ground rosemary
2 tsp. finely minced fresh parsley
2 tsp. fresh lemon juice
5 Tbs. salt butter

Wash and dry the chicken. Sprinkle both sides of each piece with salt, pepper, garlic, rosemary, parsley, and lemon juice, then set aside while you preheat the broiler, broiling pan, and rack.

Melt the butter over low heat in a small saucepan. Pour half the melted butter on the skin side of the chicken pieces, then place them skin side down on the hot broiling rack. Pour the remaining butter over and broil, about 7 inches from the flame, for 20 minutes on each side. Serve with the juice and butter that collect in the broiling pan poured over the chicken.

OLD STYLE SMOTHERED CHICKEN

An old time Creole chicken dish prepared with bacon, lemon slices, vegetables, and plenty of seasoning. Be sure to baste the chicken with liquid from the bottom of the pot frequently during cooking. *(for 4)*

---

1 large fryer or small hen (about 3¼ lb.), whole, giblets removed
½ lb. sliced bacon, cut into strips 3 inches long
10 slices fresh lemon (each about ¼ inch thick)
½ c. water
2 carrots, quartered lengthwise, then cut in half crosswise
1 large onion, sliced
½ tsp. dried thyme
½ tsp. ground bay leaf
1 tsp. finely minced fresh parsley
2 tsp. coarse salt
1 tsp. freshly ground black pepper
¼ tsp. sugar
¼ tsp. allspice
⅛ tsp. mace
2 tsp. minced chives
½ c. chicken stock

Wash and dry the chicken and truss as for roasting. Lay half the bacon strips in the bottom of a deep heavy pot or kettle about 10 inches in diameter. Distribute the lemon slices on top, then cover with the remaining bacon strips. Moisten with the ½ cup water and put the pot over low heat. Add the carrot pieces and sliced onion in another layer, then sprinkle with the thyme, bay leaf, parsley, salt, pepper, sugar, allspice, mace, and chives. Place the trussed whole chicken on top of the vegetables and bacon. Bring to a boil, then add the chicken stock. Cover the pot loosely, reduce the heat, and simmer for 45 minutes to 1 hour, or until the chicken is tender, basting the chicken with liquid from the bottom of the pot about every 10 minutes during cooking.

To serve, carve the chicken and top each portion with solids and liquid from the pot.

CHICKEN FRICASSEE

At the turn of the century Creole cooks prepared chicken this way, with onions, lots of pepper, some water, and the Creole bouquet garni—parsley, bay leaf, and thyme.

After you brown the floured chicken in hot fat, remove it to a platter while browning the onions; the fat, onions, and flour from the dredged chicken form a brown roux. When you put the chicken back in the pot and add the seasonings and liquid, a rich gravy gradually forms. We like this served with boiled rice and with some of the gravy poured over it. *(for 4)*

- 3½ Tbs. lard
- 1 fryer (3 to 3½ lb.), cut up
- Flour
- 2 c. chopped onion
- 2 c. water
- 1¼ tsp. salt
- ¾ tsp. freshly ground black pepper
- 1 whole bay leaf, crushed
- 1 tsp. finely minced fresh parsley
- ¼ tsp. dried thyme
- ⅛ tsp. cayenne
- 1/16 tsp. turmeric
- ⅛ tsp. allspice
- 1 tsp. minced chives
- ⅛ tsp. mace
- 1 tsp. Worcestershire sauce

In a large heavy kettle or pot melt the lard over medium heat. Dust the chicken parts with flour and brown on all sides in the hot lard, several pieces at a time. Remove the browned pieces to a platter. When all the chicken has been browned and the last pieces removed, add the onions to the hot lard and cook, stirring, until they are soft and brown. Add 1 tablespoon flour and brown, stirring constantly. Add the chicken and the remaining ingredients and cook over low heat for 45 minutes to 1 hour, or until the chicken is tender when pierced with a fork. Stir every few minutes to distribute the seasonings and brown the chicken evenly. When done, remove the chicken to a serving platter, turn off the heat, and stir the gravy vigorously to bring up the seasonings from the bottom of the pot. To serve, put the chicken pieces on plates, then stir the gravy well and spoon generously over each portion.

GUMBO CHICKEN

This is the chicken saved from the preparation of Shrimp Filé Gumbo (see page 21), along with bits of sliced sausage. Gumbo chicken is excellent chilled or hot.

To heat it, put the chicken and sausage into a heavy saucepan with about 3 tablespoons cold water. Bring to a boil over high heat, then cover and reduce the heat to very low. Cook until the chicken is warmed through (about 8 to 10 minutes). Serve the pieces of chicken with bits of sausage on top.

ROAST TURKEY MEUNIÈRE WITH CORN BREAD DRESSING

A New Orleans butter sauce on an old American favorite. The melted butter is combined with sausage or bacon drippings to add a slightly smoky, salty taste. To get the lovely, browned crisp skin and flavorful moist meat that distinguish the best roast turkeys, baste the bird thoroughly with pan drippings every 15 minutes. This will also give you a superb butter gravy—the juices from the turkey, the seasonings, and those lovely little browned pieces which collect in the pan, plus the butter and bacon drippings, all mixed together and browned in a saucepan after the turkey is cooked. (Use this basting procedure with turkeys labeled prebasted as well.)

We always remove the stuffing and put it in a separate dish before carving the turkey; most stuffings spoil much more quickly in warm weather than most persons realize when left in the bird after it is removed from the oven. Another delightful stuffing also popular in New Orleans is made with oysters and eggplant. (See Oyster and Eggplant Casserole, page 68.) *(for 8 or more)*

CORN BREAD DRESSING

1 c. water
1 c. (2 sticks) salt butter
2 eight-oz. bags dry corn bread stuffing
3 c. chopped onion
3 Tbs. bacon or sausage drippings
1½ tsp. salt
⅛ tsp. freshly ground black pepper
2 large eggs, lightly beaten with 2 Tbs. cold water
1⅓ Tbs. poultry seasoning

---

1 turkey (12 to 14 lb.), giblets removed
½ lemon
1½ tsp. salt
1 tsp. freshly ground black pepper
½ c. (1 stick) salt butter
½ c. bacon or sausage drippings

To make the dressing, in a large saucepan heat the water, then add the butter and let it melt. Add the dry corn bread stuffing and toss lightly to moisten thoroughly. Remove the pan from the heat. In a heavy skillet sauté the chopped onion in the bacon drippings until glazed and just beginning to brown. Remove from the heat, mix in the salt and pepper, and add to the saucepan containing the corn bread mixture. In a small bowl lightly beat the eggs and cold water with a fork. Add to the corn bread mixture, along with the poultry seasoning, and toss gently to mix.

Wash the turkey, drain, and dry thoroughly inside and out with paper towels. Rub the inside of the cavity with the cut side of the lemon half, then sprinkle it with ½ teaspoon of the salt and ½ teaspoon of the pepper. Stuff the neck and body cavities loosely with the corn bread dressing (the stuffing will expand during roasting) and truss. Sprinkle with the remaining salt and pepper, then place breast side up on a rack in a large roasting pan. Melt the butter and bacon drippings in a small saucepan and pour over the bird.

Preheat the oven to 325°, then put the turkey in to roast about 4 to 4½ hours (about 20 minutes per pound), or until a meat thermometer inserted in the fullest part of the breast reads 190°, basting with pan dripping every 15 minutes. After a while the less meaty parts such as the wings and thighs will become quite brown; cover them with pieces of heavy duty aluminum foil. When the whole outer surface of the turkey is well browned and glazed (at about 2½ hours), cover the whole bird with a large piece of aluminum foil and tuck the edges loosely over the rim of the roasting pan. Remove the foil covering at 4 hours, or when the bird is about 30 minutes short of done by weight calculation, then raise the oven temperature to 400° and baste the bird once thoroughly. Remove the turkey from the oven 30 minutes later, put on a warm platter, and let cool slightly, for about 15 minutes. Remove the trussing string and skewers and spoon out the dressing. Put it in a separate bowl, then set the bowl and the turkey platter in a 175° oven to keep warm until serving time.

To prepare the meunière gravy, pour the pan drippings and scrapings into a heavy saucepan. Heat slowly, stirring, until browned, then remove the pan from the burner and pour the sauce into a gravy boat.

Carve the turkey and serve with about 3 tablespoons of meunière sauce over each portion. Place a mound of dressing at the side of each plate, and if desired, pour a tablespoon or so of sauce over it.

ROAST TURKEY MEUNIÈRE (UNSTUFFED)

Roast turkey is just as delicious without stuffing, and the meat can have just as moist and delicate a flavor as the one that is stuffed. Prepare as directed on page 148. Season the inside as directed, and truss carefully; this will keep the inside from drying out. Season the outside and roast, allowing 15 minutes per pound; baste as directed.

BRAISED QUAIL

Most quail is now farm raised and available frozen. We particularly enjoy it prepared this way—braised with diced vegetables, then wrapped in bacon and baked. Serve two or three of these small birds to a portion. Spoon some of the butter from the baking pan over them and surround with diced vegetables. *(per portion)*

- ¼ c. (½ stick) salt butter
- 2 to 3 quail, cleaned
- ¼ c. thinly sliced shallots (scallions)
- ¼ c. finely diced carrots
- 2 strips bacon
- ⅛ tsp. salt
- ¼ tsp. freshly ground black pepper

In a heavy skillet melt 2 tablespoons of the butter over medium heat. Heat the melted butter for a minute more, then brown the quail on all sides (which should take about 5 to 7 minutes) and remove to a plate. Reduce the heat to low and sauté the shallots and carrots in the butter for 5 minutes, stirring frequently.

Cut each bacon strip in two. Wrap ½ strip around each quail from the breast side to the back and fasten with a toothpick on each side. Wrap the other half strips around from the back to the breast side and fasten in the same way. Place the quails in a shallow earthenware baking dish and pour the butter and sautéed vegetables from the skillet over the quail. Sprinkle with salt and pepper. Melt the remaining 2 tablespoons butter in a small saucepan and pour over the birds. Place the baking dish in a preheated 400° oven and bake for 30 minutes, basting frequently with butter from the bottom of the dish.

Serve the quails whole with the butter sauce over them and surrounded with the vegetables.

ROAST DUCKLING

At one time Louisiana hunters caught more wild ducks than we could consume. Things have changed and most of us have to resort to domestic birds. But we have found that if you prepare them properly the Long Island ducklings available all over America make just as delectable a feast.

Duckling is generally purchased frozen. Be sure to defrost it thoroughly according to package directions and to dry it very thoroughly inside and out with paper towels before seasoning and roasting it. Use a roasting rack or not, as you prefer. We like to roast duckling without a rack in a shallow oval baking dish, and to move the duck around a bit when we baste to keep it from sticking. The three seasonings and the use of varying oven temperatures are what make this duck special. We find that frequent basting, even with ducklings that tend to be fat, makes them much crisper.

(for 4)

1 duckling (4 to 5 lb.), cleaned and left whole, giblets removed

SEASONING FOR INSIDE OF DUCK

¾ tsp. freshly ground black pepper
¾ tsp. salt
¼ tsp. cayenne
½ tsp. dried thyme
1½ Tbs. lard

FIRST SEASONING FOR OUTSIDE OF DUCK

1 tsp. freshly ground pepper
1¼ tsp. salt
½ tsp. cayenne
2 Tbs. melted lard

SECOND SEASONING

¾ tsp. freshly ground black pepper
¼ tsp. cayenne

Wash the duck and dry it thoroughly inside and out. Season the inside as indicated and truss for roasting, then season the outside with the first seasoning. Place the duck in a shallow roasting pan and roast for 20 minutes in a preheated 475° oven. Remove from the oven and add the second seasoning. Lower the oven heat to 350° and roast for 1 hour and 20 minutes, basting frequently with drippings from the pan. Raise the oven heat to 475° again and roast for 20 minutes longer to crisp. Remove the duck from the pan with a long fork, holding it over the pan for a minute to let any excess fat drain off, then put it on a platter to cool a bit before carving.

Scrape the bottom of the pan to loosen all the crisp browned matter. Pour the drippings and scrapings into a large heatproof measuring cup; set the cup aside while you carve the duck. Pour off about ½ cup of the clear fat, which will now be at the top in the measuring cup. Pour what remains into a gravy boat and use it to sauce the portions of duck; stir well each time you spoon some out to distribute the seasonings and browned solids.

ROAST MALLARD DUCK

We use the same basic method to roast mallard duck as to roast the fatter Long Island ducklings, but add more pepper in all three phases of seasoning. Pour all the pan drippings into a gravy boat for the sauce, since mallard gives off very little fat. One mallard will feed three, so roast two ducks for four or more persons. Save any leftover duck and add it to Wild Duck Gumbo (see page 152) about 10 minutes before the end of cooking time. *(for 3)*

1 mallard duck (3 to 4 lb.), cleaned and left whole, giblets removed

SEASONING FOR INSIDE OF DUCK

½ tsp. freshly ground black pepper
½ tsp. salt
⅛ tsp. cayenne
¼ tsp. dried thyme
1 Tbs. lard

SEASONING FOR OUTSIDE OF DUCK

¾ tsp. freshly ground black pepper
1 tsp. salt
¼ tsp. cayenne
2 Tbs. melted lard

SECOND SEASONING

½ tsp. freshly ground black pepper
¼ tsp. cayenne

Wash the duck and dry thoroughly inside and out. Season the inside as indicated and truss for roasting. Season the outside as indicated for the first seasoning and place the duck in a shallow roasting pan. Roast in a preheated 475° oven for 20 minutes, basting several times, then remove from the oven and sprinkle the second seasoning on top of the duck. Lower the oven heat to 350° and roast for 60 minutes more, basting frequently, then raise the oven heat to 450° and roast for 30 minutes more. Remove the duck from the oven and allow to cool slightly before carving. Pour the pan drippings and scrapings into a gravy boat, stir well, and pour about 1½ tablespoons of gravy over each serving.

Note: Stir the gravy well each time you spoon some out.

WILD DUCK WITH VEGETABLES AND BACON

An unusual wild duck dish, roasted and then smothered. Serve this with boiled rice to soak up the gravy. If you use small wild ducks, allow three ducks for four persons. *Poule d'eau* (water hen), a local bird of the coot species, can also be prepared this way.

(for 4 to 6)

- 3 small wild ducks (about 1½ lb. each) or 2 larger ones (2 to 3 lb. each), cleaned
- 2 medium onions, thinly sliced
- 3 ripe Creole (beefsteak, Jersey) tomatoes, coarsely chopped
- 1 Tbs. finely minced garlic
- ½ tsp. dried thyme
- 1 whole bay leaf, crushed
- 2 Tbs. finely minced fresh parsley
- 6 slices bacon
- 1½ Tbs. flour, approximately
- 2 Tbs. melted lard
- ⅓ c. chopped green pepper
- 4 carrots, cut in half, then quartered lengthwise
- ¾ c. dry red wine
- 3 Tbs. brandy
- ½ tsp. freshly ground black pepper
- ¾ tsp. salt

Split the cleaned ducks in half lengthwise. Lay them side by side skin side up in a large deep roasting pan. Place the onions, tomatoes, garlic, thyme, bay leaf, and parsley around and between the ducks. Put the slices of bacon across the ducks. Sprinkle them lightly with flour, then with the melted lard, and bake in a preheated 350° oven for 1½ hours.

Remove the roasting pan from the oven and transfer the ducks carefully to a large wide pot, Dutch oven, or deep sauté pan. Pour the contents of the roasting pan over the ducks and add the remaining ingredients.

Put the pot on high heat and as soon as the liquid begins to simmer, turn the heat down just enough to keep a simmer going. Cook for 1¼ hours or until the ducks are quite tender. Serve on heated plates with about ¼ cup of sauce from the pot ladled over each portion.

WILD DUCK GUMBO

Prepare according to directions for Shrimp Filé Gumbo (see page 21), substituting 2 wild ducks, cleaned and cut up, for the fryer and omitting the shrimp. Serve with boiled rice.

FRICASSEED WILD DUCK WITH BRANDY AND WINE

A rich Cajun wild duck dish. The ducks are marinated in brandy, red wine, and seasonings for about 5 hours, then browned in hot oil and butter and cooked with fresh mushrooms, some of the marinade, and beef stock. Use a stainless steel or porcelain bowl for marinating the ducks to avoid any metallic taste, and cook them in a skillet or sauté pan you can bring to the table. Serve right from the pan, with the sauce poured over. *(for 4 to 6)*

2 wild ducks (about 2 to 3 lb. each), cleaned and cut up
Salt and freshly ground black pepper

MARINADE

¼ c. brandy
1 c. dry red wine
2 large onions, coarsely chopped
1 Tbs. finely minced fresh parsley
½ tsp. dried thyme
½ tsp. dried marjoram
¼ tsp. allspice
1 whole bay leaf, broken into quarters

3 Tbs. salt butter
3 Tbs. olive oil
1 large clove garlic, finely minced
½ lb. fresh mushrooms, thinly sliced
¾ c. beef stock

Rinse the duck pieces and dry thoroughly with paper towels. Sprinkle generously with salt and pepper. Combine the ingredients for the marinade in a large stainless steel or porcelain bowl and mix thoroughly. Put the duck into the bowl and turn the pieces several times with tongs to coat thoroughly. Cover the bowl with plastic wrap and refrigerate for at least 5 hours, turning the pieces of duck several times during marination.

When you are ready to cook the ducks, remove the pieces from the marinade with tongs and let the excess liquid drain back into the bowl. Put the duck on a platter and set aside. Strain the marinade and reserve. In a heavy skillet or sauté pan melt the butter over medium heat, then add the olive oil and mix well. Cook until quite hot, then brown the pieces of duck well on all sides (about 15 to 20 minutes). If there is too much spattering, reduce the heat a bit. Add the garlic, the mushrooms, ½ cup of the strained marinade, and the beef stock. Cook over medium heat until the liquid begins to simmer, then cover the skillet, reduce the heat to low, and cook until the duck is tender (about 1¼ to 1½ hours). Serve from the skillet, and spoon about ¼ cup of sauce from the skillet over each portion.

WILD DUCK STEWED WITH TURNIPS

A grand old Creole duck dish with a marvelous gravy. The duck is browned in hot fat, then removed. When you add flour and onion to the fat and duck drippings, you get a rich roux with a superb aroma. Brown the turnips in the roux, then add the Creole trinity—garlic, parsley, and thyme—and plenty of pepper, some salt, and water. Put the duck back in the pot and simmer for an hour or more. Be sure to use young white turnips and to serve each portion with plenty of gravy.

Try the same basic recipe using chicken and acorn squash; boil the squash for half an hour first, then peel and cut it up. Or use dark meat turkey parts and cut-up sweet potatoes. *(for 4 to 6)*

---

2 wild ducks (about 2 to 3 lb. each), cleaned and cut up
2½ Tbs. lard
1½ Tbs. flour
1 medium onion, chopped (about 1 c.)
10 young white turnips, peeled
2 c. hot water
2 tsp. finely minced garlic
1 Tbs. finely minced fresh parsley
½ tsp. dried thyme
½ tsp. freshly ground black pepper
Scant ⅛ tsp. cayenne
1½ tsp. salt

Wash the duck parts and dry thoroughly with paper towels. In a heavy 6- to 8-quart saucepan melt the lard over medium heat. Brown the duck pieces in the hot lard, turning them frequently with tongs to brown them evenly. When browned, remove the duck with tongs to a platter and set aside.

Reduce the heat under the pot to very low and add the flour gradually, stirring. Cook, always stirring, for 2 minutes more, then add the onion. Continue cooking and stirring until the onion is browned and the roux is a rich brown, about 15 to 20 minutes. Add the turnips and cook them in the roux for 2 minutes, turning them several times. Gradually add the hot water, stirring constantly, then add the remaining ingredients and mix well. Raise the heat to high. When the liquid comes to a boil, add the browned duck parts. Reduce the heat just enough to keep a simmer going and simmer for about 1¼ hours, or until the duck is tender when pierced with a fork. Serve with about ½ cup of the gravy and several pieces of turnip ladled over each portion.

DUCK SAUCE PARADIS

A delicious way to serve crisply roasted duckling, with one of our most extravagant sauces. Prepare the duck first and set it in a warm oven while you make the sauce. Be sure to stir the sauce well before spooning it over the portions. *(for 3 to 4)*

Roast Duckling (page 150)
3 c. Sauce Paradis (page 116)

After roasting the duckling, set in a 200° oven to keep warm. Pour the pan drippings into a heatproof measuring cup and allow to settle. Pour off and discard all but ½ cup. Put the cup in the oven along with the duck to keep warm while you prepare the sauce paradis.

To serve, carve the duck and put each portion on a heated plate. Spoon 2 tablespoons drippings over each portion, then cover with about ¾ cup sauce.

PIGEONNEAUX ACADIENS À LA CRÈME

Squab with a typical Cajun stuffing and a rich cream sauce with brandy in it. The squabs are roasted for a while, then stuffed and roasted some more. You can prepare the sauce during the last phase of roasting. For an even richer dish, substitute Sauce Paradis (see page 116). Allow one squab per person. *(for 4)*

½ lb. chicken livers
½ lb. baked ham, cut into ⅜-inch dice
¾ c. chopped shallots (scallions)
3 Tbs. salt butter
½ tsp. salt
¼ tsp. freshly ground black pepper
1¼ c. soaked, crumbled French bread (Italian or white may be substituted)
¼ c. finely minced fresh parsley
4 squabs, cleaned and left whole
Melted butter
Salt and pepper for sprinkling

SAUCE

1 Tbs. salt butter
1 Tbs. flour
¼ c. very finely chopped onion
1 c. rich chicken stock
½ tsp. dried marjoram
½ tsp. salt
¼ tsp. freshly ground black pepper
¼ c. brandy
½ c. heavy cream

Sauté the chicken livers, ham, and shallots in the 3 tablespoons butter in a sauté pan for 15 minutes. Add ½ teaspoon salt, ¼ teaspoon pepper, the bread, and parsley and toss with a fork to mix. Continue cooking over very low heat for 8 minutes longer, then remove the pan from the heat and set aside.

Rinse the squabs and dry thoroughly with paper towels. Sprinkle them lightly with salt and pepper, then place them in a baking dish and roast in a preheated 450° oven for 20 minutes. Remove the dish from the oven and allow the squabs to cool for about 10 minutes, then stuff them with the mixture in the sauté pan. Tie the legs together with string and set the squabs in the roasting pan again. Brush them with melted butter and roast at 450° for 30 minutes longer.

Meanwhile, prepare the sauce. In a 2- to 3-quart saucepan melt the butter over medium heat. Gradually stir in the flour, keeping the mixture smooth. Add the onion and chicken stock and cook over low heat until the sauce thickens. Add the remaining ingredients, mix well, and cook for about 10 minutes longer. Serve the squabs with about ½ cup sauce spooned over each.

RABBIT SAUCE PIQUANTE

Wild rabbit has a slightly gamy taste. Most commercially raised rabbit available in markets today has a rather bland flavor. With either kind this Cajun style of preparation is excellent. Marinate the rabbit for at least 3 hours before cooking. The marinade is very spicy; and so is the sauce piquante. If you're not used to a lot of pepper, cut the cayenne in half the first time you prepare this dish.

Another Cajun dish prepared this way is armadillo sauce piquante—should you happen upon an armadillo. *(for 4)*

MARINADE

½ c. white wine vinegar
3 Tbs. olive oil
¼ c. red wine
½ c. finely chopped onion
1 whole bay leaf, crushed
¼ tsp. freshly ground black pepper
3 whole allspice
½ tsp. salt
½ tsp. finely minced garlic

---

2 lb. rabbit meat, cut up
Flour
6 Tbs. vegetable oil

SAUCE PIQUANTE

¼ c. flour
2 c. chopped onion
1 c. chopped green pepper
1 tsp. finely minced garlic
1 tsp. salt
¼ tsp. crushed red pepper pods
½ tsp. cayenne
½ tsp. freshly ground black pepper
2 c. water
2 six-oz. cans tomato paste
1½ tsp. lemon juice
3 Tbs. finely minced fresh parsley
¼ tsp. dried thyme
2 Tbs. red wine
1 Tbs. minced chives

Combine the ingredients for the marinade in a deep bowl narrow enough at the bottom to allow the rabbit to steep in the marinade and mix thoroughly. Put the rabbit meat into the marinade and turn the pieces several times to coat thoroughly. Cover the bowl with plastic wrap and refrigerate for at least 3 hours before cooking.

At the end of the marinating time, remove the rabbit from the liquid, drain, and dust the pieces with flour. In a heavy 6- to 8-quart pot or kettle heat the oil and fry the rabbit parts in it until they are golden brown. Remove the rabbit to a platter and reserve. Gradually add ¼ cup flour to the hot oil, stirring constantly, and cook until a medium-dark-brown roux begins to form. Add the onion and green pepper and brown for about 8 minutes more, stirring constantly. Add the remaining ingredients and blend thoroughly. Cook at a simmer for about 5 minutes, then add the fried rabbit meat. Reduce the heat to low and simmer for 1 hour and 20 minutes, or until the rabbit is tender. Serve with boiled rice.

SQUIRREL SAUCE PIQUANTE

Prepare according to the directions for Rabbit Sauce Piquante (see page 156), substituting 3 to 4 pounds of squirrel meat, cleaned and cut up, for the rabbit. Increase the total cooking time by about 20 minutes.

ROAST HAUNCH OF VENISON

This is the way venison is often prepared in the Louisiana Cajun country—marinated, then larded with salt pork and garlic and roasted. The sauce is prepared last, a glorious combination of pan drippings, marinade, red wine, currant jelly, spices, and brandy. Allow about ½ pound of venison per person. *(for 10 to 12)*

---

1 haunch of venison (6 to 7 lb.)

MARINADE

- 5 Tbs. salt butter
- 1 large onion, chopped
- 2 Tbs. chopped shallots (scallions)
- 1 carrot, chopped
- 4 whole cloves
- ½ tsp. dried thyme
- ¾ tsp. dried marjoram
- ¼ tsp. dried tarragon
- ½ tsp. dried basil
- ½ tsp. dried rosemary
- ⅛ tsp. sugar
- 1 c. dry red wine

- Olive oil
- Salt, freshly ground black pepper, and cayenne
- ½ lb. salt pork, cut into thin strips
- 2 cloves garlic, sliced very thin

SAUCE

- Pan drippings
- ¾ c. dry red wine
- ¼ tsp. ginger
- ¼ tsp. cloves
- 1½ tsp. fresh lemon juice
- ½ c. currant jelly
- 3 Tbs. flour
- 1½ Tbs. brandy

Rinse the venison, dry thoroughly with paper towels, and set aside while you prepare the marinade.

In a heavy saucepan melt the butter and sauté the onion, shallots, and carrot over low heat until soft. Remove from the heat and add the cloves, thyme, marjoram, tarragon, basil, and rosemary. Mix well, then add the dry red wine and mix again. Brush the venison with olive oil and sprinkle generously with salt, black pepper, and cayenne. Put it into a large stainless steel or porcelain bowl and pour the marinade over. Cover the bowl with plastic wrap and refrigerate for 6 to 8 hours.

When you are ready to cook the venison, lift it out of the marinade with a long fork and hold it over the bowl for a minute to let the marinade drain off. Strain the marinade and reserve. Cut slashes in the meat all around and put a slice of salt pork and a thin sliver of garlic into each incision. Put the venison into a roasting pan along with ¾ cup of the strained marinade, and roast in a preheated 450° oven for 30 minutes; then turn the oven down to 325° and roast for 30 minutes per pound at that temperature (a 6-pound haunch will take 3 hours in addition to the initial 30 minutes at higher heat). Baste frequently with the pan drippings and marinade. When the meat is done, remove it from the roasting pan to a larger platter and set the platter in a 200° oven while you prepare the sauce.

Pour the liquid in the roasting pan into a heavy 3- to 4-quart saucepan. Add the remaining ingredients for the sauce and cook over low heat until the currant jelly is melted. Raise the heat slightly until the sauce begins to simmer, then lower it just enough to keep a simmer going. Cook until the sauce is reduced by about a third, then pour into a large gravy boat.

To serve, bring the venison roast to the table on the platter and slice. Pour about 2 to 3 tablespoons of the sauce over each serving.

11
VEGETABLES AND SALADS

New Orleanians love fresh vegetables. Supermarkets, small groceries, farm trucks, and French Market stalls all proudly display the vegetables of the season. We all have special favorites and wait impatiently for the new crop of yams or collard greens or eggplants to appear. Thrifty New Orleanians buy their vegetables by the bushel at the French Market. On supermarket counters in New Orleans vegetables are generally displayed loose, rather than wrapped and sealed in plastic. We like to smell and touch and weigh in our hands the quality and freshness of the produce we buy. New Orleans markets sell two kinds of tomatoes, the little hard dry unripened ones packed, sealed, and sent in from outside the state, and our great big juicy Creole tomatoes, heaped up naked and beautiful so we can squeeze them just a little to find the precise degree of ripeness we desire for a special dish. Parsley and shallots are sold in bunches tied with string, and usually there are no fresh ones left at the end of the day.

Many local dishes combine vegetable with meat or shellfish–eggplant stuffed with shrimp or oysters; zucchini stuffed with sausage; cabbage, okra, mustard, or collard greens smothered with a little meat and a lot of seasonings. A few of our vegetables are only available locally: mirlitons (chayote), pale green, pear-shaped relatives of squash, generally stuffed with shrimp; and Louisiana yams, a locally grown strain of sweet potato, used in everything from casseroles to desserts. (Any sweet potato can be substituted.) The other vegetables we use are available throughout the country, as are the dried beans and long grain white rice so important to Creole and Cajun cooking.

This chapter is divided into three parts: a selection of cooked vegetable dishes we particularly enjoy preparing at home; a section on vegetable soufflés; and some of New Orleans' favorite salads.

ARTICHOKES VINAIGRETTE

The classic way to serve fresh artichokes, cooked just until tender, then drained and chilled, with a fine tart vinaigrette dressing for dipping. Choose artichokes that are even in color, with tightly packed leaves and no dry brown spots. There are two things to remember when cooking artichokes: use very little water, no more than an inch in the bottom of the pan; and don't overcook them. If you cover the pan and keep the heat quite low, the artichokes will actually be steamed—which keeps the texture firm and the color bright and attractive. We find it simplest to cook them early in the day or the evening before, then to put them on a platter covered with plastic wrap in the refrigerator. Prepare the vinaigrette dressing about an hour before you plan to serve.

We like artichoke vinaigrette as a first course and also as a separate salad course, served French style after the main dish. As a variation, try hot melted butter seasoned with fresh lemon juice for dipping chilled artichokes. *(for 4)*

---

4 small or medium-sized fresh artichokes
Cold water
1 tsp. salt
½ tsp. finely minced garlic
1½ c. Vinaigrette Dressing (page 182)

Trim the stems off the artichokes with a sharp knife. If desired, snip off the pointed tips of the leaves with scissors. Holding the artichokes firmly with one hand, turn them leaves-down and pound on a flat surface to open them out a bit. Turn them leaves-up again and rinse quickly under cold running water. Shake to remove most of the moisture.

Place the artichokes stem end down side by side in a heavy pot large enough to hold them comfortably. Add 1 inch of cold water, then sprinkle the salt and garlic over the tops of the artichokes and into the water. Turn the heat to high and bring the water to a boil. Cover the pot loosely, reduce the heat to low, and cook for about 40 to 45 minutes, or until a leaf pulled from one of the artichokes is tender on the inside. Remove immediately from the water and drain upside down. Allow to cool at room temperature, then put them on a platter and cover with plastic wrap. Refrigerate until ready to serve.

Serve each artichoke on a large plate with vinaigrette dressing in a small glass bowl for dipping, or if you have them, use special artichoke plates with a well at the center for the dipping sauce.

STUFFED ARTICHOKES

A New Orleans favorite, Italian stuffed artichokes. To prevent the stuffing from spilling during cooking, use a pan just large enough to hold the artichokes set closely together. Prepare them in advance and refrigerate until about half an hour before you plan to serve them.

To warm them up, put the artichokes in a heavy saucepan with about 3 tablespoons of cold water; bring the water to a boil, cover the pan, then lower the heat and cook for about 12 minutes, just until they are warmed through. Or set them in a deep covered casserole with about 2 tablespoons water and warm in a 425° oven for 15 to 20 minutes. If you want the stuffing to have a pleasantly crisp crust, uncover the pan or casserole and heat for 5 minutes longer. Serve one stuffed artichoke per person, or one for two on a shared plate if you are planning to serve a substantial main dish—they're very filling. *(for 4)*

1⅓ c. Italian bread crumbs
1½ Tbs. finely minced garlic
¼ c. finely minced fresh parsley
½ c. freshly grated Parmesan cheese
4 flat anchovy fillets, drained well and chopped very fine
1½ Tbs. fresh lemon juice
1 tsp. dried basil
¼ tsp. mace
½ tsp. dried rosemary
1 tsp. salt
½ tsp. freshly ground black pepper
¾ c. olive oil
4 medium-sized fresh artichokes
4 slices fresh lemon (each about 1/16 inch thick)
Lightly salted water

In a mixing bowl combine the bread crumbs, garlic, parsley, cheese, anchovies, lemon juice, basil, mace, rosemary, salt, pepper, and ¼ cup of the olive oil. Mix thoroughly and set aside.

Clean and trim the artichokes as directed on page 161. After pounding them to open the leaves, turn them right side up and open the leaves a bit more with your fingers to make room for the stuffing. Stuff the reserved mixture into the spaces inside the opened leaves, then pour the remaining olive oil evenly over the artichokes so that it seeps down into the stuffing. Place a lemon slice on top of each artichoke, then set them carefully in a saucepan just large enough to hold them side by side. Carefully pour lightly salted water to a depth of 1 inch around the artichokes, being careful not to get water on them or into the stuffing. Set the pan over high heat and when the water comes to a boil cover the pan and turn the heat to very low. Cook for 45 to 50 minutes, or until the outer leaves pull off easily and are tender on the inside.

When they are cooked, remove the artichokes from the pan with tongs, lifting them straight up so as not to disturb the stuffing. Hold them over the pan for a few seconds to let the water drain off, then set them on a large platter. Allow to cool for about 10 minutes, then cover the platter with several layers of plastic wrap and refrigerate. Reheat for serving as directed above.

BROCCOLI HOLLANDAISE

Fresh broccoli slightly steamed and served with hollandaise sauce. Prepare the hollandaise sauce and set the blender container in warm water while you steam the broccoli. *(for 4)*

1⅓ c. Blender Hollandaise (page 114) or Handmade Hollandaise (page 115)
1 bunch fresh broccoli
Lightly salted water

Wash the broccoli and shake off the excess water. Remove the tougher bottom part of the stems, about 3 to 4 inches. Lay the pieces of broccoli flat in a large heavy skillet or sauté pan and add lightly salted water to a depth of about ¼ inch in the skillet. Turn the heat on high. When the water begins to boil, quickly cover the skillet and reduce the heat to very low. Cook for 10 to 15 minutes, or until the broccoli is just tender; test by pricking the stems with a fork. To drain, hold the skillet over the sink with the cover on, then tilt the skillet and slide the cover away from the skillet edge closest to the sink so the water can drain out. Or simply lift the broccoli out of the skillet by grasping the middle of the stem with tongs; hold over the skillet for a few seconds to let the water drain off.

To serve, put the broccoli on individual heated plates and cover each portion with ⅓ cup hollandaise sauce.

SAUTÉED BROCCOLI WITH ROSEMARY

The broccoli is cut up and sautéed in butter, bread crumbs, and rosemary. Dried leaf rosemary works very well in this dish, but if you happen to have some fresh rosemary, by all means use it; mince it very fine and increase the amount to 3 teaspoons.

The trick to getting the broccoli pieces attractively browned is to stir the contents of the pan, scrape the bottom with a wooden spatula or spoon, and lift the browned pieces from the bottom to the top. *(for 4)*

1 bunch fresh broccoli (about 3½ c. cut up)
¼ c. (½ stick) salt butter
1 tsp. salt
½ tsp. freshly ground white pepper
¼ c. Italian bread crumbs
2 tsp. crushed dried rosemary

Wash and dry the broccoli. Cut off the stem ends and discard, then trim the hard outer layer off the thick stem part and cut into small pieces about ½ inch thick. Cut the tender stalks near the florets into 1-inch pieces. Separate the florets.

In a large heavy sauté pan or skillet melt the butter over low heat. Add the cut-up broccoli, salt, pepper, bread crumbs, and rosemary. Stir with a wooden spoon to mix thoroughly, cover tightly, and cook over low heat for 20 to 25 minutes, or until the stem pieces are tender. Remove the cover, stir, and scrape the bottom every 5 minutes or so to prevent sticking and to distribute the browning crumbs, then cover again. The broccoli pieces should be nicely browned at the end of cooking time; if not brown enough, uncover the pan, raise the heat a bit, and cook, stirring frequently, for another 5 to 8 minutes.

BROCCOLI PIE

One of our favorite vegetable dishes. The broccoli is cooked with Italian bread crumbs and olive oil in a skillet, then inverted onto a serving plate. It looks like an upside-down pie with a lovely brown crust.

If, in spite of your best efforts, some of the crust sticks to the skillet when you turn the pie out, scrape the browned pieces out with a spatula and cover the bare spots. Broccoli pie tastes best if you set it in a 175° oven for about 20 minutes before serving. Bring the dish to the table, cut the pie into wedges, and serve.

(for 8)

1 bunch fresh broccoli (about 3½ c. cut up)
Lightly salted water
Salt and freshly ground black pepper
6 Tbs. plus 2 tsp. olive oil
6 Tbs. plus 2 tsp. Italian bread crumbs

Wash, trim, and cut up the broccoli as directed on page 163, then put it in a 3- to 4-quart heavy saucepan with about ¾ inch lightly salted water. Bring to a boil, cover, reduce the heat to very low, and cook for 8 minutes. Drain the broccoli in a colander, then put in a large stainless steel or porcelain bowl. Sprinkle with salt and pepper. Add 6 tablespoons of the olive oil and 6 tablespoons of the bread crumbs; mix thoroughly by tossing with a wooden spoon or spatula.

Grease the entire inner surface of a heavy 10- to 12-inch skillet by soaking a wadded-up paper towel in the remaining 2 teaspoons olive oil and spreading the oil on evenly. Then sprinkle 2 teaspoons of the bread crumbs evenly over the entire greased surface. Put the broccoli mixture into the skillet, spread it out, and flatten it down with a spatula or the back of a spoon until it is tightly packed. Put the skillet over very low heat, cover it, and cook for 20 minutes. About every 5 minutes uncover the skillet and loosen the mixture from the sides of the pan with a long narrow spatula, then shake the pan; this should keep the bottom crust from sticking. After the 20 minutes are past, uncover the skillet, raise the heat very slightly, and cook for about 7 to 8 minutes more. Remove the skillet from the heat.

Place a serving plate over the skillet, then turn the skillet over. The pie will fall onto the plate, with the browned bottom part forming a crust over the top.

SMOTHERED CABBAGE

A delicious way to prepare small young fresh cabbage, smothered with pickled pork and slab bacon. If you live outside New Orleans and can't get pickled pork, substitute salt pork, eliminate the salt indicated in the recipe, and increase the sugar to ¾ teaspoon.

(for 4)

- 1¼ Tbs. lard or vegetable shortening
- 2 small heads young white or green cabbage
- 1 c. coarsely chopped onion
- 1 tsp. salt
- ⅓ lb. pickled pork
- ½ lb. slab bacon, cut into ¾-inch cubes
- ¼ tsp. freshly ground black pepper
- ¼ tsp. crushed red pepper pods
- ½ tsp. sugar

In a large heavy pot or kettle melt the lard over medium heat. Cut the cabbages into quarters, core them, and rinse under cold running water. Shake off the excess water, then add the cabbage to the hot lard in the pot. Add the remaining ingredients, cover, and cook over low heat, stirring occasionally, for about 1 hour.

BAKED ACADIAN CUSHAW

Cushaw is a Cajun squash resembling a giant zucchini. It tastes like a cross between pumpkin and squash. If you can't get cushaw, try this recipe with a half-and-half mixture of white pattypan squash and pumpkin.

A number of Cajun vegetable dishes are prepared this way, with a blend of spices similar to those used in Indian curried vegetables. The bourbon gives this casserole a marvelous aroma. Bring the dish from the oven to the table and spoon it out with some of the lovely brown crust on top of each portion.

(for 4)

- 2 lb. cushaw (or 1 lb. white pattypan squash and 1 lb. pumpkin)
- ¾ c. water
- 2¼ tsp. salt
- 6 Tbs. (¾ stick) salt butter
- ¼ c. bourbon
- ½ tsp. allspice
- ¼ tsp. cloves
- ½ tsp. freshly ground black pepper
- 1/16 tsp. cayenne
- ¼ tsp. mace
- ¼ c. plus 1 tsp. sugar

Wash the cushaw and cut it into large pieces about 2 by 2 inches. Trim out the dark stem ends. Place in a large heavy skillet with the water and 1 teaspoon of the salt. Bring to a boil, cover tightly, then lower the heat and cook for 15 minutes. Uncover and cook for 10 minutes more, or until all the water has boiled away, stirring frequently. Add 5 tablespoons of the butter, the remaining 1¼ teaspoons salt, the bourbon, spices, and the ¼ cup of the sugar. Cook over medium heat, stirring constantly, for about 10 minutes, or until the mixture turns a rich golden-brown color, then remove from the heat.

Put the contents of the skillet into a 1½- to 2-quart casserole. Dot with the remaining tablespoon of butter and sprinkle the remaining teaspoon of sugar evenly over the top. Bake uncovered in a preheated 400° oven for 40 minutes, or until a browned crust forms on the top.

BRAISED LEEKS HOLLANDAISE

Leeks prepared with a rich beef stock and herbs, and served with piquant hollandaise sauce. Prepare the leeks first, in a skillet with a cover. If you have no cover to fit your skillet, use heavy aluminum foil cut about an inch larger than the skillet, with the edges folded loosely around the rim. Be careful not to overcook the leeks; they should be tender but not mushy. When the leeks are cooked, put the skillet in a warm oven while you prepare the hollandaise. Save the braising liquid and use it in place of water to steam other fresh vegetables. *(for 4)*

3 bunches leeks
1 c. water, more if necessary
2 Tbs. beef stock or beef tea
1 tsp. salt
3 Tbs. salt butter
¼ tsp. freshly ground white pepper
¼ tsp. dried chervil
¼ tsp. dried marjoram
¼ tsp. dried basil
2 c. Blender Hollandaise (page 114) or Handmade Hollandaise (page 115)

Cut off the top half of the leeks and discard the green leaves. Trim the stem ends and pull off the tough outer layers. Cut the leeks into quarters lengthwise and wash thoroughly to remove all sand. Drain, then place in parallel rows in a large heavy skillet. Add the water, beef stock, salt, butter, pepper, and herbs. Bring to a boil over high heat, then cover the skillet loosely and lower the heat. Simmer covered for 10 to 20 minutes, depending on the size and texture of the leeks, adding a bit more water during cooking if necessary. Test for doneness by piercing with a fork; when the leeks pierce very easily, they are done.

Put the skillet in a 175° oven while preparing the hollandaise sauce, then lift the leeks out with a slotted spoon or spatula and serve with ½ cup hollandaise spooned over each portion.

SMOTHERED EGGPLANT AU GRATIN

Fresh eggplant smothered with bacon, then covered with Swiss cheese and glazed under the broiler. We like this dish served in individual ramekins; an attractive design forms on each serving as the carefully arranged strips of cheese glaze. You can also use a single large shallow baking dish; arrange the cheese in an interesting pattern and serve the portions with even segments of the design topping each one. *(for 4)*

½ lb. lean sliced bacon
1 medium eggplant, peeled and sliced ¼ to ⅓ inch thick
1 large onion, thinly sliced
1 Tbs. finely minced fresh parsley
1 tsp. dried marjoram
¾ tsp. freshly ground black pepper
½ tsp. salt
⅓ c. hot water
½ lb. Swiss cheese, julienned

Put the bacon slices flat in the bottom of a large heavy skillet and turn the heat to low, then raise to medium after a few minutes. When the bacon barely begins to turn brown, place the eggplant slices between the pieces of bacon and cook slowly over low heat. Add the onion, parsley, marjoram, pepper, and salt. Raise the heat to high and pour the hot water slowly into the skillet, around the sides. (Don't pour it over the eggplant and bacon.) Quickly cover the skillet tightly and lower the heat to medium. Simmer for about 20 minutes, or until the onions are tender, uncovering frequently to stir. Meanwhile, preheat the broiler.

Spoon the contents of the skillet evenly into 4 individual flameproof ramekins. Place strips of Swiss cheese in a spoke design on top of each ramekin. Put the ramekins under the broiler about 4 to 5 inches from the heat and glaze until the cheese is melted and lightly browned, about 10 minutes.

CHOPPED EGGPLANT APPETIZER

An unusual appetizer, eggplant and onion baked, then marinated and chilled. Serve on crisp lettuce leaves.

(for 4)

- 1 large firm eggplant
- 1 medium onion
- 1 tsp. salt
- ¼ tsp. freshly ground black pepper
- 3 Tbs. olive oil
- 3 Tbs. white wine vinegar
- ½ tsp. sugar
- ½ tsp. dried basil
- ⅛ tsp. dried marjoram
- ¼ tsp. coriander

Wash and dry the eggplant, then trim off the stem end. Peel the onion and remove the tough outer layers. Put the eggplant in a shallow baking dish and bake in a preheated 350° oven for 45 minutes. After the eggplant has baked for 10 minutes, put the onion beside it on the baking dish; they will be done at the same time.

Remove the baking dish from the oven and let the eggplant and onion cool for 10 to 15 minutes. Peel the skin off the eggplant and dice the pulp into ½-inch cubes. Mince the onion very fine. Combine the vegetables in an attractive bowl or soufflé dish that can be refrigerated, then add the remaining ingredients and mix thoroughly with a wooden spoon. Cover the dish with plastic wrap and refrigerate for at least 4 hours before serving. Mix lightly once before serving.

For other eggplant dishes, see also: EGGPLANT SOUFFLÉ (page 180), OYSTER AND EGGPLANT CASSEROLE (page 68), and BAKED OYSTERS AND EGGPLANT (page 68).

MUSTARD GREENS AND PICKLED PORK

Fresh greens smothered with seasoning meat. Just as good with collard or turnip greens; you can substitute slab bacon for the pickled pork. *(for 4)*

½ lb. pickled pork, cut into chunks about ¾ inch across
3 bunches mustard greens (about 2 lb.)
1 c. chopped onion
½ tsp. freshly ground black pepper
¼ tsp. dried marjoram
½ tsp. sugar

In a heavy 6- to 8-quart pot brown the pickled pork over medium heat until most of the fat is rendered and the meat is lightly browned. Wash the greens carefully to remove all sand and tear off the stem ends. Shake lightly to remove some of the water, then put the still-damp greens into the pot with the pickled pork. Cover, lower the heat, and cook for about 10 minutes. Uncover and add the onion, pepper, marjoram, and sugar; stir well. Cover again and cook over low heat for about 1 hour, or until the greens are quite tender.

STUFFED MIRLITONS

One of New Orleans' favorite vegetable main dishes. The mirliton or vegetable pear, called *chayote* in Latin America, is a cousin of the cucumber and squash. Pale green and shaped like a giant size pear, it is widely grown in home gardens in New Orleans and also available in markets throughout Louisiana. Be sure to use fresh shrimp in this delicate-tasting and attractive dish. Allow two to three stuffed halves per portion, depending on the size of the mirlitons. *(for 4 or more)*

8 large or 12 small mirlitons
Boiling salted water

STUFFING

¼ lb. lean sliced bacon
1½ c. chopped onion
½ c. chopped green pepper
3 Tbs. chopped celery
1 Tbs. finely minced garlic
1 c. ripe Creole (beefsteak, Jersey) tomatoes (2 small or 1 large), coarsely chopped
½ c. chopped shallots (scallions)
1½ tsp. salt
½ tsp. freshly ground black pepper
¾ tsp. dried thyme
2 whole bay leaves, crushed
3 Tbs. finely minced fresh parsley
⅛ tsp. cayenne
1 lb. fresh shrimp, peeled, deveined, and cut into ½- to ¾-inch pieces
½ c. slightly dampened crumbled white bread, crusts removed

Slice off the stem ends of the mirlitons. Put in a heavy pot or kettle, and add about 1 inch of boiling salted water. Cover tightly, reduce the heat, and boil for about 20 minutes. Remove the mirlitons from the pot, drain, and allow them to cool at room temperature. When cooled, cut them in half lengthwise. Scoop out the pulp with a large spoon, leaving intact a shell about ⅓ inch thick. Chop the mirliton pulp and set aside in a china or stainless steel bowl.

In a large heavy skillet or sauté pan fry the bacon until almost crisp. Add the onion, green pepper, celery, garlic, tomatoes, shallots, and mirliton pulp. Sauté for about 8 minutes, or until the vegetables just begin to turn soft. Add salt, pepper, thyme, bay leaf, parsley, and cayenne and blend well with a wooden spoon. Add the pieces of raw shrimp and cook over low heat just until the shrimp turn pink. Add the dampened crumbled bread and blend well.

Preheat the oven to 350°. Fill the reserved mirliton shells with the shrimp and vegetable mixture to a raised rounded shape. Butter a large shallow baking dish lightly and bake the stuffed mirlitons for 20 to 30 minutes, or until the tops are nicely browned. Serve hot.

CANDIED MIRLITONS

Mirlitons are delicious prepared this way—sautéed lightly, then baked with butter, sugar, brandy, and spices.
(for 4)

---

3 small or 2 large mirlitons (about 2 c. cooked and diced)
Boiling salted water
4½ Tbs. salt butter
¾ tsp. salt
¼ tsp. freshly ground white pepper
4 tsp. sugar
⅜ tsp. cinnamon
⅛ tsp. freshly grated nutmeg
3¼ tsp. brandy

In a heavy, medium-sized saucepan with a tight-fitting lid, parboil the mirlitons, covered, in about 1 inch of boiling salted water for 20 minutes. Drain thoroughly, peel off the skin, trim off the ends, and cut into 1-inch dice.

In a large sauté pan or skillet melt 3 tablespoons of the butter over low heat. Add the diced mirliton pulp and sauté for 10 minutes, stirring frequently. Gradually add the salt, pepper, 1 tablespoon of the sugar, ¼ teaspoon of the cinnamon, the nutmeg, and 3 teaspoons of the brandy; mix thoroughly.

Butter a shallow baking dish and fill with the sautéed mirliton. Combine the remaining 1½ tablespoons butter, 1 teaspoon sugar, ⅛ teaspoon cinnamon, and ¼ teaspoon brandy in a small saucepan and heat for a few minutes, mixing thoroughly. Pour evenly over the mirliton in the baking dish. Bake in a preheated 350° oven for 45 minutes, then glaze under a preheated broiler for about 3 minutes. Serve hot from the baking dish.

SMOTHERED OKRA

One of New Orleans' most popular and characteristic fresh vegetables. When buying fresh okra, look for the smaller pods with a bright even green color. In this dish the okra is sautéed, then smothered with tomatoes and lots of seasoning. We like this as a vegetable side dish and also chilled as an appetizer. *(for 4)*

- 3 Tbs. lard
- 2 c. thinly sliced onion (3 small or 2 medium onions)
- 2 lb. fresh okra, stems and tips removed, sliced ½ inch thick
- 1½ tsp. salt
- ½ tsp. freshly ground black pepper
- ⅛ tsp. cayenne
- ½ tsp. mace
- ¼ tsp. sugar
- ¼ tsp. chili powder
- 1 one-lb. can whole peeled tomatoes, drained
- ¼ tsp. dried thyme
- 2 tsp. Creole mustard

In a heavy 4- to 5-quart sauté pan melt the lard over medium heat. Sauté the onion until light brown (about 15 to 20 minutes), stirring frequently. Add the sliced okra and sauté for 15 minutes more, gradually adding the salt, pepper, cayenne, mace, sugar, and chili powder. Add the drained tomatoes and thyme and continue to sauté. Break up the tomatoes with your stirring spoon as the mixture cooks. Add the mustard. Cover the pot and cook over low heat for 30 minutes longer, uncovering to stir from time to time. Serve hot or chilled as a salad.

BRAISED OKRA

The okra is stir-fried in bacon drippings first to give it a firm crisp texture. Use the small baby okra; the larger pods will be too stringy cooked this way. You can also use frozen baby okra, if you get all the extra moisture out of it (see note below). *(for 4)*

- 1 lb. small fresh okra
- ¼ c. bacon or sausage drippings
- 1 tsp. freshly ground white pepper
- 1 tsp. salt
- ½ c. finely chopped onion
- 6 Tbs. hot water

Wash the okra thoroughly and trim off the stem ends. Dry thoroughly in a soft towel.

In a large heavy skillet or sauté pan heat the bacon or sausage drippings over high heat. Add the okra and brown on all sides, turning frequently with a spatula or wooden spoon. Lower the heat to medium and add the pepper, salt, and onion. Cook for about 5 minutes, or until the onion begins to brown. Add the hot water, cover the pan, and lower the heat to a simmer. Cook for 5 minutes more, stirring and turning several times; test the okra for doneness with a fork. When the okra is cooked and the onion is brown, remove to a heated serving bowl.

Note: If substituting frozen baby okra, use 2 ten-ounce packages in this recipe. Rinse the frozen okra under cool tap water until all the surface ice is removed and the pieces of okra are separated. Roll in a thick terry towel and pat the towel firmly to remove as much moisture as possible. Proceed as above, reducing the water by 1 tablespoon.

ONION PIE

A delicious old Creole "stretching dish"—that is, a main dish using lots of vegetables, which are cheap, to stretch a very small amount of meat, which is dear. Onion pie has disappeared from restaurant menus and home tables, but we'd love to revive it. It makes a hearty side dish with a seafood supper or a delightful light main dish. We like it with the old fashioned rich biscuit dough used for oyster pie, but you can also use a simple pastry dough of flour, butter, salt, and ice water. The pie has only a bottom crust; the crisped bacon pieces provide an attractive topping. *(for 4 to 6)*

Biscuit dough (page 69)

FILLING

3 Tbs. salt butter
2 c. chopped onion
3 large eggs
1½ tsp. salt
¼ tsp. freshly ground black pepper
1 c. commercial sour cream
3 slices lean breakfast bacon

Using the first five ingredients for Creole Oyster Pie, prepare the dough as directed on page 69. Roll out to a thickness of just under ¼ inch, then use it to line the bottom of a 9-inch pie pan. Leave an overhang of about ⅝ inch at the edges when you trim the dough to fit the pie pan, then fold the overhang under. Make a decorative edge by pinching the thick overhang at 1-inch intervals between your thumb and forefinger to form a fluted rim. Bake the crust in a preheated 350° oven for 5 minutes, then remove from the oven and raise the oven temperature to 400°.

Meanwhile, melt the butter over low heat in a heavy skillet and add the onion. Cook, stirring, until the onion is soft but not brown. Remove the skillet from the heat and put the sautéed onion into a mixing bowl. Beat the eggs lightly in a separate small bowl with a wire whisk or a fork. Add the beaten eggs and the salt and pepper to the onions and mix gently with a wooden spoon. Add the sour cream and mix thoroughly, without overbeating; the mixture should remain light and airy. Pour into the partially baked crust, then cut the bacon into ½-inch squares and place evenly over the top of the pie. Bake in a 400° oven until the bacon is crisp and the crust edging turns a very light brown, about 15 to 18 minutes. To serve, cut the pie into wedges with a serrated knife and spoon any liquid remaining in the pie dish over each portion.

SAUTÉED PEARL ONIONS

Pearl onions sautéed with aromatic seasonings, then cooked with milk and Pickapeppa Sauce. *(for 4)*

- 5 Tbs. salt butter
- 1½ lb. pearl onions, skins and hard ends removed
- ½ tsp. freshly ground white pepper
- ¾ tsp. salt
- 1 tsp. coriander
- ¼ tsp. mace
- ⅔ c. milk
- 2 tsp. finely minced fresh parsley
- 2 Tbs. Pickapeppa Sauce
- ½ tsp. dried basil
- 2 Tbs. minced chives

In a large heavy sauté pan melt the butter over low heat. Add the onions, pepper, salt, coriander, and mace. Sauté, stirring frequently, until the onions begin to brown, about 8 to 10 minutes. Add the milk, parsley, Pickapeppa Sauce, basil, and chives and mix well. Raise the heat slightly and continue to cook, stirring constantly but gently, for about 5 minutes. Cover the pan, lower the heat, and cook for 10 minutes longer. Uncover and test to see if the onions are done; if you can easily pierce them with a fork, they are done. When the onions are tender, uncover the pan and cook for 5 to 8 minutes more, until the onions are nicely browned.

Serve in deep bowls or dessert dishes with about ¼ cup of sauce spooned over each portion.

STUFFED PEPPERS

Firm fresh green peppers stuffed with ground beef, cooked rice, and plenty of seasoning. Parboil the peppers first; this helps them keep their shape and avoids the odd slightly sour taste stuffed peppers often have. If you have any left over, reheat them covered in a deep saucepan with about 1½ tablespoons water for about 8 to 10 minutes. To save time, cook the rice in advance. *(for 4)*

- 8 medium-sized fresh green peppers
- Salted water

STUFFING

- 1 Tbs. vegetable oil
- 1 lb. ground beef
- 1 c. chopped onion
- 1 Tbs. finely minced fresh parsley
- ¾ tsp. finely minced garlic
- ½ tsp. dried thyme
- ¾ tsp. salt
- ½ tsp. freshly ground black pepper
- ½ tsp. dried basil (omit if the canned tomatoes are prepared with basil)
- Scant ⅛ tsp. cayenne
- 1 one-lb. can peeled whole tomatoes, drained
- 1¾ c. firm Boiled Rice (page 17)
- 2 Tbs. Worcestershire sauce
- ⅓ c. grated sharp Cheddar cheese
- ⅓ c. grated Parmesan cheese

Cut off and discard the top fourth of the green peppers. Remove the seeds and membrane. Place the peppers upright in ⅓ to ½ inch salted water in a heavy pot or saucepan. Bring the water to a boil and cover tightly, then lower the flame and cook for exactly 5 minutes. Remove the peppers, drain them thoroughly, and set aside while preparing the stuffing.

In a large heavy skillet or sauté pan heat the vegetable oil and sauté the ground meat and onion until brown (about 8 to 10 minutes). Add the parsley, garlic, thyme, salt, black pepper, basil (if used), and cayenne. Continue cooking and stirring over low heat for a few minutes, then add the drained canned tomatoes. Cook for 6 to 7 minutes longer, breaking up the tomatoes with a wooden spoon while cooking. Add the cooked rice and Worcestershire and mix well, then cover and simmer for about 10 minutes. Uncover, turn off the heat, and add the grated Cheddar and Parmesan cheeses. Blend thoroughly with a spoon.

Stuff the parboiled peppers with the meat and rice mixture and bake uncovered in a preheated 350° oven for 30 minutes, or until lightly browned on top.

See also STUFFED CRAWFISH BELL PEPPERS, page 58.

BRABANT POTATOES

A New Orleans favorite, diced fried potatoes flavored with garlic butter. We use the two-stage method of deep frying in this dish to get potatoes that are well cooked on the inside and nicely browned and crisp on the outside. The secret to Brabant potatoes with the desired taste of garlic *and* a good crisp texture is simple: put them in the oven for 20 to 30 minutes after saucing them. *(for 4)*

- Vegetable oil for deep frying
- 6 medium white potatoes, peeled and cut into 3/4- to 1-inch dice
- 6 Tbs. salt butter
- 1 tsp. finely minced garlic
- 2 Tbs. finely minced fresh parsley

Preheat the oil in a deep fryer to 320°. Meanwhile, pat the diced potatoes very dry with paper towels. Fry for about 3 minutes in the oil, just until soft and light yellow in color. Remove and drain, then raise the oil temperature to 375°. Fry the potatoes again, this time until crisp and golden brown (about 3 to 4 minutes). Remove from the oil, drain, and place on several layers of paper towels to absorb any excess oil.

In a small heavy sauté pan or skillet melt the butter over low heat. Add the garlic and 1 tablespoon of the minced parsley and sauté for about 8 to 10 minutes over low heat. Strain the butter sauce through a fine mesh strainer to remove all solids.

Put the fried drained potatoes in a deep bowl. Pour the butter sauce over them and add the remaining parsley. Toss thoroughly to mix. Put the potatoes on a large platter lined with paper towels, then put the platter in a preheated 175° oven for at least 20 minutes before serving.

FRIED POTATO POOR BOY

The cheapest, and probably the most filling poor boy sandwich—a poor man's dinner. Split a 12-inch loaf of absolutely fresh New Orleans French bread (see page 202 if you wish to make your own), warm it briefly in the oven, then spread a thin layer of mayonnaise on the inside of both pieces of bread. Heap about 1½ cups Brabant Potatoes (see above) on the bottom half, cover with the top half, then cut the sandwich in half across.

Note: This is also good with cottage fries, regular French fries, or home fried potatoes.

CREOLE RATATOUILLE

Fresh baby okra, good ripe tomatoes, and onions sautéed, then smothered. When you cover the skillet, the moisture in the tomatoes and onions combines with the butter to make a marvelous natural sauce. Serve this in small deep saucers with plenty of liquid to each portion. And if you have any left over, refrigerate it and serve it the next day chilled as a delicious and unusual salad. *(for 4)*

---

2 Tbs. salt butter
1½ c. sliced onion (2 large onions)
2 c. fresh sliced baby okra (about 1 lb.)
1 large ripe Creole (beefsteak, Jersey) tomato, sliced
4 drops Tabasco
½ tsp. dried basil
¼ tsp. chives
¼ tsp. freshly ground black pepper
¾ tsp. salt
¼ tsp. sugar

In a heavy skillet or sauté pan melt the butter over low heat. Add the onion and cook until soft and beginning to brown. Add the sliced okra and cook, stirring frequently, for 10 minutes. Add the tomatoes and the remaining ingredients and mix thoroughly. Cook slowly, stirring frequently, for 5 minutes longer, then cover the skillet tightly, lower the heat, and cook for 10 minutes. Serve very hot.

DIRTY RICE

Dirty rice is a popular Cajun dish made with chicken livers and gizzards, vegetables, long grain rice, and lots of pepper. It is served as an accompaniment to poultry and meat. If the main dish has a gravy, you pour some of it over the dirty rice. Don't use leftover rice warmed up; the dish will have an unpleasant texture.

(for 4 or more)

---

1 lb. chicken gizzards
½ lb. pork liver
¼ c. vegetable oil
2 Tbs. flour
1½ Tbs. finely minced garlic
1⅔ c. finely chopped onion
¼ c. finely chopped celery
½ c. finely chopped green pepper
¼ c. finely minced fresh parsley
½ lb. chicken livers
2 tsp. salt
1 tsp. freshly ground black pepper
⅛ tsp. cayenne
2 Tbs. water, more if necessary
3 c. Boiled Rice (page 17)

Cut the gizzards and pork liver into small pieces and pass once through the coarse blade of a meat grinder. Heat the oil in a large heavy skillet and cook the ground meat until it begins to turn brown. Add the flour and vegetables and mix well. Cook until the vegetables begin to turn soft and slightly brown. Cut up the chicken livers and add them to the skillet along with the seasonings and 2 tablespoons water. Cook over low heat until the chicken livers are done, adding a bit more water during cooking if necessary. Remove the skillet from the heat and set it in a 175° oven while you prepare the rice.

Toss the cooked rice and the contents of the skillet together in a large preheated bowl. Serve hot.

RICE DRESSING

Rice dressing is so similar to dirty rice that they are often treated as the same dish. In fact, rice dressing does not generally contain chicken livers and is a lighter, more delicate dish. Rice dressing is excellent with duck and chicken; leftover rice dressing can be used for stuffed peppers—just add some lightly cooked ground meat and a small can of peeled whole tomatoes. *(for 4 or more)*

¼ lb. lean pork
¼ lb. beef
½ lb. chicken gizzards
¼ c. vegetable oil
2 Tbs. flour
1 c. chopped onion
¼ c. chopped celery
½ c. chopped green pepper
⅓ c. thinly sliced green shallot (scallion) tops
2 Tbs. finely minced fresh parsley
1½ tsp. salt
1½ tsp. freshly ground black pepper
⅛ tsp. cayenne
2 Tbs. water
3 c. Boiled Rice (page 17)

Cut the pork, beef, and chicken gizzards into small pieces and pass twice through the coarse blade of a meat grinder. In a large heavy skillet, heat the oil and cook the ground meat until it begins to brown. Add the flour, vegetables, and seasonings and mix thoroughly. Cook until the vegetables are soft and begin to brown. Add 2 tablespoons water, and cook for 8 to 10 minutes longer, stirring constantly. Remove the skillet from the heat and set it in a 175° oven to keep warm while you prepare the rice.

Cook the rice as directed on page 17, then toss the cooked rice and the contents of the skillet together in a large, preheated bowl. Serve hot.

SPAGHETTI BORDELAISE

A pasta dish adored by New Orleanians—spaghetti with olive oil, butter, and garlic. After you add the sauce to the cooked spaghetti, mix well, cover the pot, and let the contents steep for 5 to 8 minutes. Mix again just before serving. *(for 3 or 4)*

---

1 c. Bordelaise Sauce (page 117)
12 oz. thin spaghetti
4 qt. boiling salted water, with 1 tsp. olive oil added

GARNISH

Freshly grated Romano cheese (optional)
Freshly ground black pepper

After preparing the bordelaise sauce, cover the pan and set aside. Cook the spaghetti in the boiling salted water with olive oil added for 7 to 8 minutes. Drain thoroughly in a colander, then return the spaghetti to the pot. Pour the sauce over it and mix well. Cover the pot and let the contents steep for about 8 minutes, then uncover and mix well again.

Serve in wide shallow bowls with a dish of freshly grated Romano cheese, to be added if desired at the table. Sprinkle each bowl of spaghetti with freshly ground black pepper from a mill at the table.

CURRIED SUMMER SQUASH

This is an example of a local vegetable dish similar to Indian vegetable dishes—prepared with a careful blend of many different spices. Commercially prepared curry powders are ready-mixed blends; here all the spices are added individually. This is the only true curry in this book. It is interesting to note that the only unusual spices not widely used in Creole and Cajun cooking are fenugreek and turmeric.

You can substitute buttermilk for the yogurt; if you do, use only ½ cup. If you have neither yogurt nor buttermilk, use ½ cup whole milk and add 2 teaspoons fresh lemon juice. Do not attempt to reheat this dish; it will curdle. *(for 4)*

---

2 Tbs. salt butter
1 medium-sized onion, thinly sliced
2 to 2½ lb. yellow summer squash, ends trimmed off and sliced ½ inch thick
3 Tbs. hot water
½ tsp. salt
¼ tsp. freshly ground black pepper
Scant ⅛ tsp. cayenne
⅛ tsp. fenugreek
⅛ tsp. chili powder
¼ tsp. coriander
¼ tsp. ginger
⅛ tsp. cloves
⅛ tsp. turmeric
¼ tsp. sugar
⅔ c. yogurt

In a large heavy sauté pan melt the butter over low heat. Add the sliced onion and cook, stirring frequently, until the onion is glazed but not brown. Add the squash and 3 tablespoons hot water. Bring to a boil, then cover, lower the heat, and cook for 5 minutes. Uncover pan and add all the remaining ingredients except the yogurt. Mix thoroughly, then cook uncovered for another 10 minutes over medium heat, stirring frequently. Add the yogurt and heat through without boiling. Serve immediately.

SUMMER SQUASH AND ONIONS

Young tender yellow summer squash sautéed with onions, then smothered. Almost as good with white pattypan squash; cook it about 4 minutes longer. Serve this vegetable side dish in small bowls so you can use all the delicious liquid from the skillet.

(for 4)

- ¼ c. (½ stick) salt butter
- 4 c. thinly sliced yellow summer squash (about 1½ lb.)
- 1 large onion, thinly sliced
- 1⅛ tsp. salt
- ½ tsp. freshly ground black pepper
- ¼ c. tomato juice
- Scant ⅛ tsp. sugar

In a large heavy skillet or sauté pan melt the butter over low heat. Add the squash and onion, mix thoroughly, and cook for 5 minutes, stirring constantly. Add the salt, black pepper, tomato juice, and sugar. Cover tightly and cook over low heat for 15 minutes, or until the squash and onion are tender. Uncover to stir several times during cooking.

MIXED BAKED SQUASH

For that delightful time of the year when several types of squash are available and *all* of them look so good, there's a solution—use them all. Bake this in an attractive casserole and bring it to the table from the oven. Serve the portions with some of the buttery sauce from the casserole spooned over each one.

If you can't get the three types of squash suggested, try pumpkin, rutabaga, white turnips, zucchini—firm vegetables with mild flavors and contrasting colors.

(for 4 or more)

- 3 lb. mixed squash (acorn, summer, pattypan)
- ½ c. (1 stick) salt butter
- ¼ c. heavy cream
- ¼ tsp. freshly ground black pepper
- ¼ tsp. freshly ground white pepper
- ¾ tsp. salt
- ½ tsp. dried rosemary
- ½ tsp. coriander
- ¼ tsp. mace
- ¼ tsp. freshly grated nutmeg
- 1 tsp. sugar
- 3 Tbs. thinly sliced green shallot (scallion) tops

Wash the squash and dry well, then trim off the stem ends and cut up into large chunks. Butter the inside of a 2½- to 3-quart casserole. Put the chunks of squash, the different types mixed as much as possible, into the casserole dish.

In a small saucepan melt the butter and add all remaining ingredients except the shallot tops. Pour the butter and seasonings over the squash and bake covered in a preheated 400° oven for 30 minutes. Remove the casserole from the oven, uncover, and mix thoroughly with a wooden spoon, taking care to redistribute the seasonings, which will have settled to the bottom of the dish. Add the shallot slices, cover again, and bake for another 20 minutes. Serve at the table from the casserole.

GLAZED TURNIPS

Small white turnips baked in a spicy-sweet casserole with brandy in it.

(for 4 or more)

¼ c. (½ stick) salt butter
2½ to 3 lb. small white turnips, peeled and quartered
1 tsp. salt
2 Tbs. sugar
½ tsp. freshly ground black pepper
¼ tsp. allspice
¼ tsp. cinnamon
¼ c. water
¼ c. brandy

TOPPING

1 Tbs. salt butter
¼ c. brandy
1 Tbs. sugar
¼ tsp. cinnamon
⅛ tsp. allspice
¼ tsp. salt

Melt the butter in a large heavy saucepan. Add the turnips, salt, sugar, black pepper, allspice, cinnamon, and water. Simmer over low heat for 40 minutes, or until the turnips are quite tender, stirring frequently.

Butter a 2- to 3-quart casserole. Remove the turnips from the saucepan with a slotted spoon, allowing the liquid to drain back into the pan. Put the turnips in the casserole along with ¼ cup of the liquid from the pan.

Prepare the topping by dotting the top of the casserole with the 1 tablespoon butter cut into very small pieces, then pouring the brandy over and sprinkling with the sugar, cinnamon, allspice, and salt. Bake uncovered in preheated 350° oven for 20 minutes.

BOURBON YAM CASSEROLE

One of our favorite yam dishes, festive and attractive. The yams are partially baked in their jackets first, then peeled and baked in a casserole with butter, Curaçao, bourbon, and spices. To get the flavors thoroughly distributed during baking, take the dish out of the oven after 20 minutes and stir the yams gently with a wooden spoon, bringing the bottom layers up to the top. Then pack them down with the back of the spoon and put a bit more butter on top to form a lightly glazed crust. Regular sweet potatoes will work just as well as Louisiana yams. If you have no Curaçao, use Cointreau and add 2 teaspoons of sugar. *(for 8)*

5 large or 6 medium-sized Louisiana yams or sweet potatoes
Vegetable oil
⅓ c. Curaçao
6 Tbs. (¾ stick) salt butter
¼ c. bourbon
½ c. sugar
1 tsp. cinnamon
¼ tsp. freshly grated nutmeg
⅛ tsp. cloves
½ tsp. salt
⅛ tsp. freshly ground white pepper

Wash the yams and scrub them well. Dry thoroughly. Rub the skins with a bit of vegetable oil, then place the yams in a shallow baking dish and bake in a preheated 450° oven for 30 minutes. Allow to cool slightly, then peel and cut into ¾-inch slices. In a small saucepan melt 4 tablespoons of the butter over low heat, then add the remaining ingredients and mix thoroughly. Remove the pan from the heat.

Butter a 3- to 4-quart casserole and put the yam slices in it in 3 layers, pouring

⅓ of the seasoned butter sauce over each layer. Bake covered in a preheated 350° oven for 20 minutes, then remove the casserole from the oven and uncover. With a large wooden spoon stir up the contents, cutting the yam slices in half and bringing the bottom layers to the top. When it is thoroughly mixed, press the mixture down firmly with the back of the spoon. Smooth and flatten the top surface and dot it evenly with the remaining 2 tablespoons butter, cut into small pieces. Return to the 350° oven and bake uncovered for 20 minutes longer.

STUFFED ZUCCHINI

As a change from zucchini stuffed with ground beef, white bread, and garlic, we like this version with ground sausage, French bread crumbs, heavy cream, thyme, and rosemary. It has the delicate taste of dishes from northern Italy. Pouring chicken stock into the baking pan helps cook and flavor the tougher outer part of the zucchini.

Save the liquid if you plan to reheat any zucchini the next day. *(for 4)*

---

4 small zucchini (2 to 2½ lb.)
5 Tbs. salt butter
½ lb. ground pork sausage
¼ tsp. salt
¼ tsp. freshly ground black pepper
5 Tbs. heavy cream
2 Tbs. finely minced fresh parsley
¼ c. French bread crumbs
3 Tbs. freshly grated Parmesan cheese
½ tsp. dried rosemary
⅛ tsp. dried thyme
1/16 tsp. cayenne
¼ tsp. finely minced garlic
½ c. rich chicken stock

Wash, dry, and trim off the ends of the zucchini, then cut in half lengthwise. Carefully scoop out the pulp with a teaspoon, leaving the outer skin and about ⅛ inch of flesh intact for stuffing.

Melt 2 tablespoons of the butter in a large heavy sauté pan and add the zucchini pulp. Cook slowly over low-medium heat until quite soft and wilted. While the pulp is cooking, fry the ground sausage in a small heavy skillet until it is cooked through and just turning brown. Drain off all excess fat and add the sausage to the zucchini pulp in the sauté pan. Turn the heat to low. Add the salt, pepper, 2 tablespoons of heavy cream, parsley, bread crumbs, 2 tablespoons of grated Parmesan cheese, rosemary, thyme, cayenne, and garlic. Cook about 4 minutes, stirring constantly.

Fill the zucchini halves with the cooked mixture, distributing it evenly, then butter a large shallow baking dish and carefully arrange the zucchini in it. Sprinkle with the remaining 1 tablespoon cheese and 3 tablespoons butter, and top with the remaining 3 tablespoons heavy cream. Pour the chicken stock into the pan around the zucchini, taking care not to wet the stuffing. Bake in a preheated 350° oven for about 30 minutes, or until the zucchini are tender when pierced with a fork and the filling is golden brown on top. Remove the zucchini carefully with a large slotted spoon or spatula, allowing the liquid to drain back into the pan.

VEGETABLE SOUFFLÉS

We love vegetable soufflés. They are simple to prepare once you become familiar with the basic steps for making soufflés. The few surprisingly uncomplicated tricks that produce consistently high, light, evenly cooked soufflés are described on page 196. Follow the same procedure for the vegetable soufflés that follow and you will have a light dinner for two or a lovely side dish for four to six persons. Just remember that the soufflé must be served as soon as you take it out of the oven, and time things accordingly.

EGGPLANT SOUFFLÉ

Our favorite vegetable soufflé. Pick a firm medium-sized eggplant with an even dark color. After you bake, cube, and mash it, measure out 1 cup for the soufflé. If you have any eggplant left over, add a bit of minced onion, a pinch of black pepper, and ¼ teaspoon salt, and use it as an hors d'oeuvre spread. *(main dish for 2 to 3; side dish for 6 to 8)*

---

1 medium-sized eggplant (1 c. baked and mashed)
3 Tbs. salt butter
¼ c. flour
1 c. scalded whole milk
¾ tsp. salt
¼ tsp. freshly ground black pepper
2 tsp. minced chives
1/16 tsp. cayenne
¼ tsp. dried chervil
¼ tsp. freshly grated nutmeg
4 large eggs plus 1 large egg white

Wash and dry the eggplant, then trim off the stem end. Place in a shallow baking dish and bake in a preheated 350° oven for 45 minutes. Remove and allow to cool, then peel off the skin and cut the eggplant pulp into 1-inch cubes. Drain in a colander to remove excess moisture. Put the eggplant in a bowl and mash well with the back of a wooden spoon, then set aside.

Starting with the butter and flour, proceed with the soufflé according to the directions on page 197. When the butter, flour, and milk mixture has thickened, remove the pan from the heat. Add the seasonings and blend lightly but thoroughly, then stir in 1 cup of the mashed baked eggplant. Mix well. Separate the eggs and proceed as directed on page 197, then butter and flour an 8-cup soufflé dish and bake as directed.

BROCCOLI SOUFFLÉ

(main dish for 2 to 3; side dish for 6 to 8)

Prepare according to the directions above for Eggplant Soufflé, substituting ½ bunch fresh broccoli, thick stems removed and the florets broken up, for the eggplant. Cook the broccoli, covered, in ½ inch lightly salted boiling water for 12 minutes. Drain, then cut up into small pieces. Put into a bowl and mash as directed for eggplant. Use 1 cup mashed broccoli for the soufflé.

Eliminate the minced chives and substitute ½ teaspoon dried marjoram for the chervil.

YAM SOUFFLÉ

A delightful, spicy-sweet soufflé made with baked Louisiana yams or regular sweet potatoes. We like this as a side dish with poultry and game. It also makes a festive accompaniment to Sunday brunch. *(for 6 to 8)*

---

2 medium-sized yams (1 c. baked and mashed)
3 Tbs. salt butter
¼ c. flour
1 c. scalded whole milk
½ tsp. salt
¼ tsp. cinnamon
3 Tbs. sugar
2 tsp. Cointreau
¼ tsp. cloves
⅛ tsp. allspice
4 large eggs plus 1 large egg white

Wash the yams and dry them thoroughly. Bake in a preheated 450° oven for 1 hour. Allow to cool, then peel and trim out any dark spots. Cut the yams into large cubes, put into a bowl, and mash well with the back of a wooden spoon.

Starting with the butter and flour, proceed with the soufflé according to the directions on page 197. When the butter, flour, and milk mixture has thickened, remove the pan from the heat. Add the seasonings and blend lightly but thoroughly, then stir in the mashed yam. Mix well. Separate the eggs and proceed as directed on page 197, then butter and flour an 8-cup soufflé dish and bake as directed.

PUMPKIN SOUFFLÉ

(for 6 to 8)

Prepare according to directions above for Yam Soufflé. Cut 1 small or ½ medium-sized pumpkin into large pieces and bake as directed for yams. After cutting up the pieces of pumpkin and mashing as directed, use 1 cup mashed pumpkin for the soufflé. (Put the rest into a bowl, cover with plastic wrap, and refrigerate for later use in pumpkin pie. Prepare according to the directions for Yam Pie, page 227.) Increase the sugar to 4 tablespoons and the cinnamon to ½ teaspoon.

A FEW SIMPLE RULES

☞ *TO PREPARE FRESH GREENS FOR TOSSED SALAD:* Rinse them thoroughly under cold running water. Shake off excess moisture by hand or in a salad basket. Put the damp greens in a large linen or flour sack towel and fold the towel loosely around them, then put the towel-wrapped greens in the refrigerator for at least 20 minutes to crisp them. After crisping, wipe off any excess moisture with the towel, tear the greens into large pieces, and put the pieces into a salad bowl. Leave the small leaves intact. Sprinkle lightly with salt and freshly ground pepper (black or white, depending on how strong a flavor you like).

☞ *TO DRESS THE GREENS:* Pour the dressing over the greens. Toss lightly with a long fork and a long spoon or salad tongs. Serve immediately or put the salad bowl into the refrigerator for about 5 minutes before serving.

☞ *USEFUL SUGGESTIONS FOR PREPARING SALAD DRESSING:* Use good quality olive oil and buy it in small sizes (1 pint to 1 quart); once opened it turns rancid on the shelf if not used within several weeks. Use a good quality white wine (or champagne) vinegar. Red wine vinegar tends to give salads an unattractive color. Avoid wine vinegar with garlic added; the garlic flavor does not stay fresh.

Let the dressing stand covered at room temperature after mixing for 30 minutes to an hour; this lets the flavors combine properly. Strain the dressing. (If you like some chopped garlic in the dressing for greens, as many New Orleanians do, measure out about ¼ teaspoon per ½ cup dressing and put it back into the dressing.) Make only as much dressing as you need fresh each time. Leftover dressing saved for the next day tends to get a bitter taste.

GREEN SALAD WITH VINAIGRETTE DRESSING

(salad for 3 to 4)

1 small head Boston lettuce
½ head romaine lettuce
½ head curly top (red top) lettuce
6 leaves (approximately) of chicory greens, watercress, or Chinese (celery) cabbage; *or* ½ bunch dandelion greens
Salt and freshly ground pepper

VINAIGRETTE DRESSING (½ cup)

½ c. olive oil
2 Tbs. white wine vinegar
2 tsp. fresh lemon juice
1 tsp. finely minced garlic
¼ tsp. salt
½ tsp. freshly ground white pepper
⅛ tsp. dry mustard
1 tsp. finely minced fresh parsley

To prepare the dressing, combine all ingredients in a small stainless steel or porcelain bowl. Mix vigorously with a whisk for 1 minute, then cover the bowl with plastic wrap and let it stand at room temperature for 30 minutes to 1 hour. Prepare and refrigerate the greens as indicated above. When you are ready to toss the salad, remove the chilled crisped greens from the refrigerator, dry, and sprinkle with salt and pepper. Mix the dressing and strain it, then mix again vigorously for about a minute before pouring it over the greens.

ITALIAN SALAD

Italian salad is affectionately called Wop salad by New Orleanians, including those of Italian descent, and is served not only in Italian but also in Creole and black restaurants. It combines fresh greens, ripe Creole tomatoes, and all manner of extras, such as anchovies, pickled onions, pickled green pepper pods, canned asparagus tips, hard-boiled egg wedges, olives, artichoke hearts, and pieces of chilled cooked broccoli or cauliflower.

(for 3 to 4)

½ head romaine lettuce
½ head curly top lettuce
1 small head Boston lettuce (optional)

ITALIAN DRESSING (½ cup)

6 Tbs. olive oil
2 Tbs. white wine vinegar
2 tsp. finely minced garlic
⅜ tsp. salt
½ tsp. freshly ground black pepper
2 tsp. finely minced fresh parsley
1 Tbs. thinly sliced green shallot (scallion) tops
1 Tbs. shallots (scallions), white part only, finely minced
¼ tsp. dried basil
¼ tsp. oregano

1 large ripe Creole (beefsteak, Jersey) tomato, cut into wedges
2 flat anchovy fillets, drained
At least 2 of the following:
- ¼ c. pickled onions
- 3 pickled green pepper pods
- 3 green olives
- 3 artichoke hearts
- 4 canned asparagus tips
- 4 florets cooked broccoli
- 4 pieces cooked cauliflower

Salt and freshly ground pepper

Wash, dry, and crisp the greens as directed on page 182. Prepare the dressing as for Vinaigrette Dressing (see page 182). After straining the dressing, put back 1 teaspoon of the solids. Let the dressing stand for about 30 minutes.

Tear up the dried greens and put them into a large salad bowl. Put the tomato wedges on top of the greens and sprinkle with salt and pepper. Pour ¼ cup dressing over the tomatoes and greens. Decorate the top of the salad attractively with the remaining ingredients and top with the remaining ¼ cup dressing.

OLD FASHIONED SOAKED SALAD

An old time home favorite. The salad is dressed, tossed, then refrigerated for several hours to let the greens and tomatoes soak up the dressing. The greens should be quite soft and look a trifle wilted. It is traditional to use two types of greens and medium-ripe tomatoes in this salad. *(for 4 to 6)*

- 2 heads of lettuce (romaine, Boston, curly top, iceberg)
- 2 large medium-ripe Creole (beefsteak, Jersey) tomatoes

DRESSING

- 6 Tbs. olive oil
- 1 Tbs. white wine vinegar
- 1 Tbs. fresh lemon juice
- ½ tsp. salt
- ¼ tsp. freshly ground black pepper
- ⅛ tsp. sugar
- 1 tsp. finely minced garlic
- 1 Tbs. finely minced fresh parsley
- ½ tsp. dried basil or 1 tsp. minced fresh basil

Wash and dry the lettuces. Wash the tomatoes, pare off the ends, and cut into chunks. Put the lettuce and tomatoes into a large stainless steel or porcelain bowl.

Combine the dressing ingredients in a small bowl and mix well with a wire whisk or a fork. Pour over the salad and toss to mix thoroughly. (It's all right to bruise the chunks of tomato a bit; their juice is an important part of the dressing. Just don't mash them.) Cover the bowl with plastic wrap and refrigerate for at least 3 hours.

To serve, use small dessert bowls or deep salad dishes and spoon about 2 tablespoons of the liquid from the bottom of the salad bowl over each portion.

RICE SALAD

An unusual and colorful Cajun salad made with rice cooked in chicken broth, ripe olives, chopped pickle, and plenty of seasonings. If you have no chicken broth, use bouillon made with cubes. Refrigerate the salad for about 2 hours before serving. *(for 4)*

- 1 c. long grain white rice
- 2 c. chicken broth
- 1 tsp. salt
- 1 tsp. salt butter

DRESSING

- ¼ c. olive oil or 2 Tbs. olive oil and 2 Tbs. vegetable oil
- 2 Tbs. white wine vinegar
- 2 Tbs. prepared mustard
- 1½ tsp. salt
- ¼ tsp. freshly ground black pepper
- Scant ⅛ tsp. cayenne
- ⅔ c. ripe olives, cut into large pieces
- ½ c. chopped celery
- ¼ c. chopped dill pickles
- ¼ c. chopped pimiento, drained
- ⅔ c. mayonnaise (if you want to prepare your own, see page 119)
- ¼ c. finely chopped onion

GARNISH

- 4 crisp leaves romaine lettuce
- 2 hard-boiled eggs, sliced
- 2 small ripe tomatoes, cut into wedges

Cook the rice in the chicken broth with the salt and butter, as directed on page 17. When the rice is cooked, set the pot aside.

In a large stainless steel or porcelain bowl combine the ingredients for the dressing. Add the hot rice and toss to mix thoroughly. Let cool for about 15 minutes at room temperature, then cover the bowl with plastic wrap and refrigerate for about 2 hours before serving.

To serve, put a crisp leaf of romaine lettuce on each salad plate. Put one-quarter of the rice salad on each lettuce leaf, then put 2 or 3 thin slices of hard-boiled egg on top of the rice and a wedge of tomato on each side.

SNAP BEAN SALAD

Snap bean salad is the New Orleans name for marinated string beans. Use crisp young string beans that break with a "snap" and small to medium-sized onions. Refrigerate the salad for at least 2 hours before serving. *(for 6 to 8)*

---

2 lb. fresh, young snap (string) beans, ends removed and broken into 3-inch lengths
Lightly salted boiling water

DRESSING

2 small to medium-sized onions, thinly sliced
¼ c. white wine vinegar
½ c. olive oil
1 tsp. freshly ground black pepper
2 tsp. fresh lemon juice
1½ tsp. salt
2 Tbs. finely minced fresh parsley
¾ tsp. sugar

Cook the snap beans in lightly salted boiling water just until tender, about 10 to 12 minutes. Drain thoroughly in a colander and let cool for about 10 minutes.

In a large stainless steel or porcelain bowl combine the snap beans and the dressing ingredients. Mix thoroughly with a wooden spoon. (Don't beat or you will mash the beans.) Cover the bowl with plastic wrap and refrigerate for at least 2 hours before serving. Mix thoroughly again just before serving.

OKRA SALAD

(for 6 to 8)

Prepare according to directions above for Snap Bean Salad, substituting 2 pounds fresh baby okra for the snap beans. Cook the okra whole for 20 minutes, then trim off the stem ends and tips. Slice the okra ¼ to ⅜ inch thick and combine as directed.

AVOCADO SALAD

When ripe avocados are available, we like to serve this salad as a first course. Prepare the dressing first and cut up the avocado right before putting on the dressing. It will discolor very quickly if you let it stand around cut up. *(for 2)*

½ c. Vinaigrette Dressing (page 182)

---

1 large ripe avocado
2 crisp leaves romaine lettuce
4 flat anchovy fillets, drained
2 tsp. caviar (optional)

After you prepare the dressing, peel the avocado, remove and discard the pit, and slice the flesh into thin wedges. Arrange the wedges in a fan shape over lettuce leaves on 2 salad plates. Place 2 anchovy fillets in an X-shape on top, then put a teaspoon of caviar on the anchovy fillets where they intersect. Pour ¼ cup dressing over each portion.

POTATO SALAD

New Orleans potato salad is traditionally prepared with mashed hard-boiled egg yolks added to the mayonnaise. Include some of the whites, diced fine, if you wish. Cook the potatoes in advance. This salad tastes best when it is refrigerated for 45 minutes to an hour before serving. *(for 4 or more)*

¾ c. mayonnaise (if you want to prepare your own, see page 119)

Yolks of 4 large hard-boiled eggs, mashed
3 medium-sized white potatoes, boiled, peeled, and cubed (about 3½ c.)
1 tsp. salt
¾ tsp. freshly ground white pepper
⅛ tsp. cayenne
½ c. very thinly sliced green shallot (scallion) tops
⅔ c. chopped celery
¼ c. pimiento strips, well drained

In a large stainless steel or porcelain bowl, combine the mayonnaise and mashed egg yolks and mix well. Add the cubed potatoes and all the remaining ingredients except the pimiento strips. Toss thoroughly but lightly, so as not to make the cubed potatoes mushy. Cut the pimiento strips into ⅜-inch lengths and put them on top of the salad. Refrigerate for at least 45 minutes before serving.

12

EGGS, NEW ORLEANS BREAKFASTS, AND BREADS

The tradition of the grand New Orleans breakfast originated during the late nineteenth century in the French Market, where restaurants served a hearty full meal at mid-morning to merchants and tradesmen who had begun their day before dawn. The most famous of these eating places was Madame Bégué's, which opened in 1882. French Market coffeehouses served the traditional lighter French *petit déjeuner*, café au lait with beignets (French Market doughnuts) or calas (hot rice cakes). The fame of the full meal New Orleans breakfast spread during the Cotton Exposition of 1884–1885 and it became one of the hallmarks of Creole cuisine. Sauced egg dishes and fancy omelettes were gradually added to the grand breakfast menu. Eggs Sardou, created at Antoine's in 1908 in honor of the visiting French dramatist Victorien Sardou, was the first of our elaborate poached egg dishes. Brennan's restaurant, founded in 1945, became famous for its lavish New Orleans breakfasts, as popular a feast as dinner at Antoine's.

Many of us also enjoy the typical New Orleans breakfasts at home—as Sunday meals after church, as delightful light dinners, or as special-occasion lunches. The lighter traditional breakfast specialties also remain perennial home favorites: pain perdu (lost bread), a New Orleans version of French toast made with stale French bread; Creole cream cheese, made with milk curds and heavy cream and served with fresh fruit or sugar; freshly fried hot Creole beignets.

New Orleans' favorite and omnipresent bread is the local French bread—light, deliciously crusty, served hot, and eaten plain or with butter in enormous quantities—at home, in restaurants, or at poor boy stands—with all meals of the day. They say that in New Orleans one can always judge the success of a dinner party or a grand restaurant meal by the quantity of French bread crumbs left scattered over the table linens and the floor.

All our grand egg dishes are quite simple to prepare; they are based on poached eggs or omelettes. What makes them special is the way we add unusual ingredients and lavish sauces. Beignets, calas, and pain perdu are fun to make at home, and very little trouble. Serve them with plenty of good hot New Orleans café au lait and you'll understand why we think the New Orleans style breakfast is one of life's greater pleasures.

EGGS SARDOU

The first of New Orleans' grand egg dishes and one of our favorites. Prepare the creamed spinach ahead of time. Use fresh, frozen, or good quality canned artichoke bottoms; warm them up and set the pan in a 175° oven; do the same with the creamed spinach. Prepare the hollandaise sauce and set the container in warm water while you poach the eggs. Assemble on warm plates. *(for 6)*

---

3 c. creamed spinach (page 193)
6 large or 12 small artichoke bottoms
12 poached eggs (see note below)
3 c. Blender Hollandaise (page 114) or Handmade Hollandaise (page 115)

Put ½ cup warm creamed spinach on each warmed plate. Place 1 or 2 warm artichoke bottoms on the bed of spinach, then set 2 poached eggs on the artichoke bottoms. Cover each portion with ½ cup hollandaise sauce.

Note: To poach the eggs, break the number of eggs you wish to poach carefully into individual saucers. (If you need to poach more eggs than you have saucers, you can keep reusing the same saucers if you move quickly and keep track of which eggs were lowered into the water first.) In a skillet or sauté pan bring about 1 to 1½ inches of water with 1 teaspoon vinegar in it to a boil. Reduce the heat just enough to keep a low boil going. Slide each egg into the water from the saucer by lowering the saucer almost to the surface of the water and tipping it. Cook each egg for about 2 to 2½ minutes in the boiling water, spooning some of the water over the surface of the egg during cooking. (There will be some wispy and stringy egg white around the poached egg. Don't worry about it; you can trim this off after you remove the egg from the water.) When the egg is cooked, lift it out of the water with a mesh or slotted spoon. Hold the spoon over the pan for a few seconds to let the water drain off.

EGGS NOUVELLE ORLEANS

Poached eggs with sautéed lump crabmeat and a béchamel sauce laced with brandy, a spectacular breakfast dish. Prepare the béchamel sauce first and set the pan aside (add the brandy to it when you reheat it, just before saucing the eggs); poach the eggs last. Use preheated individual gratin dishes for serving. *(for 6)*

---

2 c. New Orleans Béchamel Sauce (page 117)
½ c. (1 stick) salt butter
1½ lb. choice lump crabmeat
1 tsp. salt
⅔ tsp. freshly ground white pepper
12 eggs
3 Tbs. brandy

In a large heavy skillet melt the butter over medium heat, then add the crabmeat, salt, and pepper. Lower the heat and sauté the crabmeat for about 5 minutes, until it is heated through. Remove the skillet from the heat and set it in a 175° oven along with six gratin dishes.

Poach the eggs according to the directions given above. When all are poached, put 6 tablespoons sautéed crabmeat in the bottom of each preheated gratin dish. Place 2 poached eggs over the crabmeat. Cover the eggs with another 6 tablespoons crabmeat. Add the brandy to the béchamel and warm for a few seconds over medium heat, stirring to mix. Spoon ⅓ cup sauce over each portion, then set the gratin dishes on plates and serve immediately.

EGGS HUSSARDE

Hollandaise and marchand de vin sauce over grilled ham and poached eggs, a classic New Orleans egg dish. It is most practical to prepare this dish for at least 6 persons. Of course, if you are making tournedos marchand de vin the day before, you can easily prepare enough marchand de vin sauce for eggs Hussarde the next day.

(for 6)

6 slices toasted white bread, crust trimmed off
6 slices grilled baked ham
1½ c. Marchand de Vin Sauce (page 116)
12 slices grilled tomato
12 poached eggs (page 189)
2 c. Blender Hollandaise (page 114) or Handmade Hollandaise (page 115)

Prepare the marchand de vin sauce and set aside. Preheat the oven to 175°, then toast the bread and put it at one end of a large platter set in the warm oven. Pan grill the baked ham and tomato slices (use a bit of butter for the tomatoes) and put them on the platter with the toast; prepare the hollandaise sauce and set the blender container in warm water; poach the eggs; warm the marchand de vin sauce.

Now assemble the ingredients on warm plates. Place a slice of toast on each plate and cover with a slice of grilled ham. Pour ¼ cup marchand de vin sauce over each slice of ham, then place 2 slices grilled tomato side by side and overlapping slightly on the marchand de vin sauce. Place 2 poached eggs on top of the tomato slices. Cover each portion with ⅓ cup hollandaise sauce and serve.

CRAWFISH OMELETTE

Rich and delicious, a folded omelette filled with crawfish cooked in butter and cream. Combine the ingredients for the omelette batter first, then prepare the filling. Leave the filling in the pan while you begin to cook the omelette—it will stay warm for that short length of time—then fill the omelette across the middle just as it begins to set. Fold the edges over from each side, break the omelette in half, and serve. Filled omelettes are simple to prepare and can be varied almost infinitely. *(for 2)*

OMELETTE BATTER

4 large eggs
3 Tbs. milk
½ tsp. salt
¼ tsp. freshly ground white pepper
3 drops Tabasco

FILLING

2 Tbs. salt butter
¼ c. heavy cream
⅛ tsp. freshly ground black pepper
1/16 tsp. cayenne
⅛ tsp. salt
1/16 tsp. freshly grated nutmeg
1 c. crawfish tails (about 20 tails)

1½ Tbs. salt butter

First prepare the batter. In a mixing bowl, combine the eggs, milk, salt, pepper, and Tabasco. Beat lightly with a fork or a wire whisk just until well blended, then set aside.

To prepare the filling melt the 2 tablespoons butter in a medium-sized heavy sauté pan or skillet. Keep the heat low. Add the cream and seasonings and blend thoroughly, then mix in the crawfish tails. Continue cooking over low heat, stirring frequently, until the crawfish are tender (about 8 to 10 minutes). Remove the pan from the heat.

In a 10-inch omelette pan, melt the 1½ tablespoons butter over medium heat. When butter begins to sizzle, add the omelette batter and spread it evenly across the inside of the omelette pan by tilting the pan with a circular motion. Cook over medium heat just until the mixture begins to set and the omelette begins to turn brown at the edges. Lower the heat and add the crawfish filling in a band about 2 inches wide across the diameter of the omelette. When the inner surface of the omelette appears almost dry, fold the edges across the filling from each side so that they overlap about 1 inch. With the edge of a spatula break across into 2 portions; then slide each portion onto a preheated plate.

YAM OMELETTE

Peel and dice the yams or sweet potatoes first and sauté them until they are soft and lightly browned. Some minced chives add an attractive touch of color to the filling. *(for 2)*

FILLING

3 Tbs. salt butter
1 c. peeled, diced yams or sweet potatoes (about 2 small yams, cut into ½-inch dice)
¼ tsp. salt
⅛ tsp. freshly ground black pepper
2 Tbs. minced chives

OMELETTE BATTER

4 large eggs
3 Tbs. milk
½ tsp. salt
¼ tsp. freshly ground white pepper

2 Tbs. salt butter

To prepare the filling, melt the butter in a large heavy sauté pan or skillet over low heat. Add the yams, salt, and pepper and sauté over low heat for about 20 minutes, stirring constantly and turning the pieces of yam over frequently, until they are soft and browned. Add the chives during the last 5 minutes of sautéing.

Prepare, fill, fold, and divide the omelette as directed on page 191, then slide onto heated plates and serve immediately.

ONION OMELETTE

A home favorite. Use small or medium-sized onions rather than large ones, which tend to have too strong a flavor. *(for 2)*

FILLING

2 Tbs. salt butter
⅔ c. onions cut in half, then thinly sliced
¼ tsp. salt
⅛ tsp. freshly ground white pepper

OMELETTE BATTER

4 large eggs
3 Tbs. milk
½ tsp. salt
¼ tsp. freshly ground white pepper

2 Tbs. salt butter

To prepare the filling, melt the butter in a medium-sized heavy sauté pan or skillet over low heat. Add the onion, salt, and pepper and sauté for 12 to 15 minutes over low heat, stirring frequently, until the onion is soft and lightly browned. (If you prefer the onion browner, sauté for 20 minutes.) Remove the pan from the heat and set aside.

Prepare the omelette according to the directions on page 191. Fill, fold, and divide as directed, then slide onto heated plates and serve immediately.

NEW ORLEANS SHALLOT OMELETTE

A filled omelette made with those green onions we love so much. Sauté the shallots just until they are soft; don't brown them. *(for 2)*

Prepare according to the directions for Onion Omelette (page 192), substituting 1 cup thinly sliced shallots (scallions) for the onions and increasing the butter for sautéing to 3 tablespoons.

OMELETTE FLORENTINE

A classic grand breakfast omelette, filled with creamed spinach and garnished with fresh parsley. Prepare the béchamel sauce first, then add the chopped spinach. Set the pan in the oven to keep warm while you mix the omelette batter.

We also like this as a light dinner. *(for 2)*

FILLING

- 2/3 c. well-drained and finely chopped cooked spinach
- 5 Tbs. New Orleans Béchamel Sauce (page 117)
- 1/8 tsp. freshly ground black pepper
- 1/8 tsp. salt

OMELETTE BATTER

- 4 large eggs
- 3 Tbs. milk
- 1/2 tsp. salt
- 1/4 tsp. freshly ground white pepper

- 2 Tbs. salt butter
- 1 tsp. finely minced fresh parsley

Add the chopped spinach to the béchamel sauce and warm for a few minutes over low heat, stirring constantly. Mix in the salt and pepper, then set the pan in a 175° oven to keep warm while you prepare the omelette batter.

Mix the batter and cook, using the 2 tablespoons butter, according to the directions on page 191. Fill, fold, and divide the omelette as directed, then slide the portions onto heated plates and sprinkle each one with 1/2 teaspoon minced parsley. Serve immediately.

CREOLE OKRA OMELETTE

An omelette filled with sautéed baby okra, onion, and pimiento. If you can't get fresh baby okra, use frozen. Defrost it thoroughly, dry it carefully, and sauté a few minutes less than you would fresh. *(for 2)*

OMELETTE BATTER

4 eggs
3 Tbs. milk
½ tsp. salt
⅛ tsp. freshly ground white pepper
3 drops Tabasco

FILLING

2 Tbs. salt butter
1 c. sliced baby okra
½ c. chopped onion
½ tsp. finely minced garlic
½ tsp. salt
⅛ tsp. freshly ground white pepper
3 drops Tabasco
2 Tbs. chopped pimiento
1½ tsp. minced fresh parsley

2 Tbs. salt butter

Prepare the omelette batter by combining all the ingredients in a bowl and beating lightly with a whisk or fork just until blended.

To prepare the filling, melt the butter in a heavy skillet or sauté pan over low heat. Add the okra, onion, and the rest of the ingredients and sauté over low heat for about 20 minutes, stirring frequently, or just until the okra and onion are tender and slightly browned. Remove the skillet from the heat and set aside.

Prepare and fill the omelette as directed on page 191, divide in half, and serve on warmed plates.

OYSTER OMELETTE

An old Creole favorite, a fluffy pancake style omelette made with fresh oysters. We like it with the oysters cut up and a bit of meunière sauce poured over each portion. You will need a 10-inch omelette pan to prepare an omelette for two persons. If you want to serve more, repeat the process in the same pan. It takes only a few minutes to make an omelette and you can set the first omelette in a warm oven for just a few minutes. Or use two pans. *(for 2)*

---

4 large eggs
3 Tbs. milk
½ tsp. salt
¼ tsp. freshly ground white pepper
⅔ c. fresh shucked oysters (about 1 doz. medium-sized oysters), cut into 1-inch pieces
¼ c. (½ stick) salt butter

Combine the eggs, milk, salt, and pepper in a mixing bowl. Beat with a rotary egg beater or a balloon whisk for about 2 minutes, or until the mixture becomes quite light and airy. Drain the oysters thoroughly and fold gently into the egg batter with a wooden spoon.

Melt 2 tablespoons of the butter in a 10-inch omelette pan and pour in the batter. Cook over medium heat until the omelette begins to set, then turn it over carefully with a large spatula and cook just until the bottom turns light brown. Cut the omelette in half with the edge of the spatula and slide the halves onto prewarmed plates. Add the remaining 2 tablespoons butter to the omelette pan and cook over medium heat until the butter turns a rich hazelnut color, then pour half over each portion.

SHIRRED EGGS WITH CREAM

Oeufs sur le plat were popular in New Orleans at the turn of the century. We particularly like them this way, with a bit of heavy cream added. Serve 2 eggs per person in individual gratin dishes or ramekins. *(for 4)*

---

4 tsp. butter
8 large eggs
Salt and freshly ground white pepper
8 tsp. heavy cream

Preheat the oven to 350°. Using 1 teaspoon of butter for each, butter 4 individual gratin dishes or ramekins. Break 2 eggs into each one, sprinkle with salt and pepper, and pour 2 teaspoons heavy cream over each portion. Cover the dishes with aluminum foil and tuck the foil loosely around the edges of the dishes, then cut 4 small slits in each foil cover to allow the steam to escape during baking. Bake in the preheated oven for 6 minutes. Remove the foil and serve sizzling hot.

A FEW SIMPLE RULES

☞ *EGGS:* Eggs should be at room temperature; take them out of the refrigerator ½ hour ahead or warm in a bowl of tepid water.

☞ *EGG WHITES:* Separate carefully so there is no yolk in the whites. Beat the whites to get the greatest possible volume. We prefer using a large balloon whisk or hand mixer in a copper bowl; if you use a plain bowl, add a pinch of cream of tartar; if the mixer is stationary— unless it is a heavy-duty appliance with rotary action— scrape down the whites from the sides of the bowl with a rubber spatula several times while beating.

☞ *FOLDING WHITES:* Incorporate the beaten whites in three parts: mix the first third of whites in firmly; fold the second in gently with a lifting motion, bringing the mixture up from the bottom of the bowl in large amounts with a wooden spoon; fold the third part very, very gently, leaving the final mixture a bit streaky.

☞ *BAKING:* Use the middle rack of the preheated oven and don't open the door for the first 30 minutes. The soufflé will be done when the crust is browned and cracked and when it has risen at least an inch above the sides of the dish. A cake tester inserted in the middle should come out dry; if it doesn't, bake for an additional 5 to 8 minutes.

CHEESE SOUFFLÉ

(for 2)

3 Tbs. salt butter
3 Tbs. flour
1 c. scalded whole milk
1 c. freshly grated cheese (Swiss Emmenthal, French Gruyère, American Swiss)
1 tsp. salt
1/8 tsp. freshly ground white pepper
1/8 tsp. freshly grated nutmeg
4 large eggs plus 1 large egg white

In a heavy 2- to 3-quart saucepan melt the butter slowly over a very low flame. Carefully blend in the flour a little at a time, stirring constantly with a wooden spoon to keep lumps from forming. Remove the pan from the heat and gradually stir in the scalded milk. Return the pan to heat and cook very slowly, stirring constantly, until the mixture thickens to the texture of a medium-heavy white sauce. Remove the pan from the heat again and stir the cheese and seasonings into the still-warm mixture. Blend until smooth, then set aside.

Separate the 4 eggs, putting the yolks into a large mixing bowl and the whites into another large bowl (preferably of solid copper) along with the extra white. Beat the yolks until they are light and lemon colored. Pour the white sauce mixture into the yolks and blend thoroughly. Beat the whites with a balloon whisk or rotary hand beater until they are stiff but still moist; stiff peaks should form at the ends of the lifted whisk or beater. Using a wooden spoon or spatula, gently fold the egg whites into the yolk mixture in three stages, as described in the preceding Simple Rules.

Butter the entire inner surface of a 6-cup soufflé dish, then dust the buttered surface lightly with flour. Pour the soufflé mixture into the dish and bake on the middle rack in a preheated 375° oven for 30 to 35 minutes. At the end of 30 minutes, check to see if the soufflé is done; it should have risen about 1½ inches above the rim of the soufflé dish and the top should be browned and cracked in a few places. A cake tester inserted into the center of the soufflé should come out clean. If necessary, bake for 5 to 8 minutes longer. Remove the soufflé from the oven and serve immediately.

CREOLE CREAM CHEESE EVANGELINE

Creole cream cheese with fresh fruit, the traditional first course for a grand New Orleans breakfast. Creole cream cheese is prepared by all the local dairies and packed in 11-ounce containers similar to those used for cottage cheese. It consists of a single large curd made from milk surrounded by cream. The culture that produces Creole cream cheese cannot be duplicated successfully outside southwestern Louisiana, so if you live elsewhere, for 2 portions substitute a 7-ounce chunk of farmer cheese or about 7 ounces of large curd cottage cheese pressed together, and pour ½ cup heavy cream over it.

Use soft fresh fruit such as peaches, plums, and strawberries. *(for 2)*

---

1 eleven-oz. container Creole cream cheese (or 7 oz. farmer cheese or large curd cottage cheese plus ½ c. heavy cream)
1 c. cut-up fresh fruit (use 2 or more different fruits)
2 tsp. sugar (optional)

Put the contents of the container of Creole cream cheese into two breakfast bowls, with equal amounts of curd and cream in each. Top each serving with ½ cup fruit and sprinkle with 1 teaspoon sugar, if desired.

RAISED CALAS (RICE CAKES)

Hot calas were carried through the French Quarter by black cooks in the nineteenth century to the cry of "*Belles calas tout chauds.*" The name appears to have originated from an African word for rice. These fluffy sweetened fried cakes made with cooked rice and yeast are rarely sold here today, but they're simple to prepare at home and add an authentic touch to an old fashioned Creole breakfast. Cook the rice the night before and mix it with the yeast, then set it to rise overnight. The rice is cooked with more water and for a longer time than usual, so it will be soft enough to mash easily. The batter cannot be saved and the calas can't be reheated, so eat hearty. *(for 4)*

½ c. long grain white rice
1½ c. cold water
1 tsp. salt
½ tsp. salt butter
1 package dry yeast or ½ oz. compressed yeast, softened in ½ c. lukewarm water
3 large eggs, well beaten
¼ c. sugar
¼ tsp. freshly grated nutmeg
½ tsp. salt
1¼ c. flour
Vegetable oil for deep frying
Confectioners' sugar

Combine the rice, water, salt, and butter and cook according to the directions on page 17, increasing the cooking time to 25 minutes. Drain the rice in a colander and put it in a large deep mixing bowl, then mash it with the back of a wooden spoon. Let it cool just until it is lukewarm, then add the dissolved yeast. Beat thoroughly with a wooden spoon for about 2 minutes. Cover the bowl with a towel and set in a warm place to rise overnight.

In the morning, add the eggs, sugar, nutmeg, salt, and flour. Beat again for about 1 minute, then cover the bowl again and set in a warm place to rise for 20 to 30 minutes.

Heat oil in a deep fryer to 375°. Drop the batter by heaping tablespoons into the hot oil and fry about 3 or 4 at a time, until golden brown. Drain and place on a platter lined with paper towels. Set the platter in a preheated 175° oven and keep adding fried batches of calas to it until all the batter is used up. Serve hot, sprinkled with confectioners' sugar.

ACADIAN COUSH-COUSH

Coush-coush is a Cajun corn meal fritter. The coush-coush batter is also served as a cereal, cooked slowly in an iron skillet. The version given here resembles hush puppies without the onions, These fritters are inexpensive, easy to prepare, and *not* highly seasoned; they provide a kind of cushion for the very spicy Cajun sausages and the marvelous "burnt roast" Cajun pure coffee they accompany. Serve them immediately after frying; they get leaden as they cool. *(for 8)*

---

2 c. yellow corn meal	2 tsp. sugar
1½ tsp. salt	1½ c. water
1 tsp. baking powder	Vegetable oil for deep frying

Mix the dry ingredients together in a large bowl, then add the water and blend thoroughly. Shape into balls about 1¾ inches in diameter and fry in oil preheated to 375° until golden brown, about 8 to 10 minutes. Drain on paper towels and serve very hot, with cane or pancake syrup.

For other New Orleans breakfast dishes, see also: GRILLADES AND GRITS (page 129), PANÉED VEAL (page 128), CHAURICE (page 136), NEW ORLEANS CAFÉ AU LAIT (page 238).

BEIGNETS (FRENCH MARKET DOUGHNUTS)

Beignets are the rectangular doughnuts served fresh and hot around the clock at the French Market coffeehouses. They are simple to prepare at home and make a delightful breakfast bread or a delicious snack at any hour of the day. The yeast dough must be prepared in advance and refrigerated overnight. We have found that for home preparation the dough works best in the large quantity given here, enough for more than 5 dozen beignets. But that's no problem—the dough keeps beautifully under refrigeration for almost a week. Just cut off some dough when you want to make beignets; roll it out, cut it up, and fry for about 3 minutes per batch, then sprinkle the beignets with confectioners' sugar and serve piping hot.

We wondered for a long time why homemade beignets lacked the special flavor of those served in the French Market. Then one day we figured out the secret—using canned evaporated milk. And it made sense. Many older New Orleanians consider canned evaporated milk a great delicacy and, in fact, refer to it fondly as "pet cream."

Serve freshly fried beignets with good hot café au lait.

(about 5 dozen beignets)

- 1½ c. warm water
- 1 package active dry yeast
- ½ c. sugar
- 1 tsp. salt
- 2 large eggs
- 1 c. undiluted canned evaporated milk
- 7 c. flour
- ¼ c. vegetable shortening
- Oil for deep frying
- Confectioners' sugar

Put the warm water into a large bowl, then sprinkle in the dry yeast and stir until thoroughly dissolved. Add the sugar, salt, eggs, and evaporated milk. Gradually stir in 4 cups of the flour and beat with a wooden spoon until smooth and thoroughly blended. Beat in the shortening, then add the remaining flour, about ⅓ cup at a time, beating it in with a spoon until it becomes too stiff to stir, then working in the rest with your fingers. Cover the bowl with plastic wrap and refrigerate overnight.

Roll the dough out on a floured board or marble pastry surface to a thickness of ⅛ inch, then cut it into rectangles 2½ inches by 3½ inches with a sharp knife. Preheat oil in a deep fryer to 360°. Fry the beignets about 3 or 4 at a time until they are puffed out and golden brown on both sides (about 2 to 3 minutes per batch). Turn them over in the oil with tongs once or twice to get them evenly brown, since they rise to the surface of the oil as soon as they begin to puff out. Drain each batch, place on a platter lined with several layers of paper towels, and put the platter in a 200° oven to keep warm.

Sprinkle the beignets heavily with confectioners' sugar and serve hot.

PAIN PERDU (LOST BREAD)

The local version of French toast, made with stale French bread. Pain perdu originated as a way of using up leftover bread. We like it so much that we buy extra French bread and set it on the kitchen counter to get stale so we can prepare this old time favorite. If you live outside New Orleans and can't get our local French bread, substitute thick slices of white bread or Italian bread. Let the butter and oil get sizzling hot in the skillet before adding the soaked slices. Keep the fried slices warm in a 200° oven while you finish cooking the rest; we find that the brief drying-out in the oven makes pain perdu taste even better.

Provide a pitcher of Louisiana cane syrup or pancake syrup for those who want additional sweetening. *(for 4)*

1 c. milk
2 large eggs, well beaten
¼ c. granulated sugar
¼ tsp. vanilla extract
4 slices stale French bread (each about 1¼ inches thick)
2 Tbs. salt butter
2 Tbs. vegetable oil
½ tsp. cinnamon mixed with 2 tsp. confectioners' sugar

In a large bowl combine the milk, beaten eggs, granulated sugar, and vanilla and mix thoroughly. Soak the slices of stale French bread in the milk and egg mixture for a few minutes.

Meanwhile, melt the butter in a heavy skillet and add the vegetable oil. When the butter and oil mixture is quite hot, fry the soaked bread slices one or two at a time on each side, until golden brown. Sprinkle with the cinnamon and confectioners' sugar mixture just before serving. Serve with Louisiana cane syrup or pancake syrup, if desired.

BAKED PAIN PERDU

For cooks who are too sleepy early in the morning to cope with frying, this is another way to prepare an old favorite. It's not as crisp and brown as the classic version, but it's very good. *(for 4)*

1 c. milk
2 large eggs, well beaten
¼ c. granulated sugar
¼ tsp. vanilla extract
4 slices stale French bread (each about 1¼ inches thick)
½ tsp. cinnamon mixed with 2 tsp. confectioners' sugar

Preheat the oven to 400°. Proceed as for regular pain perdu (see above) through the soaking of the bread. Grease a large baking pan with butter or shortening and place the soaked bread slices on it. Bake in the oven until the slices are dry and browned, about 20 minutes. Sprinkle with cinnamon and confectioners' sugar and serve with Louisiana cane syrup or pancake syrup, if desired.

NEW ORLEANS FRENCH BREAD

The marvelous light crusty bread basic to good New Orleans eating. Most New Orleanians buy their French bread at markets supplied by local bakers who make it fresh several times a day. You can bake good New Orleans French bread at home using all purpose flour and dry yeast. However, if you plan to bake it regularly you'll find that bread flour—that is, hard wheat flour—fresh compressed yeast, and yeast food—all of which can be obtained through bakeries or wholesale grocery supply houses—will give you higher, lighter loaves with a finer flavor and texture. French bread works best baked in the minimum quantity given here and freezes well. Frozen loaves should be set on the counter about 10 minutes ahead of time, then warmed in a 400° oven for about 6 minutes. We find that 8- to 9-inch loaves are perfect for individual poor boy sandwiches and for two persons at the dinner table. New Orleans French bread is traditionally served hot, wrapped in a linen napkin, and replenished frequently.

(8 loaves, 8 to 9 inches long, about 2½ to 3 inches wide, and weighing 4 ounces each)

- 1½ oz. fresh compressed yeast or 3 packages active dry yeast
- 2 tsp. sugar
- 4 tsp. salt
- ½ c. warm water (90° for fresh yeast, 110° for dry yeast)
- 5 to 6 c. bread flour or all purpose flour
- ½ tsp. Arkady yeast food (optional)
- 2 tsp. Crisco
- 1½ c. warm water (see note, page 204)
- ⅓ c. white corn meal, approximately, pulverized in a blender or electric grinder
- Crisco for greasing mixing bowl

To begin fermentation, put the yeast, sugar, and salt into a 5- to 6-quart mixing bowl. (Fresh yeast should be crumbled before it is added.) Add the ½ cup warm water, stir once with a wooden spoon, and set the bowl aside. Put 5 cups of the flour, yeast food if used, and 2 teaspoons Crisco into a smaller bowl. Mix lightly. (It is not necessary to mix the shortening in thoroughly.) Add ½ cup of the flour mixture to the dissolved yeast and wait about 30 seconds. The mixture will begin to bubble, indicating fermentation.

To mix the dough, add ½ cup of the warm water to the yeast mixture and stir. Add ½ cup flour and stir. Repeat, stirring after each addition, until all the warm water has been added. Add all but 1 cup of the remaining flour gradually, stirring it in at first, then, as the dough gets stiff, working it in with your hands.

To prepare the dough for the first rising, flour a marble pastry surface or wooden surface and turn the dough out onto it. Scrape out any dough or flour that clings to the bowl and pat it into the wad of dough. Dust your hands with flour and begin to knead, gently at first, then more vigorously, until the dough forms a smooth elastic ball that springs back when you poke it with two fingers; the surface of the ball of dough should be moist and slightly blistery. (Kneading will take from 6 to 12 minutes, depending on how vigorously you knead, the flour you use, and the temperature of your kitchen.) Add flour from the remaining cup as necessary during kneading. If the dough seems to stick to the work surface and tear, dust the surface and your hands with flour, keeping the addition of flour to a minimum. When the dough is sufficiently kneaded, let it rest while you wash and dry the large mixing bowl.

To set the dough to rise, grease the bowl lightly with Crisco. Place the ball of dough gently in the bowl and turn it several times to coat evenly with shortening. Cover the bowl with plastic wrap and set to rise in a warm draft-free place. (A closed unlit gas oven is excellent; the heat from the pilot provides just enough warmth for proper rising. With an electric oven, turn it to 150° for about 3 minutes, then turn off the heat and open the door for about 3 minutes. Put the bowl of dough in the oven and quickly shut the door; this will give you an approximate temperature of 85°, just right for even and fairly quick rising.) Allow to rise until doubled in bulk (about 1 to 1½ hours). To check for sufficient rising, dust one finger lightly with flour and poke the dough very gently. If it falls away from your finger and appears to deflate slightly, it's ready.

To divide the dough into loaves, clean the kneading surface and dust it lightly with flour. Turn the bowl of dough upside down over the surface to drop the dough onto it. Flatten the dough gently but firmly with the palms of your hands to a thickness of ⅔ to 1 inch, then cut it into 8 equal-sized pieces with a sharp knife. Fold each piece in half and move it to one side of the work surface. Cover the folded pieces of dough immediately with a single large piece of plastic wrap to keep the exposed surfaces from forming a hard outer surface, which would hamper the rising of the loaves.

Prepare 2 large heavy baking sheets by dusting them evenly with pulverized corn meal. Cut 2 sheets of plastic wrap large enough to cover the pans loosely with the edges tucked under all around, or use 2 eight-gallon plastic bags. (Translucent wastebasket liners are perfect.)

To shape the loaves, remove the folded pieces of dough one at a time from the plastic covering. Flatten each piece, with your palms into a circle 8 to 9 inches in diameter. Fold the top half of the circle down a bit more than halfway and flatten the folded part firmly with your palms. Fold the bottom half of the circle up so that it overlaps the folded-down top edge about ⅜ inch and flatten firmly with your palms. You now have in front of you a piece of dough 8 to 9 inches across and about 4 inches from top to bottom. Fold down from the top to within ¼ inch of the bottom edge. Seal the seam along the bottom edge by pressing down firmly with the edge of your hands. The dough is now in the shape of a loaf about 8 to 9 inches by 2¼ inches. Roll the loaf toward you a quarter turn; the sealed seam is now at the bottom. Seal the ends by pressing down firmly with the edge of your hands. Carefully lift the shaped loaf and place it on one of the prepared baking sheets. Immediately cover the pan with plastic wrap or a plastic bag. Shape the remaining folded pieces of dough in the same way, setting the shaped loaves on the baking sheets with about 3 inches between each loaf and between the end loaf and the edge of the sheet, to allow for rising and further expansion during baking. (You may find it most practical to place the loaves diagonally on the baking sheets to make best use of the space. The narrow ends may be closer to the edges, since the loaves will get much wider and higher, but will lengthen very little.)

To set the loaves to rise, place them, covered, in a warm draft-free place until almost doubled in bulk (about 1 hour). To check for sufficient rising, dust one finger with flour and poke a loaf near one end. The dough should give just a little bit, but *not* begin to fall away from your finger as the dough did after the first rising. (If you let the loaves rise a bit more than necessary, they will not puff up as much during baking, but will taste just as good. It takes a bit of practice to learn precisely when the loaves are ready for baking.)

Preheat the oven to 475° soon after you set the loaves to rise. Place an iron skillet two-thirds filled with water on the floor of your oven, to provide humidity during baking. Keep the oven door closed during preheating.

To bake the loaves, slash each one lengthwise along the top with a thin sharp knife or a single-edged razor blade. The slash should be about ⅛ inch deep and at a

45° angle. Brush the loaves with cold water immediately after slashing and set the baking pans on the middle and upper racks in the oven. Spray or brush the loaves once more with cold water after 5 minutes. Bake for another 20 minutes, or until the loaves are golden brown and crisp. They will rise further during baking and appear puffed up and attractively cracked along the slash line. (You will find that loaves on the upper rack will not always puff and crack as much as those on the lower racks; this is normal. If you wish more uniform-looking loaves, reverse the pans after about 14 minutes; do so quickly and shut the oven door quickly to prevent excessive heat loss.) Remove the finished loaves from the oven and set to cool on cake racks. To serve, heat in a 400° oven for 5 to 6 minutes.

Note: If your kitchen is cool in winter, use water a bit warmer than you normally would; if it gets hot during the summer, use slightly cooler water. These adjustments will counterbalance the lower or higher temperatures of your utensils, counter surfaces, and hands, all of which affect the temperature of the dough as you mix it.

CORN BREAD

Old fashioned corn bread, baked in a heavy iron skillet. For a special flavor touch, use sausage or bacon drippings to grease the skillet instead of shortening.

(for 4 or more)

- 1 c. yellow corn meal
- 1 c. flour
- 1 Tbs. sugar
- 4 tsp. baking powder
- 1 tsp. salt
- 1/8 tsp. allspice
- 1/8 tsp. freshly ground white pepper
- 1 large egg
- 1 c. milk
- 1/4 c. vegetable shortening
- 1 1/2 Tbs. shortening or bacon or sausage drippings, approximately

Sift the dry ingredients together into a large mixing bowl. Add the egg, milk, and 1/4 cup shortening and beat with a wooden spoon or spatula until smooth, about 1 minute. Grease an 8- or 9-inch iron skillet (or a heavy 8-inch square baking pan) with the shortening or drippings, pour in the batter, and bake in a preheated 425° oven for 25 to 30 minutes, until light golden brown on top. Bring the skillet to the table and cut into wedges to serve.

Note: For a moist interior and a nice crisp crust, put an iron skillet two-thirds filled with water on the floor of your oven before you begin to preheat it. This old Creole trick works well with all home baked bread.

YAM BREAD

An old Creole favorite, delicious still warm from the oven or chilled, then thinly sliced and toasted. Bake the yams or sweet potatoes ahead of time, refrigerate them, then mash them just before beginning to bake. If you use canned yams, be sure to drain them thoroughly. Home baked bread seems to come out better with more loaves in the oven—they create their own humid atmosphere. If you have enough loaf pans, double or triple the recipe. For the best possible texture and flavor, put an iron skillet two-thirds full of water on the oven floor before turning on the heat and preheat for at least 20 minutes. Yam bread keeps for weeks in the refrigerator and about 8 months in the freezer. *(2 loaves, 9 by 5 by 3, or 8½ by 4½ by 3⅛ inches)*

---

2 to 3 medium-sized yams or sweet potatoes (2 c. baked and mashed)
1 oz. fresh compressed yeast or 2 packages active dry yeast
1½ Tbs. sugar
1 Tbs. salt
½ c. warm water (about 90° for fresh yeast, 110° for dry yeast)
6 to 7 c. bread flour or all purpose flour
⅛ tsp. allspice
⅛ tsp. freshly grated nutmeg
⅛ tsp. freshly ground white pepper
1 c. warm water
2 Tbs. melted salt butter
1½ Tbs. salt butter, approximately, for greasing pans and mixing bowl
Cold milk

Wash the yams thoroughly, dry well, and rub with vegetable oil. Bake in a preheated 450° oven for 1 hour, then allow to cool. Peel, cut into pieces, then mash in a bowl with a wooden spoon or potato ricer just until smooth.

In a 4- to 5-quart mixing bowl dissolve the yeast in ½ cup warm water. Sift the dry ingredients together and add about ½ cup immediately to the dissolved yeast to begin the fermentation. Mix with a wooden spoon.

Gradually add the remaining flour and dry ingredients about ½ cup at a time, followed by about ¼ cup of the remaining water. Repeat, mixing well after each addition. When all the water has been mixed in, add all but 1 cup of the remaining flour all at once. Mix briefly, then add the mashed yams and melted butter. Stir briefly with the spoon; the dough will be rather thick at this point. Dust a pastry surface or board and your hands with flour. Turn out the contents of the bowl, scraping out any of the mixture that clings to the bowl. Begin to knead the dough. It will tend to get moist as the yams are mixed in more thoroughly, so add flour as necessary and knead for 10 to 15 minutes; the dough should be elastic and slightly moist, but not sticky. (If you use canned yams, more flour than indicated above may be necessary.)

Let the ball of dough rest while you wash and dry the bowl and grease it thoroughly with butter. Place the ball of dough in the bowl, then turn it over gently several times to coat it all over with butter. Cover with plastic wrap and set to rise in a warm draft-free place until doubled in bulk (about 1 hour). Clean the pastry surface or board and dust with flour. Turn out the risen ball of dough. Flatten it with the palms of your hands to about ⅓ inch thick. Cut the dough in half with a sharp knife, then fold each piece over and cover with a piece of the plastic wrap. Let the pieces rest for a few minutes while you set the oven to 425° and butter the loaf pans.

Uncover the pieces of dough one at a time and flatten them into ovals as wide as the length of your bread pans and about twice as long. (For example, for a 9-by-5-by-3-inch pan, you should form an oval about 9 inches by 16 to 18 inches.) With the oval of dough lengthwise on the surface in front of you, fold it down from the top a bit more than halfway. Flatten the folded part with your hands, then fold up from the bottom to overlap the folded top edge about ½ inch. Again flatten the folded section with your hands. Now you have in front of you a rectangle of dough about 9 inches across and 7 to 8 inches from top to bottom. Fold the rectangle in half from top to bottom by lifting the top edge and bringing it down to meet the bottom edge. Seal the edges together tightly by pressing down firmly with the side of one hand. Then roll the piece of dough forward toward you about a quarter turn, so that the sealed edge is at the bottom. Seal the ends at each side by pressing down with the sides of your hands, then carefully lift each shaped loaf and set it in a loaf pan. The pans should be about two-thirds full. If necessary, pat the loaves down gently so that the dough touches the narrow edges of the pan.

Cover the pans with plastic wrap, then set to rise again until the dough reaches the top or about ½ inch above the edge of the pan (about 30 minutes). Uncover the loaves, make 4 or 5 slashes across the top with a sharp knife, brush with cold milk, then bake in the preheated oven for 30 to 35 minutes. Test for doneness by inserting a cake tester; if it comes out dry, the loaves are probably done. To make the final check, turn a loaf out onto your hand (use insulated gloves) and rap on the bottoms: if you get a slightly hollow sound the loaves are done. If not, put them back into the pans and bake for 5 to 10 minutes longer. Turn the finished loaves out and set to cool on a rack for at least 15 to 20 minutes before slicing.

YAM BISCUITS

A breakfast bread from the Cajun country, delicious served hot with butter. Leftover biscuits can be wrapped in plastic, then unwrapped and reheated for 4 to 5 minutes in a hot oven.

(1 dozen)

- 1 large or 2 small yams or sweet potatoes (½ c. baked and mashed)
- 2 c. flour
- 1 Tbs. baking powder
- 1 tsp. salt
- 2 tsp. sugar
- ¼ c. vegetable shortening
- ½ c. milk

Bake and mash the yams according to the directions on page 181. Sift the dry ingredients together into a large mixing bowl. Mix in the shortening and mashed yams with an electric beater (at medium-low speed) or a whisk, until they are evenly distributed and the mixture appears light and crumbly (about 2 minutes). Gradually add the milk, continuing to mix just until the ingredients are evenly dampened; do not beat.

Flour a marble pastry surface or board and turn the contents of the bowl out onto it. Knead lightly for about 30 to 45 seconds, just until a slightly moist, streaky-looking dough is formed. Roll out gently to a thickness of ¾ inch and cut out biscuits with a biscuit cutter. As the biscuits are cut, place them about 1½ inches apart on an ungreased heavy baking sheet. Pat the leftover pieces of dough together gently with your hands and again roll out lightly, as indicated above. Cut the remaining biscuits from the patted-together dough. If necessary, pat any leftover dough together once again, then roll out and cut, until all the dough is used up.

Bake on the middle rack of a preheated 450° oven for 12 to 15 minutes, or until the biscuits are lightly browned on top and appear flaky. Set to cool for about 5 minutes on a cake rack. Serve warm, with butter.

13

DESSERTS

New Orleanians love dramatic desserts for special occasions—crêpes Suzette or bananas Foster flamed at the table, baked Alaska ceremonially served. And they also love simpler desserts, ones made with leftover bread or cake, home-baked puddings, pies, cakes, and fresh fruit compotes. New Orleans' most popular dessert, prepared in home kitchens and in almost every restaurant in the city, is bread pudding with whiskey sauce. Originally devised as a way to use up stale French bread, bread pudding has become a local art form. Every good local cook has his or her own version, and crowns it with a special rich sauce prepared from a jealously guarded secret recipe.

Most New Orleans desserts are wholly or largely prepared in advance, which makes them ideal for home eating and entertaining. Crêpes freeze beautifully and defrost almost instantly, so you can whip up a dramatic New Orleans crêpe dessert at a moment's notice. And many of our traditional family desserts are prepared in one large dish, then divided up at the table—"pot desserts" in the same tradition as our beloved pot dinners.

CARAMEL CUSTARD (CUP CUSTARD)

An old fashioned Creole dessert that has never gone out of style. Chill the unmolded custards for at least an hour before serving. *(for 6)*

---

1 c. sugar
3 large eggs plus 2 large egg yolks
1/8 tsp. salt
1/4 tsp. vanilla extract
2 c. milk
1/4 c. water

In a mixing bowl combine 1/2 cup of the sugar, the eggs, egg yolks, salt, and vanilla. In a small saucepan scald the milk, then stir it gradually into the egg mixture. Make caramelized sugar by combining the remaining 1/2 cup sugar with the 1/4 cup water and cooking them in a small saucepan over high heat, stirring from time to time with a wooden spoon, until golden brown in color. Pour some of the caramel mixture into each of 6 small (4- to 5-ounce) custard cups, then fill with the custard.

Set the custard cups in a baking pan with about 1 to 1 1/2 inches of water in it. Set the baking pan in a preheated 325° oven and bake for 40 to 45 minutes, or until a knife inserted in the center of a custard cup comes out clean. Place the cups to cool on a cooling rack.

When cool, unmold by covering each cup with a small plate and turning it upside down. (It may be necessary to first loosen the custard by sliding a thin knife around the edges of the custard.) Chill before serving.

CREOLE RICE CUSTARD

This nineteenth-century favorite makes a delightful dessert for a large group. Pour it into a shallow baking dish about 1 1/2 inches high. Let it cool for a while, then cover and refrigerate. Bring the chilled dish to the table. If you don't have a single baking dish large enough, use two. Leftover rice custard can be left in the dish and refrigerated for several days. *(for 8 or more)*

---

1 c. long grain white rice
2 c. cold water
1 tsp. salt
1 tsp. salt butter
1 qt. whole milk
6 large eggs
3/4 c. sugar
4 tsp. finely chopped orange rind
1/4 tsp. vanilla extract
3/4 tsp. freshly grated nutmeg

Put the rice, cold water, salt, and butter in a large heavy pot or kettle and bring to a boil over high heat. Stir once with a fork, cover tightly, lower the flame to very low, and cook for precisely 15 minutes without uncovering. After 15 minutes, remove the pan from the heat, uncover, and stir with a fork to fluff the rice. Return the pan to the heat, add the milk, and bring slowly to a boil, stirring frequently.

In a bowl beat the eggs and sugar together with a wire whisk until light and lemon colored. Add the chopped orange rind and the sugar and egg mixture to the boiling custard. Cook over low heat for about 5 minutes, or until the rice is very soft and the mixture begins to thicken. Add the vanilla and nutmeg and stir to blend, then remove from the heat. Pour into a large shallow baking dish about 1 1/2 inches high and allow to cool at room temperature. When cooled, cover the dish with plastic wrap and refrigerate. Serve chilled.

BANANAS FOSTER

One of our most popular festive desserts and surprisingly simple to prepare. You will need a flambé pan (used to heat crêpes) or a large heavy skillet. To get a good flame, use this simple trick: heat half of the rum, which is added last, in a separate small saucepan until it begins to boil. Quickly pour it into the flambé pan and ignite. (If you get the match wet by accident and no flame appears, heat a bit more rum to boiling, separately, and try again. Most of the alcohol burns off as it flames.) Add the ice cream and sauce just before you serve; the ice cream softens and blends with the sauce as you eat. *(for 2)*

---

2 Tbs. salt butter
3 Tbs. brown sugar
½ tsp. cinnamon
2 bananas, sliced lengthwise
¼ c. banana liqueur
¼ c. rum
2 scoops vanilla ice cream

In a flambé pan or a large skillet melt the butter over low heat. Add the sugar and cinnamon and mix well. Put the bananas in the pan and sauté until they begin to turn soft. Pour in the banana liqueur and half of the rum and continue to cook over low heat. Heat the remainder of the rum in a small saucepan until it begins to boil, then quickly pour it into the flambé pan and ignite. Distribute and prolong the flame by tipping the pan with a circular motion with one hand and basting the bananas with flame, using a long-handled spoon, with the other hand. When the flame dies out, serve two slices of banana to each portion and top each with a scoop of vanilla ice cream. Spoon the sauce remaining in the pan over the ice cream.

FLAMED BANANAS WITH CREOLE CREAM CHEESE ICE CREAM

Creole cream cheese ice cream is a New Orleans specialty, an ice cream with a rich taste that is both sweet and slightly tart. One evening when we ran out of vanilla ice cream for Bananas Foster we tried this dessert and loved it. *(for 2)*

Prepare according to the directions above for Bananas Foster, substituting 2 scoops Creole cream cheese ice cream for the vanilla ice cream.

DESSERT CRÊPES

A number of New Orleans' elegant desserts are made with crêpes. The pyrotechnics and bustling about that accompany the preparation of crêpe desserts in good restaurants lead many people to believe it's far too difficult to try these dishes at home. Quite the contrary. Few fancy dessert dishes are simpler to prepare. The only time-consuming part is making the crêpes. Once that's done, the rest takes just a few minutes. We include here a basic recipe for dessert crêpes, which yields about 2 dozen crêpes. Crêpes keep perfectly in the freezer for months and defrost within a few minutes. Prepare them in large batches and wrap them flat in stacks of 6 to 8 (or whatever multiple will suit the needs of your family) in aluminum foil. Put them in some spot in the freezer where you don't risk breaking them.

As for cooking crêpes, it takes a bit of practice, but once you get the hang of it, it's easy and it's fun. You will need an 8-inch black iron crêpe pan (diameter measured across the top). Season it when it's new and never wash it; just rub it clean with paper towels. You will become quite attached to that inexpensive little skillet rather quickly. Keep the things you'll need nearby: a pitcher or a bowl with a spout or a special crêpe ladle, for getting the small amount of batter into the pan; a thin flexible spatula or spreader for loosening the crêpes and turning them over; a potholder or an insulated sleeve for the handle of the crêpe pan, which you will be holding most of the time; a wooden spoon for stirring the batter so it doesn't get thick and lumpy at the bottom; a small pan or bowl with melted butter in it and a paper towel wadded up for rubbing the pan with butter along the way; a flat plate about 10 inches across for stacking the finished crêpes. And get yourself comfortably arranged. We have a high stool in front of the range in our kitchen, so one can sit down to cook some things that take time. There's no way of explaining it, but the crêpes seem to come out better when you're relaxed.

One last comment. No one turns out 24 or 26 absolutely perfect, symmetrical crêpes, with no holes or tears or folds that refuse to come unstuck. The batter actually makes about 32 to 34 crêpes. We just eat the imperfect ones along the way. They're delicious fresh from the pan. *(about 2 dozen 6-inch crêpes)*

- 7/8 c. flour
- 1/8 tsp. salt
- 1 Tbs. sugar
- 3 large eggs
- 1 tsp. vanilla extract
- 2 Tbs. Cognac
- 2 Tbs. melted salt butter
- 1½ c. milk, approximately
- Melted butter in a small pan or bowl (4 to 5 tsp., approximately)

Sift the flour, salt, and sugar together 3 times. Put them in a mixing bowl. Add the eggs one at a time, stirring constantly to keep lumps from forming, then add the vanilla, Cognac, and 2 tablespoons melted butter and mix well. Add the milk, a bit at a time, stirring constantly first with a wooden spoon, then with a wire whisk when the mixture becomes quite liquid. When you have added all but ¼ cup of the milk, check the consistency of the batter, which should have the texture of light cream; if necessary, add some or all of the remaining ¼ cup milk. Put the batter into a pitcher (unless you are using a special crêpe ladle).

Heat an 8-inch black iron crêpe pan and rub it with a paper towel soaked in some melted butter you will keep on hand during the making of the crêpe. The pan should be kept lightly greased, but not running with butter, and should be almost smoking hot when the batter is poured in. Holding the handle of the crêpe pan with a potholder in your left hand, pour about 1½ tablespoons of the batter into the pan with your right hand. (Reverse if you are left-handed, of course.) Tilt the pan with a circular motion to spread the batter evenly and thinly over the bottom of the pan; any excess should be poured back into the pitcher or bowl of batter. Cook the crêpe until the edges begin to turn brown, and it can be loosened easily from pan with a thin narrow spatula or by shaking the pan.

Turn the crêpe over with a spatula or with your fingers and cook on the other side for about 30 seconds. Put the cooked crêpe on a plate kept near the burner. (All the cooked crêpes will be stacked, one on top of the other, on this plate.) A properly done crêpe will be quite thin, a golden color with a tinge of light brown at the edges and perhaps a few flecks of light brown across the surface. Be sure to stir the batter every few crêpes to keep it smooth and remember to rebutter the pan lightly about every other crêpe.

CRÊPES SUZETTE

The queen of crêpe desserts and absolutely delicious. We have simplified the preparation of the heady, orangy sauce by using Curaçao liqueur (in place of orange rind rubbed with sugar cubes), which produces a consistently rich, flavorful sauce that doesn't depend on the sweetness and juiciness of the oranges you buy. Heat the Cognac separately for a dramatic flame. *(for 4)*

---

3 Tbs. salt butter
1 Tbs. sugar
¼ c. Curacao
¼ c. Grand Marnier
12 Dessert Crêpes (page 211)
3 Tbs. Cognac

In a flambé pan or large skillet melt the butter over low heat. Add the sugar, Curaçao, and Grand Marnier. Mix well and continue to heat slowly. Fold each crêpe in thirds and lay the folded crêpes flat in the bottom of the flambé pan, in the liqueur and sugar mixture. To heat the top of the crêpes, spoon some of the hot liquid in the pan over the top of each one, or turn them over carefully with a thin spatula. When the crêpes are warmed through, place the flambé pan over an alcohol burner on the dining table.

Heat the Cognac in a small saucepan over a stove burner until it is bubbling. Quickly bring the Cognac to the table, pour it into the flambé pan, and ignite the sauce. (It is essential that the Cognac be very hot, much hotter than the sauce already in the flambé pan, and that it be ignited immediately. Otherwise the match will fizzle and the sauce will not flame.) Keep tilting the flambé pan with a circular motion to keep the flames going as long as possible. When the flame dies out, serve 3 folded crêpes per portion with sauce from the flambé pan poured over them.

CRÊPES AUX FRAISES

A marvelous crêpe dessert for the strawberry season. Remove the strawberries with a slotted spoon after they have cooked in the sauce and put them in a warm bowl. Then spoon them over the crêpes and cover them with the sauce just before serving.

(for 4)

- 1 pt. fresh strawberries
- 1/4 c. (1/2 stick) salt butter
- 6 Tbs. kirsch
- 3 Tbs. Fraises des Bois liqueur
- 2 1/2 Tbs. sugar
- 1 tsp. cinnamon
- 1/4 tsp. ginger
- 12 Dessert Crêpes (page 211)
- 1/4 c. brandy

Wash and dry the strawberries carefully. Cut off the stem ends and pare off any bad spots, then slice in half lengthwise. In a flambé pan melt the butter over low heat. Add the strawberries and sauté until they begin to turn soft, then add the kirsch, Fraises liqueur, sugar, cinnamon, and ginger and mix well. When the strawberries have become quite soft, but not mushy, remove them from the pan with a slotted spoon and set aside in a warm bowl.

Fold the crêpes in thirds and place them in the sauce in the flambé pan. Warm for about 1 1/2 minutes, then turn them over carefully and warm on the other side. Place the flambé pan on an alcohol burner on the dining table.

In a small saucepan on the stove heat the brandy till it bubbles. Bring it immediately to the table, pour into the flambé pan, and ignite. Tip the pan with a circular motion to distribute and prolong the flaming. Serve the crêpes with some of the sautéed strawberries over them and sauce from the flambé pan over both berries and crêpes.

CRÊPES MAISON

A delicious crêpe dessert made famous by Galatoire's. It's not flamed, probably because there was never enough room between the aisles for the necessary paraphernalia. Glaze the filled and garnished crêpes under the broiler for 30 seconds before serving.

(for 4)

- 1 1/2 Tbs. salt butter
- 1/2 c. Cointreau
- 8 Dessert Crêpes (page 211)
- 1 c. apple or grape jelly or preserves
- 2 Tbs. grated orange rind

Melt the butter over low heat in a large heavy skillet. Add the Cointreau and heat. Put the crêpes two at a time, unfolded, in the sauce. Warm for about 30 seconds, then spoon 2 tablespoons jelly or preserves across each crêpe in a band about 1 inch wide. Fold the crêpe over from each side so the edges overlap about 3/4 of an inch. Move the filled and folded crêpes to one side of the skillet as you complete the rest, keeping the heat at very low all the while; turn it off if the sauce begins to bubble. When all the crêpes are filled and folded, sprinkle 1 1/2 teaspoons grated orange rind over each one. Pass the skillet under a preheated broiler for 30 seconds, just until the rind browns a bit.

Using a spatula, place 2 crêpes on a heated plate (a salad plate is the right size) for each portion. Lift carefully to keep the rind on top. Spoon equal amounts of the sauce from the pan over each portion and serve immediately.

PANNEQUETS SOUFFLÉS NORMANDS

These souffléed crêpes with a Calvados (apple brandy) sauce were a popular dessert course for elegant New Orleans dinners in the nineteenth century. Their puffy lightness comes from separating the eggs and beating the whites until they are very light and airy. If you have no Calvados, use applejack. Keep the finished crêpes warm in the oven.

(for 4)

- 3 large eggs
- ½ to ¾ c. flour
- Grated rind of ½ medium-sized lemon
- ½ tsp. salt
- ½ tsp. cinnamon
- ¼ tsp. ginger
- ½ c. sugar
- ⅔ c. applesauce
- ½ c. (1 stick) salt butter, approximately
- ⅓ c. Calvados

Separate the eggs into 2 large bowls, the whites in a copper bowl if you have one. Beat the yolks with a whisk until they are thick and lemon colored. (Rinse the whisk thoroughly under cold running water and dry it well if you plan to use it for beating the whites.) Beat the whites with a balloon whisk or a hand rotary beater until they are very light and almost dry. Add the flour (start with ½ cup), lemon rind, salt, cinnamon, ginger, and sugar to the egg yolks and mix well. Slowly add the applesauce and fold gently to mix. Check the consistency of mixture; it should be fairly thick but not gummy. If it seems too wet, add as much of the remaining ¼ cup flour as seems necessary, bit by bit, blending as you go. Then fold in the beaten egg whites, about a heaping tablespoon at a time, until they are all added; the mixture should be fairly well blended, but not mixed so thoroughly that it loses its airiness.

In a large heavy skillet melt about 2 tablespoons of butter over medium heat, then lower the heat to very low. Cook about 3 heaping tablespoons of the batter at a time to form the souffléed crêpes, which should be about 4 to 5 inches in diameter, until golden brown on the bottom. Turn each crêpe over carefully with a spatula and fry on the other side till it, too, is golden. Add butter as necessary to the skillet. Stack the completed crêpes on a platter and put the platter in a preheated 175° oven to keep warm until ready to serve.

When all the crêpes are cooked, add sufficient butter to make about 4 tablespoons in the skillet. Allow to melt, then add the Calvados and stir to mix. Let warm for a minute or so, then remove from the heat. Serve one or two pannequets per portion on heated plates with sauce from the skillet spooned over them.

BREAD PUDDING

New Orleans French bread gets stale very quickly—so one easily accumulates leftovers to make our favorite pudding. This is the version of bread pudding we prepare at home. The bread should be dry and slightly hard, to give the pudding the proper slightly chewy texture after it is baked. And we use canned fruit—that's the local touch—it is sweeter than fresh and its syrup becomes part of the pudding. If you live elsewhere, substitute stale cubed unsliced white or Italian bread and if you insist, fresh soft fruit for canned (add quite a bit of sugar to the indicated amount). Serve bread pudding warm or chilled, with brandy sauce. *(for 8 or more)*

---

3 c. milk
1 twenty-four-inch loaf day-old French bread, cut into 1½- to 2-inch cubes (12 c. bread cubes)
1 one-lb. can fancy fruit cocktail, cherries removed, drained
1 twenty-nine-oz. can peach halves, drained and cut into large chunks
⅔ c. raisins
¼ c. (½ stick) melted salt butter
4 large eggs
1 c. sugar
½ tsp. vanilla extract
1 tsp. cinnamon
¾ tsp. freshly grated nutmeg
¼ tsp. allspice
½ tsp. salt

Scald the milk in a heavy 4- to 5-quart saucepan. Remove from the heat and allow to cool for about 5 minutes, then add the bread, fruit cocktail, canned peaches, raisins, and melted butter and mix thoroughly. In a separate bowl, beat the eggs and add the sugar, vanilla, cinnamon, nutmeg, allspice, and salt. Mix until thoroughly blended, then add to the bread mixture and blend well.

Butter a 3- to 4-quart earthenware or china casserole thoroughly on all inner surfaces (or use a baking dish about 3 to 4 inches deep). Pour the mixture into it and stir to distribute the ingredients thoroughly. Bake uncovered in a preheated 350° oven for 1 hour and 10 minutes or until a knife inserted in the center comes out clean and the top begins to brown and form a rough crust. Allow to cool at room temperature. Serve warm or chilled, with Brandy Sauce (see below).

BRANDY SAUCE

(about 1 cup)

---

3 large eggs
¼ c. sugar
¼ tsp. vanilla extract
¼ c. (½ stick) melted salt butter
¼ c. brandy
⅛ tsp. cloves
½ c. milk

In a heavy 2- to 3-quart saucepan beat the eggs thoroughly. Add the sugar, vanilla, and melted butter and heat slowly, stirring constantly, until the mixture begins to thicken. Remove the pan from the heat and add the brandy, cloves, and milk, stirring constantly. When well mixed, place the sauce in an electric blender and blend at high speed for about 1 to 1½ minutes or until the sauce has the texture of very heavy cream. Serve over bread pudding.

NEW ORLEANS POUND CAKE

The favorite local cake, eaten plain, topped with fruit or whipped cream sliced into layers, filled with candied fruit and rum, iced for birthday cakes, and used in puddings and in Creole style trifles. We love this rich, hand-mixed version made with butter—the kind you can't find these days in bakeries. Baking the cake at a low heat for a longer than usual time seems to produce a lighter, more even texture.

(a 2-pound, 10-ounce pound cake)

1 c. (2 sticks) salt butter
2 c. sugar
2¼ c. flour
½ tsp. baking powder
½ tsp. salt
¼ c. milk
5 large eggs
1 tsp. vanilla extract

Cream the butter and sugar together in a large mixing bowl. Sift the flour, baking powder, and salt together twice and add to the butter and sugar. Gradually pour in the milk, beating the mixture slowly and regularly with a wooden spoon as you pour, then add the eggs, one at a time, mixing thoroughly after each one. Add the vanilla and stir several times to distribute it evenly.

Butter the inside of a tube pan, or an 8-inch round or square cake pan, then dust the buttered surface lightly with flour. Fill the pan with the cake batter and bake in a preheated 300° oven for 1 hour and 15 minutes or a bit longer; the cake is done when the top is golden brown and a cake tester or toothpick inserted into it comes out dry. Cool on a cake rack at room temperature before turning out of the pan.

Note: Take the butter and eggs out of the refrigerator about 45 minutes ahead; having all the ingredients at room temperature gives you the smoothest possible batter.

POUND CAKE PUDDING WITH CUSTARD SAUCE

An offbeat variation on our beloved bread pudding, made with crumbled pound cake. A bit of brandy in the custard sauce makes this rich dessert even more delicious. Prepare the sauce just before serving.

(for 4)

3 c. large chunks of New Orleans Pound Cake (above)
½ c. sugar
4 large egg yolks plus 1 large egg
1 tsp. vanilla extract
1 c. milk
¼ c. heavy cream
3 Tbs. brandy

Place the chunks of pound cake in individual dessert dishes. Prepare the sauce in a medium-sized saucepan lightly beating the sugar and egg yolks together. Beat the whole egg in lightly, then add the vanilla, milk, and cream and mix thoroughly. Set the pan over very low heat and cook until the mixture thickens, stirring constantly with a wooden spoon or spatula to keep it smooth. When the custard becomes thick enough to adhere to the stirring spoon in a thick even coating that barely drips, remove the pan from the heat. Add the brandy, stir lightly, and allow to cool for about 10 minutes; the custard sauce should be warm but not hot when it is poured over the portions of pound cake. Serve immediately after saucing.

CARROT CAKE

An old time favorite, beautiful to look at and delightful to eat. Refrigerate any leftover cake to keep the frosting from spoiling. Carrot cake tastes best at room temperature, so take it out of the refrigerator about 30 to 40 minutes before serving.

(3 eight-inch layers, or 1 eleven-by-fifteen-inch cake, or 1 ten-inch tube-mold cake)

2¼ c. flour
2 c. sugar
2¼ tsp. baking powder
1 tsp. salt
1 tsp. cinnamon
⅛ tsp. freshly grated nutmeg
⅛ tsp. allspice
5 large eggs
1 c. (2 sticks) well-softened salt butter
3 c. grated fresh carrots
½ c. chopped pecans or walnuts

FROSTING

1 eight-oz. package Philadelphia cream cheese
¼ c. (½ stick) salt butter
1 lb. confectioners' sugar

Sift the dry ingredients together twice. In a large mixing bowl beat the eggs with an electric mixer or a wire whisk for 2 minutes. Add the butter and mix lightly but thoroughly. Gradually add the dry ingredients, mixing gently but constantly with a wooden spoon or spatula. Add the grated carrots and chopped nuts and mix to blend thoroughly.

Butter 3 eight-inch layer pans, an 11-by-15-inch cake pan, or a 10-inch tube mold, then dust the buttered surface lightly with flour. Pour the batter into the pans and bake in a preheated 350° oven for about 30 minutes for layers, 50 minutes for a single rectangular cake, or 1 hour and 10 minutes for a tube-mold cake. Test for doneness by inserting a cake tester or toothpick into the center of the cake; if it comes out dry, the cake is done. Set to cool on a rack.

To prepare the frosting, cream the cream cheese and butter together with a pastry blender or spatula until smooth. Add the sugar and blend thoroughly by mixing with a wooden spoon, wire whisk, or electric mixer at low speed for 2 minutes. For a layer cake, frost the top of each layer, stack, then cover the sides with frosting. For a single rectangular cake, frost the top and sides and make patterned swirls on the top with any leftover frosting. For a tube cake, spread the entire surface evenly with frosting, using a spatula.

BABAS AU RHUM

An old time Creole favorite, these classic French individual yeast cakes are delightful served warm with hot rum sauce. Freeze the babas you don't plan to serve for another day; they will keep perfectly when individually wrapped soon after they come from the oven. The use of a sponge, which is allowed to rise before the eggs and butter are added, gives the babas the lightest possible texture. *(1 dozen babas)*

---

1 oz. fresh compressed yeast or 2 packages dry yeast
½ c. lukewarm milk
2½ c. sifted flour
2 Tbs. sugar
1 tsp. salt
2 large eggs
¼ c. (½ stick) melted salt butter, cooled

RUM SYRUP

½ lb. cube sugar
1 c. water
½ c. rum

To make the sponge, put the yeast (crumbled, if fresh is used) into a large 4- to 5-quart mixing bowl. Add the milk and half of the flour. Mix with a wooden spoon or spatula until a dough, or sponge, begins to form. Turn out onto a floured surface and knead with your fingers for about 2 minutes. Let the sponge rest while you rinse and dry the bowl. Put the sponge into the bowl, cover with plastic wrap, and place in a warm draft-free place to rise for 20 to 30 minutes, or until the sponge has almost doubled in bulk.

To mix the dough, add the sugar, salt, and remaining flour to the bowl containing the sponge. Add the eggs one at a time, mixing thoroughly after each addition. Add the melted butter last. Knead the dough in the bowl with your hands or with an electric beater at low speed, taking care to gradually incorporate the dough that clings to the sides of the bowl, for 5 to 8 minutes, just until a very soft and silky smooth dough is formed. Cover the bowl and let the dough rest for 10 minutes. Begin preheating the oven to 425°

Butter 12 baba tins or a 12-muffin pan thoroughly, then dust the buttered inner surfaces evenly with flour. Spoon the dough into the molds to fill them just half full. Set to rise uncovered in a warm draft-free place until the dough rises just to the rim of the molds (about 15 to 20 minutes). Check the molds frequently, since rising time can vary considerably. If allowed to rise too much before baking, the cakes may collapse on contact with the oven heat.

To bake, set the molds or muffin tin on a baking sheet and put the sheet on the middle rack of the preheated 425° oven. Close the oven door and immediately reduce the heat to 375°. Bake for about 15 minutes, until the babas are golden brown on top and domed at the center, then set the molds to cool on a rack for about 5 minutes. Unmold by turning upside down and catching the cakes in your hand; then set them side by side, puffed side up, in a shallow baking dish just large enough to hold them comfortably.

To prepare the syrup, combine the sugar cubes and water in a heavy saucepan. Cook over medium heat, stirring, until the sugar is dissolved. Raise the heat and bring to a boil, then lower the heat just enough to keep a low boil going. Cook for 10 minutes, then remove the pan from the heat and add the rum. Stir to mix.

To sauce the babas, prick the tops with a fork. Ladle the syrup evenly over them, then let them stand in the dish for about 25 minutes to soak up the syrup.

Baste with syrup from the bottom of the dish several times, using a bulb baster or a large spoon. To serve, carefully remove the babas to individual dessert plates, using a wide spatula or pie server. Spoon any syrup remaining in the dish over the portions.

SAVARIN

A variation of babas au rhum baked in a large ring mold and served with fresh whipped cream. *(1 eight- to ten-cup ring-mold cake)*

- Dough and syrup for Babas au Rhum (page 218)
- 1 pt. heavy cream, chilled

Prepare the sponge and dough as directed on page 218. Butter an 8- to 10-cup savarin or shallow ring mold tin thoroughly and dust evenly with flour. Fill half full with dough and set to rise uncovered in a warm draft-free place.

When the dough rises to the rim of the mold (in about ½ hour), set the mold on a heavy baking sheet and put in a preheated 425° oven. Reduce the oven temperature to 375° immediately after closing the oven door and bake for 20 to 30 minutes, or until the cake is golden brown and puffed up. Set the mold to cool on a rack while preparing the rum syrup as directed for babas.

Unmold the cake by placing a large plate upside down over the mold, then inverting. Prick the rounded top of the savarin with a fork all around and spoon the hot rum sauce over it. Allow to soak in the sauce for about 20 minutes; baste with sauce from the dish several times. Just before serving, whip the cream with an electric mixer or whisk until stiff and spoon over the top and into the center well of the savarin. Serve at the table.

KING CAKE (TWELFTH NIGHT CAKE)

This large brioche-type cake shaped like a thick oval crown and decorated with candied fruit and colored sugar is prepared in New Orleans bakeries for the period between Twelfth Night (January 6) and Ash Wednesday. A bean or tiny china baby doll is baked into it and the person who gets the slice containing the bean or doll is king or queen for a week and must also provide a new King cake to be served at the week's end. And so every week brings a new cake and a new king or queen. This ritual is a popular custom in family groups and in offices, a way of making all the weeks leading up to Lent festive. The tradition appears to have been introduced to New Orleans by its earliest French settlers, who continued a custom dating back to the Middle Ages. In recent years the King cake has come to be associated with the series of Carnival balls held in New Orleans during the weeks from Twelfth Night to Mardi Gras, the day before Lent begins.

New Orleanians do not bake their own King cakes, since they are available freshly baked in a wide range of sizes and prices, but if you know how to make a coffee cake, you should have no trouble following these general instructions for putting the King cake together. The principal points to keep in mind are: the shape, an oval ring about 2½ inches thick and about 3 inches high at the highest point; and the decoration, as elaborate and colorful as possible in order to make the cake look like a jeweled crown. As for the bean or doll, it can be baked into the batter or pushed into the finished cake from underneath—just so long as it's done secretly, so no one knows in advance which slice will designate the monarch for the week.

(1 King cake)

Dough of your choice for one large coffee cake (approximate proportions: 2 oz. fresh compressed yeast or 4 packages active dry yeast; 4 to 5 c. flour; 1 c. lukewarm scalded milk; ¾ c. sugar; 1 tsp. salt; 5 eggs; 1 tsp. vanilla extract; ¾ c. salt butter)

---

1 dried bean or tiny (about ¾ inch long) china baby doll
1 c. sugar
5 or more small bottles of assorted food coloring
1 c. candied fruit (preferably small pieces, with at least 60 percent citron)

After mixing the dough (adding the bean or doll now, if desired) and letting it rise, shape it into an oval ring, following the description given above for the approximate dimensions. Sprinkle the top of the cake evenly with sugar and make swirls with food coloring all over the top, with the swirl of one color slightly overlapping the next. Imbed the pieces of candied fruit in the top of the cake, concentrating most of them in a band about 1¼ inches wide all the way around. If you wish, make a rosette shape with a piece of fruit of one color surrounded by a circle made with alternating pieces of two other colors, to give the impression of a lavishly bejeweled crown. Set the cake on a baking sheet and bake according to instructions in the recipe you use. The finished cake should be lightly browned wherever the dough shows through; the parts covered with colored sugar should appear slightly crusty.

RUSSIAN CAKE (CREOLE TRIFLE)

New Orleanians have always been thrifty. They use leftover cake the way they do bread to make a marvelous dessert with a character all its own. Russian cake is a moist delicious icebox cake made with whatever baked things you happen to have around that aren't pretty enough or fresh enough to serve by themselves. We use stale pound cake, leftover birthday cake, end slices of sweet breads, broken pieces of coffee cake, crumbled bits of pie crust—as long as it's sweet and crumbly. Everything is mixed together, then moistened with a sweet liquid such as pineapple juice or the syrup from fruit cocktail and some red wine, and the "cake" is then packed down and refrigerated for at least 4 hours to let the liquid soak in. Russian cake is served plain or topped with ice cream or whipped cream. As for the name, it probably comes from the exotic appearance of the arabesques of mixed cakes and textures.

(1 cake, 8 inches square and 3 inches high)

---

5 to 6 c. broken mixed cake, sweet breads, etc., approximately
1 c. sweet juice (pineapple, fruit cocktail syrup, etc.)
¾ c. red wine
Ice cream or whipped cream (optional)

Mix the broken pieces of cake together in a large mixing bowl with a wooden spoon. Put the mixture into a deep 8-inch-square cake pan (or a round baking dish, if you prefer). Pack down very lightly with the back of the spoon. Pour the sweet juice evenly over the top of the cake and let it soak in for about 4 minutes, then pour the red wine evenly over the cake. Pack it down firmly this time. Cover the pan or dish with plastic wrap and refrigerate for at least 4 hours. To serve, cut the cake into rectangles (or wedges if you use a round dish) and lift them onto cake plates with a spatula or pie server. Top each portion with 1 scoop vanilla ice cream or ⅓ cup whipped cream, if desired. Save any leftover cake by covering the pan again and refrigerating.

DOBERGE CAKE

This rich delicious seven-layer cake with chocolate cream filling is a distant relative of the famous Hungarian *Dobostorte.* When first introduced by a local bakery in the early 1940s, it was called "d'auberge cake" (country inn cake) on the assumption that anything so good to eat had to be French, and in characteristic New Orleans style, it was spelled "doberge." Fairly easy to prepare at home and very festive to serve, this cake *does* require seven 8-inch layer pans, so be prepared to borrow if necessary. (Foil pans are too thin; the layers come out too flat.) The chocolate cream filling should be at room temperature for filling the layers, so prepare it first. The same is true of the milk, butter, and eggs, so take them out of the refrigerator about 35 minutes before you mix the batter. After the layers are filled, the cake is refrigerated for 1½ hours to firm it before icing. *(1 eight-inch seven-layer cake)*

FILLING

½ c. water
3 Tbs. flour
2 Tbs. cornstarch
3 large egg yolks
2 one-oz. squares bitter chocolate
¼ c. (½ stick) salt butter
1½ c. milk
⅔ c. sugar
1 tsp. vanilla extract

BATTER

(for 7 round 8-inch layers about ⅜ inch thick)

6 Tbs. (¾ stick) salt butter
⅔ c. plus 1 Tbs. sugar
¼ tsp. salt
2 large eggs
1 tsp. vanilla extract
½ c. milk
1½ c. sifted cake flour
1¼ tsp. baking powder

ICING

1 lb. confectioners' sugar
2 Tbs. clear corn syrup
⅓ c. water
2 one-oz. squares melted bitter chocolate
½ tsp. vanilla extract

To prepare the filling, put the water into a small bowl, then add the flour and cornstarch. Stir until thoroughly mixed, then mix in the egg yolks. In a small saucepan melt the chocolate and butter over low heat.

In another 3-quart saucepan combine the milk and sugar and bring to a boil over medium heat. Reduce the heat slightly and add the flour and cornstarch mixture while stirring vigorously. Raise the heat again, bring to a boil, and immediately remove the pan from the heat. Stir in the melted chocolate and butter mixture, plus the vanilla. Mix until well blended and set the pan aside to cool at room temperature for about 45 minutes.

To prepare the batter, cream the butter, sugar, and salt together very well, until they are quite fluffy. Add the eggs, one at a time, stirring well after each one is added; then add the vanilla. Cream the mixture again for about 1½ minutes. Add one-third of the milk, flour, and baking powder. Mix well. Add the second third and mix, then the last third and mix.

Grease 7 round 8-inch layer pans evenly with butter and dust them lightly with flour. Distribute the batter evenly among the pans by spooning about 3 tablespoons at a time into each one consecutively until all the batter is used up. Bake in a preheated 375° oven for 10 to 12 minutes, until the layers are firm and very lightly browned on top. Set the pans on cake racks to cool, then turn them out carefully so as not to break the layers. The layers will be about ⅜ inch thick and rather dry.

To fill the layers, score the top of the pan containing the filling with the tip of a knife, as if you were marking off 6 even slices of pie; this will guide you in using even amounts of filling on each of the first 6 layers. Place what will be the bottom layer of the cake on a flat plate about 10 inches across. Cover evenly with ⅙ of the filling. Put the next layer on top and repeat the process until you have covered 6 layers with filling. Cover with the seventh layer and place in the refrigerator for 1½ hours. When the cake is firm, remove it to a cake rack and set on a large piece of waxed paper or a cookie sheet to catch the icing that will drip off the cake. Then make the icing.

To prepare the icing, sift the confectioners' sugar into a large bowl. In a small saucepan combine the corn syrup and water. Bring to a boil. Remove from the heat and mix into the bowl of sugar. Add the melted chocolate and vanilla and mix again. The icing should be fairly thin and still warm, so that it will flow easily over the cake. Pour the warm icing slowly over the cake from the center to cover the top and sides as evenly as possible, using about two-thirds of the icing. Then, before the icing cools, dribble spoonfuls of it over any spots you wish to cover more evenly and with a spatula pat more icing over any bare or thin spots on the sides. Leave the cake undisturbed on the rack for about 15 minutes; the icing will get firm as it cools. Cover the cake with a dome or cake cover until you serve it or set it in the refrigerator; remove it about 30 minutes before serving.

Variations: Use apricot preserves in place of the chocolate filling. Spread the preserves in very thin layers, ⅛ inch thick. This will give you a Viennese-type seven-layer cake.

Use lemon cream filling in place of chocolate. Ice with either the flowing chocolate icing given above or the frosting used for Carrot Cake (see page 217).

Prepare the batter as for a two-layer cake. Bake the layers about 25 minutes. Fill with chocolate cream and ice with the frosting given for Carrot Cake (see page 217), flavored with 3 tablespoons rum.

LES OREILLES DE COCHONS (PIGS' EARS CAKES)

A Cajun delicacy, deep fried twists of dough coated with cane syrup and encrusted with nuts—a cookie or a candy, depending on one's mood. Let the twists cool before coating them with the thickened cane syrup, then quickly sprinkle on the chopped nuts. *(about 3 dozen cakes)*

¼ c. (½ stick) melted salt butter
2 large eggs, lightly beaten
2 c. flour
½ tsp. salt
Oil for deep frying

COATING

2 c. cane syrup or dark corn syrup
1½ c. chopped pecans

Melt the butter in a small saucepan. In a large mixing bowl beat the eggs lightly, then stir in the melted butter. Sift the flour and salt together and put in the bowl. Mix with a wooden spoon until a dough begins to form. Turn out onto a floured surface and knead just until well blended. Pinch off pieces of dough about the size of walnuts and roll them out individually quite thin (about ⅛ inch or less), into circles 3 to 4 inches in diameter. Heat oil in a deep fryer to 360°. To form the swirl or "ear" in each circle of dough, put the tines of a fork at the center of each circle, just piercing the dough, and twist the fork a quarter turn. Drop the twists into the hot oil from the fork. Fry about 3 ears at a time until light brown and crisp, about 2 to 3 minutes. Remove from the oil and place on paper towels to drain. Allow the twists to cool, then place them on a large heatproof platter for coating. In a saucepan heat the corn syrup until it is partially thickened (a few drops poured into cold water will form a soft ball), then pour it over the twists. Sprinkle with chopped nuts before the syrup dries.

AMBROSIA

A simple nineteenth-century dessert made with fresh oranges, grated coconut, and confectioners' sugar. We use those incredible navel oranges grown in Louisiana's Plaquemines Parish, but any large sweet juicy ones will do. Refrigerate the individual dessert bowls for about an hour before serving. *(for 4)*

3 large navel oranges
½ c. confectioners' sugar, approximately
⅓ c. grated coconut, approximately

Peel the oranges and slice them about ¼ inch thick. Put a layer of 2 or 3 orange slices at the bottom of 4 deep individual dessert bowls. Sprinkle about 1½ tablespoons sugar over each one, then sprinkle each with about 1 tablespoon grated coconut. Repeat the layers until you have used up all the orange slices. Cover with sugar and a layer of coconut. Set the bowls in the refrigerator to chill for an hour or more before serving.

PRINCESS CUP

Some New Orleanians (including one of us) absolutely adore this dessert made famous by Galatoire's—ice cream with diced fruit cocktail and Cointreau served in a parfait glass. *(for 4)*

- 1½ c. diced sweetened fruit (canned fruit cocktail or fresh soft fruit such as peaches, plums, or pineapple), juice reserved
- ¾ c. Cointreau
- ¾ qt. vanilla ice cream, approximately

Put the diced fruit and about ⅓ cup of its juice into a stainless steel or porcelain bowl and pour ½ cup of the Cointreau over it. Mix thoroughly. Cover the bowl and refrigerate for 1 hour.

To serve, put about 3 tablespoons of the fruit mixture at the bottom of each of 4 parfait glasses. Add 2 scoops of ice cream. Cover each portion with one-quarter of the remaining fruit mixture and pour 1 tablespoon of Cointreau over. Set the parfait glasses on small flat plates and serve.

RUM OMELETTE

This fluffy pancake style flamed dessert is an old Creole favorite. *(for 2)*

- 4 large eggs
- 2 Tbs. milk
- ¼ tsp. salt
- ⅛ tsp. freshly ground white pepper
- 3 Tbs. plus 2 tsp. sugar
- ½ c. rum
- 3 Tbs. salt butter

In a mixing bowl combine the eggs, milk, salt, pepper, and 3 tablespoons sugar and beat with a wire whisk until thoroughly mixed and airy. In a 10-inch omelette pan melt the butter until it begins to sizzle, then pour in the egg mixture. Cook over high heat for about 1 minute, then lower the heat to medium. Keep tilting the omelette pan from side to side with a circular motion to keep the omelette from sticking. Cook until the top is no longer wet, then sprinkle with 2 teaspoons sugar. Pass the pan under a preheated broiler for about 30 seconds to caramelize the sugar.

Heat the rum in a small pan until it bubbles. Pour it over the omelette and ignite, then spoon the burning rum over the omelette until the flame dies out. Divide in half and serve immediately, with the liquid from the pan poured over.

BAKED ALASKA

A favorite New Orleans version of this classic dessert, prepared with pound cake and rectangular in shape. Cake about 2 to 3 days old works best because it doesn't absorb too much ice cream. It should be prepared in advance and frozen.

(for 6 to 8)

MERINGUE

4 large egg whites	¼ tsp. vanilla extract
¼ tsp. fresh lemon juice	1 c. confectioners' sugar

1 lb. New Orleans Pound Cake (page 216), 2 to 3 days old	1 qt. vanilla ice cream (in brick form)
	1 c. brandy

To make the meringue, put the egg whites into a large mixing bowl (copper, if you have one) and beat with a balloon whisk or a rotary hand beater until they are very light and frothy, but not at all dry. Add the lemon juice and vanilla and beat until stiff. Gradually beat in the sugar until the meringue is quite thick and glossy; it should stand in firm peaks.

On a flameproof plate about 10 inches in diameter put a ¾-inch-thick slice of pound cake of the same dimensions as the wide side of the ice cream brick. Put the brick of ice cream on top of the cake. Cut the remaining pound cake into pieces, one to cover the top of the ice cream and four others to cover the sides. (The ice cream should be completely covered with cake. Trim any edges which stick out to give a neat effect.) Cover the top and sides of the cake with a 1-inch layer of meringue, using a flexible spreader or thin spatula. Put the remaining meringue on top of the cake and make decorative swirls with the spreader.

Immediately cover the Alaska with plastic wrap or aluminum foil, taking care not to crush the meringue crust, and put it in the freezer. When you are ready to serve it, preheat the broiler to very hot, then place the Alaska on a rack so that the top of the meringue shell is about 5 inches from the heat. Cook for about 3 minutes, just until the merinque is lightly browned. Watch carefully so it doesn't burn. Remove immediately from the oven.

Heat the brandy in a small saucepan until it boils, then bring the plate with the Alaska and the hot brandy to the table. Pour the brandy over the Alaska and ignite. When the flame dies out, cut into slices and serve on individual dessert plates.

PECAN PIE

Very sweet and absolutely delicious, pecan pie has been a New Orleans favorite from the earliest days of pecan growing in Louisiana. The combination of sugar and thick corn syrup gives the filling its soft, candylike texture. *(for 6 to 8)*

½ c. sugar
½ c. (1 stick) salt butter
3 large eggs
1½ c. pecan meats
⅛ tsp. salt
1 tsp. vanilla extract
1 c. dark corn syrup
1 unbaked 9-inch pie shell

In a large mixing bowl cream the sugar and butter together. Add the eggs one at a time, beating thoroughly after each addition. Add pecans, salt, vanilla, and corn syrup and mix lightly but thoroughly, then pour into the pie shell and bake in a preheated 450° oven for 10 minutes. Reduce the oven temperature to 350° and continue baking for 30 minutes more, or until a knife inserted in the center of the pie filling comes out clean. Set the pie on a cake rack to cool and serve at room temperature.

Note: If you refrigerate the pie for later use, take it out of the refrigerator about 30 minutes before serving.

YAM PIE

We like this pie with baked mashed Louisiana yams or regular sweet potatoes, but in a pinch you can substitute canned sweet potatoes. Just be sure to drain them thoroughly and to remove any excess moisture by rolling the potato segments in several layers of paper towels. *(for 6 to 8)*

---

3 medium-sized yams or sweet potatoes (1½ c. baked and mashed)
⅔ c. brown sugar
½ tsp. salt
¼ tsp. allspice
½ tsp. cinnamon
⅛ tsp. nutmeg
2 large eggs, lightly beaten
1 c. light cream or half-and-half
½ tsp. vanilla extract
1 unbaked 9-inch pie shell

Bake and mash the yams or sweet potatoes as directed on page 181, then combine with all the other ingredients except the pie shell. Mix thoroughly, pour into the pie shell, and bake in a preheated 450° oven for 15 minutes. Reduce the oven temperature to 325° and bake for 30 to 35 minutes more, or until a knife inserted in the center of the pie filling comes out clean. Serve warm or chilled.

PUMPKIN PIE

Prepare according to the directions for Yam Pie (see page 227), substituting 1½ cups mashed baked pumpkin for the yams (prepare 1 small or ½ medium-sized pumpkin as directed for Pumpkin Soufflé, page 181). Add ¼ cup sugar and ¼ teaspoon cinnamon to the amounts given for Yam Pie.

PLANTAIN PIE

Prepare according to the directions for Yam Pie (see page 227), substituting 2 cups sliced plantains (about 2 medium-sized plantains) for the yams. Cook the sliced plantains in a heavy 3- to 4-quart saucepan with about ⅓ cup sugar and ¼ teaspoon salt until soft (about 8 to 10 minutes). Drain thoroughly and proceed as directed.

FIG SOUFFLÉ

Our favorite dessert soufflé, prepared with mashed fresh ripe figs, available in season at the French Market and from many New Orleanians who have fig trees in their back yards. Use the ripest ones you can find; they should be just about to burst open, or already oozing their sweetness just a bit. *(for 4)*

---

3 Tbs. salt butter
¼ c. flour
1 c. milk, scalded
¼ c. sugar
4 large eggs, separated, plus 1 large egg white
1 c. mashed ripe figs
½ tsp. salt
¼ tsp. freshly ground white pepper
1½ Tbs. kirsch
1½ Tbs. brandy
¼ tsp. freshly grated nutmeg
Confectioners' sugar

Prepare according to the directions for Cheese Soufflé (see page 197). When the butter, flour, and milk mixture has thickened, remove the pan from the heat. In a large bowl, beat the sugar in with the egg yolks. Fold the thickened butter-flour mixture into the bowl containing the yolks and sugar, then add the mashed figs and all the remaining ingredients except the egg whites. Beat the egg whites as directed, then fold into the mixture in the bowl as for cheese soufflé.

Butter an 8-cup soufflé dish and dust evenly with confectioners' sugar. Pour the soufflé mixture into the dish and bake in a preheated 350° oven for 35 to 45 minutes. Check at 35 minutes as directed and bake for 5 to 10 minutes longer, if necessary. Serve immediately.

TARTE AUX POMMES

A fruit tart in the classic French style, with no top crust. It's fun to prepare this type of pastry with different seasonal fruits and to vary the liqueur. *(for 6)*

THIN PASTRY CRUST

1¼ c. sifted flour
½ tsp. salt
¼ c. (½ stick) salt butter
¼ c. ice water, more if necessary

FILLING

6 to 7 firm red apples
½ c. sugar
¼ tsp. salt
1¼ tsp. cinnamon
⅛ tsp. freshly grated nutmeg
1 Tbs. salt butter
Scant ⅛ tsp. cloves
¾ tsp. vanilla extract
¼ c. kirsch
¼ c. water

To prepare the crust, sift the flour and salt into a large bowl. Cut in the butter with a spatula or a knife, then blend by flaking gently with your fingertips until the butter is evenly distributed through the flour. When the flour is mealy, add the ice water and work the mixture into a ball with your hands. (The pastry should stick together but not be too doughy. If more ice water is needed, add a bit at a time by sprinkling it in with your fingers just until the pastry sticks together.) Roll the pastry into a ball and wrap it in waxed paper. Refrigerate for 20 to 30 minutes.

When you are ready to roll out the pastry, flour a rolling pin and a board or marble pastry surface. Press down into the center of the ball of pastry with the rolling pin and roll out, turning the pastry every few rolls and always rolling from the center outward, so that the pastry assumes a circular shape. Roll out to a thickness of about ⅛ inch or less, adding flour to the board or the rolling pin if the pastry begins to stick to either one. (If pieces of pastry tear off, reattach them by moistening the edges, then joining them by kneading them together with your fingers. Dust with a small amount of flour, and roll outward evenly until the seam disappears.) Cut the rolled-out crust into a 10-inch circle, so that it will overhang the edges of a 9-inch pie pan about ½ inch. Fold the extra ½ inch under and flute the edges all around by pinching at ½-inch intervals between your thumb and forefinger.

Peel and core the apples, then cut into thin slices. Put a layer of apples over the bottom of the crust, sprinkle with part of the sugar, salt, cinnamon, and nutmeg. Dot the layer with tiny pieces of butter. Repeat in layers until all the apple slices and sugar are used up. Sprinkle the cloves and vanilla over the top. Mix the kirsch with the water and pour evenly over the filling. Bake on a rack near the bottom of a preheated 350° oven for 1 hour, or until the filling is bubbling and the crust has turned golden. Remove from the oven and allow to cool at room temperature. When serving, use a serrated knife for slicing.

FLAMED APPLES CALVADOS

A flaming dessert made with fresh apples and apple brandy, topped with a little vanilla ice cream.

(for 4)

- 3 firm red apples
- 1/4 c. (1/2 stick) salt butter
- 2 tsp. cinnamon
- 3/4 tsp. freshly grated nutmeg
- 1/4 tsp. cloves
- 1/4 c. sugar
- 2 Tbs. fresh lemon juice
- 1/3 c. Calvados
- 1/4 c. rum
- 4 scoops vanilla ice cream

Core and peel the apples, then cut into 3/8-inch slices. In a heavy skillet melt the butter over low heat. Add the apple slices, cinnamon, nutmeg, cloves, sugar, lemon juice, and Calvados. Cook slowly, stirring constantly, until the apples are tender when pricked with a fork and the liquid in the skillet is beginning to get syrupy.

Heat the rum in a separate small saucepan until it begins to boil, then pour over the apple mixture and ignite. Continue to flame by stirring gently and tilting the skillet with a circular motion. When the flame dies out, pour into prewarmed individual dishes and top each portion with a scoop of vanilla ice cream just before serving.

FRUIT COMPOTE

A delightful way to serve fresh fruit of the season, as a light dessert or in the old fashioned way as an accompaniment to meat or poultry. Any fresh fruit will do. Adjust the amount of sugar according to the sweetness of the fruit you use.

(about 5 cups)

- 1 qt. diced fresh fruit (peaches, apples, pears, plums, etc.), washed, cored or pitted, and peeled, if desired
- 2 c. cold water
- 1/2 tsp. salt
- 3/4 c. sugar
- 2 tsp. fresh lemon juice
- 1/8 tsp. freshly ground white pepper
- 1/4 tsp. cinnamon
- 1/8 tsp. allspice
- 3 Tbs. brandy
- 1/8 tsp. cloves

In a large heavy saucepan combine all the ingredients and bring to a boil over high heat. As soon as the mixture begins to boil, cover and reduce the heat just enough to keep a low simmer going. Cook for 30 to 40 minutes, or until the diced pieces of fruit are tender but not mushy. Remove the pan from the burner and allow to cool to room temperature, then put the compote into a stainless steel or porcelain bowl, cover with plastic wrap, and refrigerate.

Remove the compote from the refrigerator at least half an hour before serving to allow it to come to room temperature. If you prefer it warm, heat the amount you plan to serve over low heat in a saucepan for a few minutes before serving.

SWEET POTATO AND PEACH CHANTILLY

An unusual and delicious combination, a favorite local vegetable with fresh ripe peaches. Serve this hot, with plenty of homemade whipped cream put on at the last minute.

(for 8)

- 6 medium-sized sweet potatoes or yams (about 3 c.), baked and diced
- Salad oil
- 2 lb. fresh ripe peaches (about 3 c.), pitted and diced
- ½ c. cold water
- 1 c. corn syrup
- ¼ tsp. salt
- ⅛ tsp. freshly ground white pepper
- ¼ c. brandy
- 5 Tbs. salt butter
- ½ tsp. cinnamon
- ¼ tsp. freshly grated nutmeg
- Whipped cream for topping

Wash and dry the sweet potatoes. Rub them lightly with salad oil and bake in a 450° oven for 35 minutes. Allow them to cool, then peel and dice into 1-inch cubes. Wash the peaches, remove the pits, peel off the skin, and dice as for the potatoes. Butter a 3-quart baking dish and preheat the oven to 375°.

In a saucepan combine the potatoes, peaches, water, syrup, salt, pepper, and brandy. Bring to a boil and cook for about 10 minutes, or until the liquid in the pan begins to turn quite thick. Remove the potato and peach segments with a slotted spoon and put some of them in a layer in the prepared baking dish. Pour some of the syrup from the pan over the layer. Cut the butter into small pieces and use about 6 pieces to dot the layer, then sprinkle with some of the cinnamon and nutmeg. Repeat the layers until all the peach and potato mixture is used up. Cover the top with the remaining butter and a bit more syrup than the other layers. Bake uncovered in the preheated oven for 35 to 40 minutes, or until the top turns brown and the liquid in the baking dish is well candied.

Serve hot with about ½ cup whipped cream over each portion.

SAUTÉED PEARS WITH ICE CREAM

Fresh ripe pears sautéed in butter, seasoned with spices and kirsch, and topped with vanilla ice cream. As the ice cream melts over the warm fruit, a delicious sauce forms. Serve with soup spoons.

(for 4)

- 3 to 4 ripe pears, cored and peel left on, sliced ¼ inch thick
- 2 Tbs. salt butter
- 2 Tbs. sugar
- 1 tsp. cinnamon
- ⅛ tsp. cloves
- ¼ tsp. freshly grated nutmeg
- ¼ c. kirsch
- 4 scoops vanilla ice cream

In a heavy skillet sauté the sliced pears in melted butter over low heat. Gradually add the sugar, cinnamon, cloves, and nutmeg. When the pears are almost tender (after about 12 to 15 minutes), add the kirsch and mix. Serve hot topped with a scoop of vanilla ice cream.

PRALINES

The classic Creole candy, made with choice pecan halves. A candy or deep fat thermometer will tell you the point at which to add the pecans.

You can make rum pralines by adding ½ cup rum and reducing the milk to ⅔ cup.

(about 2 dozen pralines)

- 1½ c. brown sugar
- 1½ c. sugar
- ½ tsp. salt
- 1 c. milk
- ¼ tsp. cream of tartar
- ¼ c. (½ stick) salt butter
- 1 tsp. vanilla extract
- 2½ c. pecan halves

Combine the sugars, salt, milk, and cream of tartar. Stir over low heat until the sugar dissolves, wiping the crystals from the sides of the pan with a rubber spatula. Cook to 236-238° on a candy thermometer, then cool to 220°. Add the butter, vanilla, and pecans and beat until creamy with a wire whisk.

While still soft, drop by spoonfuls onto a piece of buttered waxed paper, with about 4 inches of space between each spoonful. When the pralines cool and get firm, cut up the waxed paper halfway between each one and wrap them individually.

14

DRINKS

New Orleans' favorite drinks are elaborate, rich, full of surprises, and are served with a dramatic flair. Just as in the nineteenth century New Orleans' restaurants became famous for their food, so its cafés and saloons came to be identified with unique alcoholic drinks. In the heat of the semitropical afternoon, an hour spent on a tree-shaded patio or inside a pleasantly dim bar savoring a Ramos gin fizz or a Sazerac or an absinthe Suissesse was and still is a splendid way to relax.

And most famous of all is New Orleans coffee, made from a complex blend of coffee and chicory and traditionally served with hot milk as café au lait. As a dramatic conclusion to a grand dinner we like café brûlot, a combination of coffee, spices, citrus peel, brandy, and liqueur flamed at the table and ladled into tall narrow brûlot cups. All these drinks can be prepared at home, and are fun to serve and to savor.

RAMOS GIN FIZZ (NEW ORLEANS GIN FIZZ)

Invented in the 1880s by Henry C. Ramos in his bar at Meyer's Restaurant, this is one of New Orleans' most famous drinks. The secrets of its delightful taste and texture are orange flower water and egg whites. When Huey Long was governor of Louisiana he brought with him to New York's Roosevelt Hotel the bartender from the New Orleans Roosevelt just so he could have New Orleans gin fizzes whenever he was in New York.

(per drink)

1½ oz. dry gin
2 drops orange flower water
2 egg whites
5 tsp. confectioners' sugar
½ tsp. lemon juice
2 oz. half-and-half
1 drop vanilla extract
½ c. coarsely cracked ice

Combine all the ingredients in an electric blender. Cover the blender and turn on high speed for 1½ minutes. (The mixture should become quite thick and airy, so blend some more if the texture is still too thin.)

To serve, pour into a tall thin glass, or a double-sized old fashioned glass.

OJEN

(per drink)

2 oz. Ojen
1 dash Peychaud bitters
2 oz. club soda
4 oz. cracked ice

Combine all the ingredients in a cocktail shaker, cover, and shake for 30 seconds. Pour into a prechilled cocktail glass, straining out the ice.

SAZERAC

Named for the New Orleans bar where it was invented. The Sazerac is made with an absinthe derivative, bourbon or rye whiskey, sweetening, and lots of showmanship. An impressive way to coat the glass with absinthe is to twirl it in the air and catch it. Recommended only on the first drink.

(per drink)

1 oz. bourbon or rye whiskey
2 drops Angostura bitters
2 drops Peychaud bitters
1 tsp. sugar syrup
1 tsp. Pernod
1 twist lemon peel

Combine all ingredients except the Pernod and lemon peel in a cocktail shaker. Put the Pernod into a prechilled old fashioned glass, then tilt the glass in all directions to thoroughly coat the inside with Pernod. Pour off any excess. Mix the ingredients in the shaker thoroughly with a cocktail spoon; do not shake. Strain into the chilled coated glass and place the twist of lemon peel on top.

ABSINTHE SUISSESSE

A potent absinthe milkshake. The texture resembles a brandy Alexander.

(per drink)

1 oz. Pernod
1¼ tsp. confectioners' sugar or
¼ tsp. orgeat syrup
2 egg whites
2 oz. light cream
½ c. coarsely cracked ice
Nutmeg

Combine all the ingredients in an electric blender and turn on high speed for 20 to 30 seconds. Pour into a large prechilled old fashioned glass and sprinkle lightly with nutmeg.

ABSINTHE FRAPPE

(per drink)

Cracked ice
1½ oz. Pernod
1¼ tsp. sugar syrup
Club soda (optional)

Fill a cocktail shaker with cracked ice. Add the Pernod and sugar syrup, then add water or half water and half club soda slowly while stirring vigorously with a cocktail spoon. Cover the shaker and shake vigorously for a few seconds. Pour into a tall prechilled glass, straining out all but about 3 tablespoons of the cracked ice.

MILK PUNCH

(per drink)

1½ oz. bourbon
2 oz. whole milk
2 oz. heavy cream
¾ tsp. confectioners' sugar
1 drop vanilla extract
2 oz. cracked ice, approximately

Combine all the ingredients in a cocktail shaker. Shake for 20 to 30 seconds, then pour into a highball glass, straining out the ice.

MINT JULEP

A traditional Southern drink that accounted for much of the ice-shipping business in the old days. Ice was brought down the Mississippi River on flatboats from colder climes and then stored in specially insulated icehouses in the city. By the end of the New Orleans summer there was generally not a sliver to be had, no matter what one was willing to pay.

(per drink)

1½ oz. bourbon
3 to 4 sprigs fresh mint
2 tsp. sugar syrup
4 oz. cracked ice

Combine all the ingredients in a tall highball glass and mix vigorously with a cocktail spoon until the outside of the glass becomes frosted. Put an extra sprig of mint on top before serving.

NEW ORLEANS CHICORY COFFEE

Traditional New Orleans coffee is a rich very strong dark roasted blend of many different beans mixed with roasted ground chicory root. The dark roasting and special blend of beans give the coffee its characteristic strength and bite; the chicory gives it the thickness and special flavor. The coffee made by New Orleans coffee blenders is not available elsewhere. Proportions of coffee to chicory vary considerably; Union Coffee and Chicory and CDM with Chicory are the heartiest blends, French Market and Luzianne with Chicory the lighter ones (Union and Luzianne are also available as dark roasted pure coffee)—and all are easily found in markets in and around New Orleans. If you live elsewhere, order your coffee from one of the sources listed in the Shopping Guide on pages 239-40. All you need to make good New Orleans coffee is an inexpensive 6-cup Neapolitan coffee pot or the kind of drip pot available in dime stores, and paper coffee filters or paper towels cut to fit. (See note below.) A couple of useful suggestions: turn off the heat under the kettle once the water comes to a full boil; overboiled water will alter the flavor of the coffee. And you can keep on dripping boiled water through the same grounds until the coffee begins to look pale; the drip method in this recipe uses a great deal of coffee, but makes it go quite a long way.

(6 to 12 cups)

1 six-c. Neapolitan coffee pot or drip pot
1 paper coffee filter (3-inch diameter for the Neapolitan pot)
7 heaping coffee measures chicory coffee (or 1 c., level)
2 to 3 qt. freshly boiled water

Set a large kettle of cold water to boil. Discard the small screw-on coffee container which comes with the Neapolitan pot or drip pot. (If you use a regular drip pot, make a great many extra holes in the bottom of the top section with an awl or an ice pick.) Put a coffee filter over the perforated bottom of the upper part of the pot and set it over the bottom section. (It will stay upright and just fit into the rim of the bottom section.) Fill the upper part with 7 heaping coffee measures or 1 cup chicory coffee. When the water comes to a full boil, turn off the heat. Pour a small amount of freshly boiled water (about 3 tablespoons) over the coffee just to dampen the grounds. Wait 30 seconds. Then fill the upper container with water. When it drips through, fill again. The bottom section will be full after you fill the top section two or three times; pour the coffee into cups to serve or into a coffee server set on a warming tray as the bottom fills. Serve with cream and sugar to be added if desired.

Note: With a few modifications Chemex and other drip coffee makers using paper filters will produce excellent New Orleans style coffee, as will the new electric drip coffee makers.

NEW ORLEANS CAFÉ AU LAIT

The thick rich coffee New Orleanians traditionally drink in enormous quantities every day, at breakfast, at lunch and dinner, and at the French Market coffeehouses with hot beignets. *(6 to 8 large cups)*

6 to 8 c. hot New Orleans Chicory Coffee (page 237)
3 c. whole milk
⅓ to ½ c. heavy cream

Combine the milk and cream in a saucepan. Bring just to a boil, then immediately remove the pan from the heat. Using large coffee or breakfast cups (or mugs), fill one-third full with hot chicory coffee. Add the hot milk and cream until the cups are two-thirds full. (If desired, make the café au lait a bit darker by increasing the amount of coffee. Always pour the coffee first.)

CAFÉ BRÛLOT

We like to make high drama of café brûlot at the end of a grand meal, with special brûlot bowls, ladles, and cups. Café brûlot can also be made in a chafing dish and served in demitasse cups. *(for 8)*

1 two-inch stick cinnamon
6 whole cloves
¼ c. thinly slivered orange peel
¼ c. thinly slivered lemon peel
3 lumps of sugar
½ c. brandy
2 Tbs. Curaçao
3 c. hot, strong black coffee (page 237)

Combine the cinnamon, cloves, orange and lemon peel, and lumps of sugar in a brûlot bowl or chafing dish. Mash together with the back of a ladle. Add the brandy and Curaçao and mix well. When the mixture begins to boil, ignite and keep stirring to dissolve the sugar. Add the black coffee very gradually, so as to keep the flame going as long as possible. Serve in brûlot or demitasse cups.

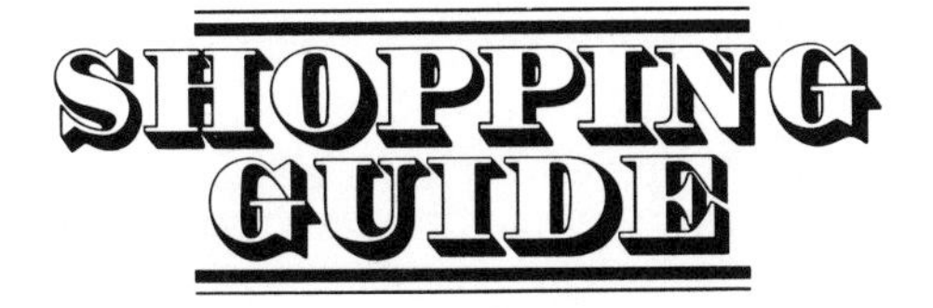

Except where noted, the stores listed below will fill mail orders for New Orleans specialties.

COFFEE

We have never been able to duplicate the best New Orleans coffee elsewhere. If you want the real thing, order it directly. Some types of New Orleans coffee are available across the country in fancy food stores, but they are generally the lighter chicory blends or a lighter roast packed for "export."

Luzianne Coffee Co., Box 60296, New Orleans, La. 70160. Telephone (800) 692-7895. Luzianne ships all of their blends by the case. Our preferred blends are CDM Dark Roast Coffee with Chicory (a rich chicory blend) and RT Dark Roast Coffee and Chicory (a very rich dark roast coffee with lots of chicory). Luzianne White Label Dark Roast Coffee with Chicory (a lighter chicory blend) is also available. Write to Luzianne for a mail order list.

COOKWARE

La Cuisine Classique, 439 Decatur Street, New Orleans, La. 70130, is the finest cookware shop in the city. Run by Thomas E. Long, the shop stocks a wide range of cooking implements, cookbooks, and baking and serving pieces. The attention is personal and careful.

Gentry, 714 South Carrolton Avenue, New Orleans, La. 70118, has a large selection of cookware and serving pieces.

GROCERIES

New Orleans still has many fine small neighborhood grocery stores with individual specialties. The two most useful larger specialty groceries are located in uptown New Orleans; they cater primarily to local clientele, but will also ship certain items upon request.

Langenstein's Super Market, 1310 Arabella Street, New Orleans, La. 70115, is the grand emporium of New Orleans fancy food. Here one finds all the elements of crawfish cooking, a daily supply of fresh seafood, and countless specialty items from cochon de lait to special cuts of meat for any cooking applications. For special attention ask for Buddy, and trust his judgment, which is impeccable. Langenstein's will ship nonperishable items out of the city; write for information on the items you desire.

Whole Food Company, 3125 Esplanade Avenue, New Orleans, La. 70119, specializes in quality fruit, vegetables, spices, cheese, meat, and unusual specialty items. Also at Riverwalk.

SEAFOOD

Battistella's Sea Foods, Inc., 910 Touro Street, New Orleans, La. 70116. Telephone: (504) 949-2724. Battistella's will ship any desired New Orleans seafood in fresh or frozen form anywhere in the country. As we have already indicated, we like expertly frozen seafood and often find it preferable to fresh seafood, which may encounter several time delays between catching and eating. The common prejudices against frozen seafoods stem from improper freezing, poor shipping, and carelessness. Most seafoods flash-frozen at the moment of perfect freshness will yield better cooking results than fresh seafood that has been kept on ice for several days. (Lump crabmeat and oysters are the notable exceptions.) When you have seafood shipped to you, critical points in transit arise if the cargo is transferred from one flight to another and if it must make a long journey between the airport and your home. Be sure it is marked "frozen—perishable."

From Battistella's you can order crawfish live, boiled, or prepicked; shrimp in the shell with the heads removed; oysters in the shell in sacks or shucked by the gallon; soft shell crabs live, hard shell crabs live or boiled; redfish, speckled trout, and pompano in season. Battistella's is expert at packing and shipping, and will discuss personally with you the best way to get the seafood you desire to your kitchen in perfect condition. When you phone, ask for Cathy.

WINE AND SPECIALTY ITEMS

Martin Winde Cellar, 3827 Baronne Street, New Orleans, La. 70115. Telephone: (504) 899-7411. The oldest and largest wine and liquor store in New Orleans, Martin's has one of best stocks of wine in the country. New Orleans food calls for much more white wine than is common in other regions of America; in fact, New Orleans grand restaurants sell anywhere from 70 to 90 percent white wine, rather than the more usual red. Martin's is particularly well stocked with the wines that go well with New Orleans food. We are especially fond of California Chardonnays and the dry French Alsatians, which handsomely complement our seafood and are relatively inexpensive.

Martin's also carries a large selection of cheeses, fancy groceries, and local specialties which they will ship anywhere in the country. Creole mustard, filé powder, crab and shrimp boil, Louisiana navel oranges, and Louisiana orange wine are all available here, in addition to usual and unusual wines and liquors.

INDEX

A NOTE ABOUT THE AUTHORS

Rima and Richard Collin live in an 1889 Victorian house in New Orleans' historic Garden District. As food writers the Collins have written *The Pleasures of Seafood* and *The New Orleans Restaurant Guide*. Richard Collin is the author of the *New Orleans Underground Gourmet* and wrote a weekly restaurant column for the New Orleans *States-Item* for ten years. Rima Collin, who learned to cook while on a Fulbright Scholarship in France, founded her New Orleans Cooking School in 1975.

Rima Collin is Rima Drell Reck, Professor of Comparative Literature at the University of New Orleans and the author of *Literature and Responsibility* and numerous articles on modern French literature, art, and culture. She has been a Guggenheim Fellow and Associate Editor of the *Southern Review*.

Richard Collin, Professor of American History at the University of New Orleans, is a specialist in twentieth century and cultural American history and the author of *Theodore Roosevelt, Culture, Diplomacy, and Expansion* and articles on recent American history.

A NOTE ON THE TYPE

The text of this book was set in film in Souvenir, a typeface originally drawn by Morris Fuller Benton for American Type Founders in 1914. The film version of Souvenir was designed by Edward Benguiat and was brought out by International Typeface Corporation in 1970. Although the original Souvenir consisted of a single roman face, Benguiat transformed it into four weights—Light, Medium, Demi, and Bold—and created a full range of italic for the different weights. With its easy, open curves and its gentle, flowing quality, Souvenir has been widely accepted as one of the finest and most useful contributions to type design since the introduction of film composition.

The text for each of the chapter openings was set in Linotype in Bodoni Bold, a typeface named after Giambattista Bodoni (1740-1813), a celebrated printer and type designer of Rome and Parma. As Bodoni grew older, his types became rather too rigidly perfect in detail with his later designs still further contrasting the thick and the thin wiry lines. The Bodoni types of today were designed not as faithful reproductions of any one of the Bodoni fonts but rather as a composite conception of the Bodoni manner. Used with care, they can produce results both pleasing and effective.

Film composition by Superior Type, Champaign, Illinois. Linotype composition by The Haddon Craftsmen, Scranton, Pennsylvania, and Maryland Linotype Composition Company, Baltimore, Maryland. Printed and bound by The Haddon Craftsmen, Scranton, Pennsylvania. Wood engravings by James Grashow. Design by Stephanie Tevonian.